Pocket PARIS

TOP SIGHTS • LOCAL LIFE • MADE EASY

Catherine Le Nevez

In This Book

QuickStart Guide

Your keys to understanding the city – we help you decide what to do and how to do it

Need to Know
Tips for a smooth trip

Neighbourhoods
What's where

Explore Paris

The best things to see and do, neighbourhood by neighbourhood

Top Sights
Make the most of your visit

Local Life
The insider's city

The Best of Paris

The city's highlights in handy lists to help you plan

Best Walks
See the city on foot

Paris' Best...
The best experiences

Survival Guide

Tips and tricks for a seamless, hassle-free city experience

Getting Around
Travel like a local

Essential Information
Including where to stay

Our selection of the city's best places to eat, drink and experience:

⊙ **Sights**

⊗ **Eating**

⊖ **Drinking**

⊛ **Entertainment**

🔒 **Shopping**

These symbols give you the vital information for each listing:

☑ Telephone Numbers	👪 Family-Friendly
⊙ Opening Hours	🐾 Pet-Friendly
P Parking	🚌 Bus
⊖ Nonsmoking	🛳 Ferry
@ Internet Access	M Metro
📶 Wi-Fi Access	🚊 Tram
🥗 Vegetarian Selection	🚆 Train
📖 English-Language Menu	

Find each listing quickly on maps for each neighbourhood:

Bar Hemingway

16 ⊖ Map p233, B2

Legend has it that Hemi
self, wielding a machine
...rate this timber-pan
...ered bar during
...showpiece is a
...en by Papa ar
...town. Dress
...s.com; Hôtel Rit
... ⊙6.30pm-2a

6 ⊙ Plac
Vc

Lonely Planet's Paris

Lonely Planet Pocket Guides are designed to get you straight to the heart of the city.

Inside you'll find all the must-see sights, plus tips to make your visit to each one really memorable. We've split the city into easy-to-navigate neighbourhoods and provided clear maps so you'll find your way around with ease. Our expert authors have searched out the best of the city: walks, food, nightlife and shopping, to name a few. Because you want to explore, our 'Local Life' pages will take you to some of the most exciting areas to experience the real Paris.

And of course you'll find all the practical tips you need for a smooth trip: itineraries for short visits, how to get around, and how much to tip the guy who serves you a drink at the end of a long day's exploration.

It's your guarantee of a really great experience.

Our Promise

You can trust our travel information because Lonely Planet authors visit the places we write about, each and every edition. We never accept freebies for positive coverage, so you can rely on us to tell it like it is.

QuickStart Guide   7

Paris Top Sights 8
Paris Local Life 12
Paris Day Planner 14
Need to Know 16
Paris Neighbourhoods 18

Explore Paris   21

22 Eiffel Tower & Les Invalides

36 Arc de Triomphe & Champs-Élysées

48 Louvre, Tuileries & Opéra

70 Sacré-Cœur & Montmartre

86 Centre Pompidou & Le Marais

108 Notre Dame & the Islands

126 The Latin Quarter

146 Musée d'Orsay & St-Germain des Prés

Worth a Trip:

Exploring the Canal St-Martin 84
Père Lachaise 104
Southeastern Discovery 144
Versailles 166

The Best of Paris 171

Paris' Best Walks

Left Bank Literary Loop 172
Seine-Side Romantic Meander 174
Right Bank Covered Passages 176

Paris' Best ...

Museums 178
Architecture 180
History 182
Parks & Gardens 184
Of the Seine 185
Churches 186
Panoramas 187
Eating 188
Markets 190
For Kids 191
Drinking 192
Nights Out 194
Gay & Lesbian Paris 196
For Free 197
Fashion 198
Multicultural Paris 200
Tours 201
Cooking & Wine-Tasting Courses ... 202

Survival Guide 203

Before You Go 204
Arriving in Paris 205
Getting Around 208
Essential Information 210
Language 215

QuickStart Guide

Paris Top Sights 8

Paris Local Life 12

Paris Day Planner 14

Need to Know 16

Paris Neighbourhoods 18

Welcome to Paris

Paris is renowned for its magnificently preserved cityscapes awash with icons including the Eiffel Tower, Arc de Triomphe and Notre Dame, and museums filled with priceless works of art. Exploring the surrounding Parisian streets takes you into the heart of the city's *quartiers* (quarters), where time-honoured restaurants and enchanting boutiques coexist alongside creative neobistro kitchens, fashion ateliers and street art.

Montmartre street with Sacré-Cœur (p72) in the background
JULIAN ELLIOTT PHOTOGRAPHY/GETTY IMAGES ©

Paris
Top Sights

Eiffel Tower (p24)

No other monument is as synonymous with a place as this graceful wrought-iron spire is with Paris. Head to the top for panoramic views over the city, day and night.

MAJANA/GETTY IMAGES ©

Notre Dame (p110)

A vision of stained-glass rose windows, gothic gargoyles and flying buttresses, Paris' glorious cathedral lies at the heart of the city. Climbing its 400-oddspiralling steps takes you up into its towers.

Louvre (p50)

The *Mona Lisa* and the *Venus de Milo* are just two of the priceless treasures among the 35,000 works of art housed inside this resplendent fortress turned palace turned France's first national museum.

Arc de Triomphe (p38)

Standing sentinel on the Champs-Élysées, this intricately carved triumphal arch epitomises Paris' pomp and ceremony, especially during festivals and celebrations. And yes,you can climb to the top of it too.

Sacré-Cœur (p72)

In the fabled artists' neighbourhood of Montmartre, climb staircased, ivy-clad streets or catch the funicular that glides up to reach the dove-white domes of Paris' crowning basilica.

Centre Pompidou (p88)

Richard Rogers and Renzo Piano's striking building, with exposed pipes and plumbing, has an exceptional collection of modern, postmodern and contemporary art, topped off by a panorama radiating from the roof.

Jardin du Luxembourg (p150)

Do as Parisians do: grab a 1923-designed metal chair and find your own favourite part of the city's loveliest park, filled with chestnut groves, ponds and children's activities.

Musée d'Orsay (p148)

Works by some of the most famous artists to have painted in Paris – including Van Gogh, Renoir and Monet – are spectacularly showcased in this turn-of-the-20th-century former railway station.

Musée Rodin (p26)

Rodin's seminal sculptures, including *The Thinker*, are placed in the rose gardens, while the 18th-century mansion's interior demonstrates that Rodin's talents encompassed myriad other art forms.

Musée National du Moyen Âge (p128)

A Roman-era bathhouse (c AD 200) and 15th-century mansion, the Hôtel de Cluny, house France's National Museum of the Middle Ages, famed for its medieval tapestries.

Versailles (p166)

It's worth venturing outside central Paris to marvel at the extraordinary opulence of this colossal château, which was the seat of the royal court until the start of the French Revolution.

Père Lachaise (p104)

Paris is a collection of villages, and this 44-hectare cemetery of lanes and elaborate tombs qualifies as one in its own right. Famous 'residents' include Oscar Wilde, Jim Morrison and Édith Piaf.

Paris Local Life

Insider tips to help you find the real city

Paris' star attractions certainly justify the hype. But to discover the 'Parisians' Paris', you need to delve into the city's *quartiers*. These quarters are like a patchwork of villages, each with its own evolving character and timeless sense of community.

The Spirit of Les Halles (p56)

▶ Cookware shops
▶ Late-night bistros

In the streets where Paris' wholesale markets were located, their spirit lives on, with grocers' stalls, virtually unchanged bakeries, and late-opening and 24-hour bistros, as well as cookware shops where Parisian chefs still buy the tools of their trade.

A Heads-Up on the Haut Marais (p90)

▶ Emerging designers
▶ Covered markets

The southern Marais used to attract all the hype, but the *haut* (upper, ie northern) part of Paris' hippest *quartier* continues to explode as an art and fashion hub, with edgy boutiques and galleries popping up amid long-standing neighbourhood haunts enjoying a revival.

Exploring the Canal St-Martin (p84)

▶ Offbeat boutiques
▶ Cool cafes

The banks of picturesque Canal St-Martin and its surrounds are the epicentre of the city's *bobo* (bohemian bourgeois) culture, where artists, musicians and other creative types catch cutting-edge music and shop at offbeat new and secondhand boutiques.

Art in Montmartre (p74)

▶ Windmills
▶ Village squares

Picasso, Renoir and Van Gogh were just some of the seminal artists who once lived and worked in Montmartre, and although this quaint, village-like neighbourhood of higgledy-piggledy streets now teems with visitors, you can find tangible reminders of its artistic legacy that still thrive today.

A Stroll along Rue Mouffetard (p130)

▶ Market stalls
▶ Lively bars

This old Roman road in the Latin Quarter is lined with colourful food-

Canal St-Martin (p84)

market stalls, cheap eateries, quirky shops and student-filled bars. You can easily spend several hours here, but give it a miss on Monday, when the markets are closed.

St-Germain des Prés' Historic Shops (p152)

▶ Antique dealers
▶ Storied shops

You'll find a trove of history-steeped shops and designer boutiques in the soulful Left Bank neighbourhood of St-Germain des Prés, as well as the city's first-ever department store and its magnificent food hall, which draws Parisians from across the city.

Southeastern Discovery (p144)

▶ National library
▶ Floating bars

There are lots of reasons to explore this up-and-coming area off the tourist radar, including exhibitions at the book-shaped national library, the national cinema institute and the national fashion institute, as well as floating bars and nightclubs and even a floating swimming pool.

Other great places to experience the city like a local:

Rue Cler (p34)

Place de la Madeleine (p68)

Rue des Martyrs (p80)

Pletzl (p97)

Marché d'Aligre (p102)

Rue de Lappe (p100)

'Little Brittany' (p160)

Rue Daguerre (p164)

Les Berges de Seine (p156)

Paris
Day Planner

Day One

This one-day itinerary covers the very top sights of the city. Start your visit at the emblematic **Eiffel Tower** (p24) for stupendous views across the city. Back on solid ground, make your way to the **Louvre** (p50), which holds some of the world's greatest art treasures, including the *Mona Lisa* and *Venus de Milo*.

You'll want to spend at least a couple of hours at the Louvre. Once you're finished, head to **Angelina** (p66) for outrageously decadent hot chocolate. Walk it off with a stroll along the Seine, finishing at the Île de la Cité to visit the island's beautiful churches, **Notre Dame** (p110) and **Sainte-Chapelle** (p118). Spend the rest of the afternoon wandering the laneways and poking through the quirky shops of the Île St-Louis, stopping to savour a **Berthillon** (p119) ice cream.

Dine on French classics at **La Tour de Montlhéry – Chez Denise** (p63) or cutting-edge neobistro cuisine at **Frenchie** (p62). After dinner, order the ultimate Bloody Mary at the place it was invented, **Harry's New York Bar** (p66).

Day Two

Start your second day at the **Sacré-Cœur** (p72), taking in vistas from the steps out front and up inside its dome. Spend some time strolling Montmartre's backstreets, checking out bustling **place du Tertre** (p75) and works by the surrealist master at the **Espace Dalí** (p77), before lunch at local favourite **Le Miroir** (p80).

After lunch, head to the **Centre Pompidou** (p88) to gaze at its eye-popping exterior and explore its fabulous modern art museum. Spend the rest of the afternoon absorbing the atmosphere of Le Marais, checking out the **boutiques** (p90) and galleries in the Haut Marais, visiting the **Musée National Picasso** (p94) and getting lost in the maze of medieval streets before a stroll along the elevated park **Promenade Plantée** (p95).

Le Marais and its eastern neighbour Bastille are the epicentre of Paris' nightlife. Start off with a glass of wine at **Le Baron Rouge** (p102), before moving on to dinner at the beautiful art nouveau **Brasserie Bofinger** (p100). Afterwards, kick off a bar crawl on **rue de Lappe** (p100).

Short on time?
We've arranged Paris' must-sees into these day-by-day itineraries to make sure you see the very best of the city in the time you have available.

Day Three

☼ Spend your third day on Paris' Left Bank. Start at the vast **Hôtel des Invalides complex** (p30), incorporating a **military museum** (p31), an exhibition on de Gaulle, and **Napoléon's tomb** (p30). Then visit the **Musée Rodin** (p26), where the artist's sculptures are displayed in a mansion and its rose-filled gardens. Continue the artistic theme at the **Musée d'Orsay** (p148), which holds the nation's incredible impressionist and postimpressionist collections.

☼ Wander east through chic St-Germain des Prés, stopping for lunch at **Bouillon Racine** (p160) and checking out the area's historic shops. Linger over a coffee at legendary literary hang-out **Les Deux Magots** (p162) and stroll through the beautiful **Jardin du Luxembourg** (p150). Then mingle with **Sorbonne** (p136) students on the Latin Quarter's **rue Mouffetard** (p130) and visit the **Panthéon** (p134) mausoleum, the resting place for many of France's great thinkers.

☾ After dinner at romantic **Le Coupe-Chou** (p138), head to charming local wine bar **Café de la Nouvelle Mairie** (p138), before catching jazz in the medieval cellars of the **Caveau de la Huchette** (p141).

Day Four

☼ Take in panoramic city views from the top of Paris' iconic **Arc de Triomphe** (p38), then promenade along the grand **av des Champs-Élysées**. Detour for high-end window-shopping in the *haute couture* heartland of the **Triangle d'Or** (Golden Triangle; p46), then meander through the World Heritage–listed **Jardin des Tuileries** (p60) to the wonderful **Musée de l'Orangerie** (p60) to view Monet's stunning *Water Lilies*.

☼ Spend the afternoon exploring the buzzing, bohemian Canal St-Martin neighbourhood, starting with lunch on the canalside terrace at **Chez Prune** (p85), before checking out the area's offbeat boutiques. Then make your way to the world's most visited cemetery, **Père Lachaise** (p105), to visit famous graves including those of Édith Piaf, Oscar Wilde and Jim Morrison.

☾ After dinner at hip bistro **Yard** (p105), or **Chatomat** (p85) in up-and-coming Belleville, check out the area's bars, catch the cancan dancers at the famous **Moulin Rouge** (p82) cabaret or take in a performance at the lavish **Palais Garnier** (p66) opera house.

Need to Know

For more information,
see Survival Guide (p204)

Currency
Euro (€)

Language
French

Visas
Generally no restrictions for EU citizens. Usually not required for most other nationalities for stays of up to 90 days.

Money
ATMs widely available. Visa and MasterCard accepted in most hotels, shops and restaurants; fewer accept American Express.

Mobile Phones
Check with your provider about roaming costs before you leave home, or ensure your phone's unlocked to use a French SIM card (available cheaply in Paris).

Time
Central European Time (GMT/UTC plus one hour)

Plugs & Adaptors
Plugs in France have two round pins. Voltage is 220V AC, 50Hz. Appliances rated US 110V need a transformer to work safely.

Tipping
Already included in prices under French law, though if service is particularly good, you might tip an extra 5% to 10% in restaurants. Round taxi fares up to the nearest euro.

① Before You Go

Your Daily Budget

Budget: Less than €100
► Dorm bed: €25–50
► Coffee/glass of wine from: €3/3.50
► Self-catering
► Frequent free concerts and events

Midrange: €100–250
► Double room: €130–250
► Two-course meals: €20–40
► Museums: free to around €12
► Admission to clubs: free to around €20

Top End: More than €250
► Historic luxury hotel double: from €250
► Gastronomic restaurant menus: from €40
► Designer boutiques

Useful Websites

Lonely Planet (www.lonelyplanet.com/paris) Destination information, hotel bookings, traveller forum and more.

Paris Info (www.parisinfo.com) Comprehensive tourist-authority website.

Secrets of Paris (www.secretsofparis.com) Loads of resources and reviews.

Paris by Mouth (www.parisbymouth.com) Foodie heaven.

Advance Planning

Two months before Book accommodation, organise opera, ballet or cabaret tickets, check events calendars, and make reservations for high-end/popular restaurants.

Two weeks before Sign up for a local-led tour and choose museums, pre-purchasing tickets online where possible.

2 Arriving in Paris

Paris' two main airports are its largest, Charles de Gaulle, and the smaller Orly; the quickest and easiest transport options are listed below. Some budget carriers such as Ryanair use Beauvais airport, linked by shuttle bus. Gare du Nord train station is also a major entry point for UK travellers.

✈ From Charles de Gaulle Airport

Destination	Best Transport
Champs-Élysées, Arc de Triomphe	Air France bus 2
St-Germain des Prés (Gare Montparnasse)	Air France bus 4
Bastille (Gare de Lyon)	Air France bus 4
Châtelet–Les Halles, Notre Dame	RER train B
St-Germain des Prés, Latin Quarter (Denfert Rochereau)	RER train B
Opéra	Roissybus

✈ From Orly Airport

Destination	Best Transport
Les Invalides	Air France bus 1
Champs-Élysées, Arc de Triomphe	Air France bus 1
St-Germain des Prés (Gare Montparnasse)	Air France bus 1
St-Germain des Prés, Latin Quarter (Denfert Rochereau)	Orlybus
Châtelet–Les Halles, Notre Dame	Orlyval, then RER train B
Latin Quarter	Orlyval, then RER train B

3 Getting Around

Walking is a pleasure in Paris, and the city also has one of the most efficient and inexpensive public transport systems in the world, making getting around a breeze.

Ⓜ Metro & RER

The fastest way to get around. Runs from about 5.30am and finishes around 12.35am or 1.15am (to around 2.15am on Friday and Saturday nights), depending on the line.

᚛ Bicycle

Virtually free pick-up, drop-off Vélib' bikes operate across 1800 stations citywide.

🚌 Bus

Good for parents with prams/strollers and people with limited mobility.

🚢 Boat

The Batobus is a handy hop-on, hop-off service stopping at nine key destinations along the Seine.

🚕 Taxi

You'll find ranks around major intersections.

Paris
Neighbourhoods

Arc de Triomphe & Champs-Élysées (p36)

This neighbourhood sees glamorous avenues flanked by flagship fashion houses, excellent museums and elegant restaurants.

👁 Top Sights

Arc de Triomphe

Eiffel Tower & Les Invalides (p22)

Zipping up the spire is reason enough to visit, but this stately neighbourhood also has some unmissable museums.

👁 Top Sights

Eiffel Tower

Musée Rodin

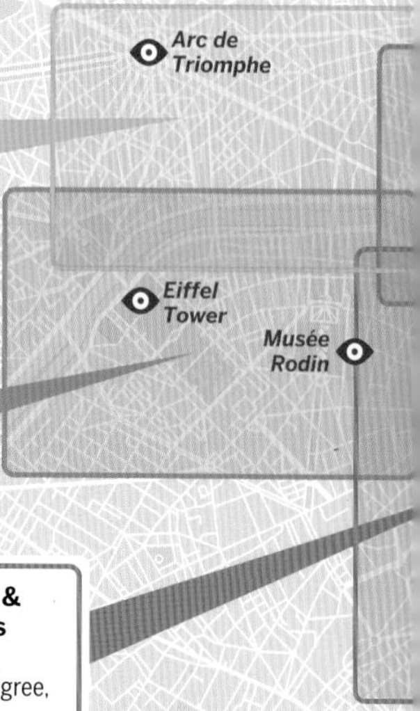

Musée d'Orsay & St-Germain des Prés (p146)

With a literary pedigree, cafe terraces and exquisite boutiques, this gentrified neighbour-hood retains a soulful, cinematic quality.

👁 Top Sights

Musée d'Orsay

Jardin du Luxembourg

Latin Quarter (p126)

The lively Latin Quarter is home to vast gardens, intriguing museums, a mighty mausoleum and spirited Sorbonne university students.

👁 Top Sights

Musée National du Moyen Âge

Arc de Triomphe

Eiffel Tower

Musée Rodin

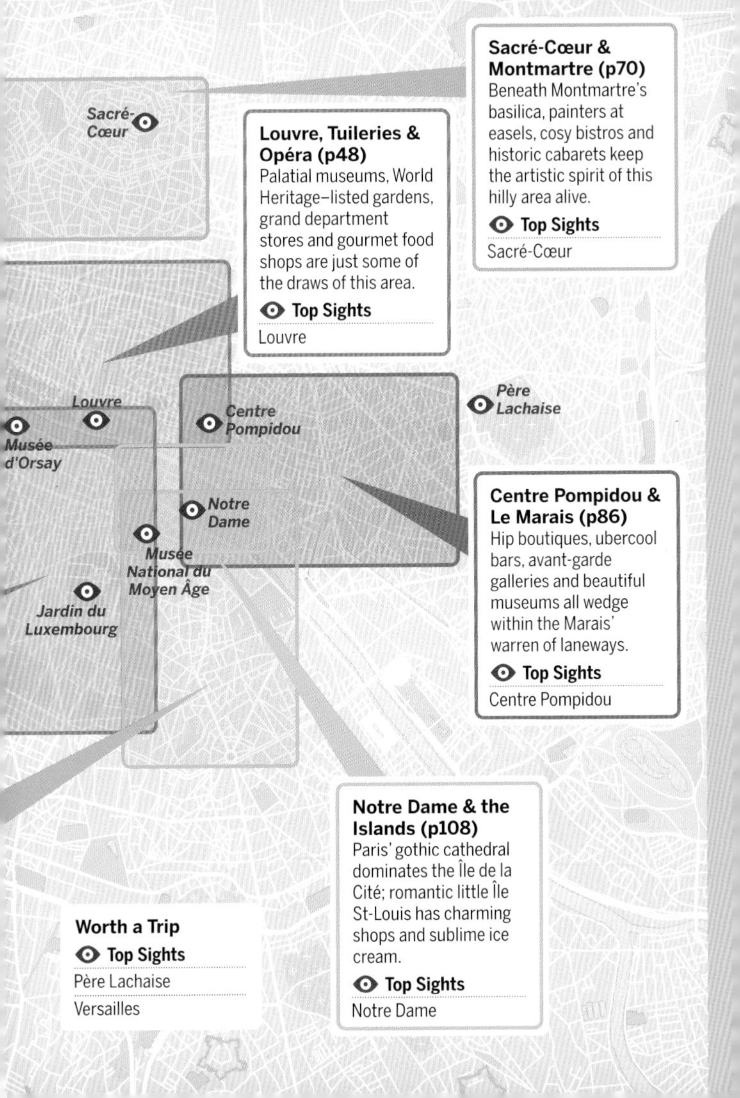

Sacré-
Cœur

Louvre, Tuileries & Opéra (p48)

Palatial museums, World Heritage–listed gardens, grand department stores and gourmet food shops are just some of the draws of this area.

⊙ Top Sights

Louvre

Sacré-Cœur & Montmartre (p70)

Beneath Montmartre's basilica, painters at easels, cosy bistros and historic cabarets keep the artistic spirit of this hilly area alive.

⊙ Top Sights

Sacré-Cœur

Louvre

Centre
Pompidou

Père
Lachaise

Musée
d'Orsay

Notre
Dame

Musée
National du
Moyen Âge

Jardin du
Luxembourg

Centre Pompidou & Le Marais (p86)

Hip boutiques, ubercool bars, avant-garde galleries and beautiful museums all wedge within the Marais' warren of laneways.

⊙ Top Sights

Centre Pompidou

Worth a Trip

⊙ Top Sights

Père Lachaise

Versailles

Notre Dame & the Islands (p108)

Paris' gothic cathedral dominates the Île de la Cité; romantic little Île St-Louis has charming shops and sublime ice cream.

⊙ Top Sights

Notre Dame

Explore
Paris

Eiffel Tower
& Les Invalides 22

Arc de Triomphe
& Champs-Élysées..................... 36

Louvre, Tuileries
& Opéra.................................... 48

Sacré-Cœur
& Montmartre 70

Centre Pompidou
& Le Marais................................ 86

Notre Dame
& the Islands 108

The Latin Quarter....................... 126

Musée d'Orsay &
St-Germain des 146

Worth a Trip

Exploring the Canal St-Martin................ 84
Père Lachaise 104
Southeastern Discovery....................... 144
Versailles 166

Arc de Triomphe (p38) amid the Parisian cityscape
COMPASSANDCAMERA/GETTY IMAGES ©

Explore

Eiffel Tower & Les Invalides

Stretching west along the Seine's southern bank, the broad boulevards and imposing architecture of the Eiffel Tower and Les Invalides area are Paris at its most bombastic. In this *grande dame* of a neighbourhood you can get up close and personal with the city's symbolic tower and discover its evolving history.

The Sights in a Day

A river cruise is the ideal way to start (and/or end) a day in this iconic area, with several companies stopping near the Eiffel Tower. Spend the morning exploring the **Musée Rodin** (p26), allowing time to soak up the serenity of its sculpture garden, then head to the **Hôtel des Invalides** (p30; pictured left) to learn about French military history through the ages and pay homage at Napoléon's tomb.

After lunch at **Le Casse Noix** (p32) or a picnic in the **Parc du Champ de Mars** (p31) beneath the Eiffel Tower, check out the indigenous art and striking architecture of the **Musée du Quai Branly** (p30). If you and your olfactory senses are game, you could take a walk below ground in the Paris sewers at the **Musée des Égouts de Paris** (p32).

Sunset is the best time to ascend the Eiffel Tower, to experience both the dizzying views during daylight and then the glittering Ville Lumière (City of Light) by night. For mind-blowing mystery degustation menus, head to **Restaurant David Toutain** (p32).

Top Sights

Eiffel Tower (p24)

Musée Rodin (p26)

♥ Best of Paris

Architecture
Eiffel Tower (p24)

Musée du Quai Branly (p30)

Museums
Musée Rodin (p26)

Eating
Restaurant David Toutain (p32)

Drinking
Coutume (p35)

Panoramas
Eiffel Tower (p24)

Île aux Cygnes (p30)

Multicultural Paris
Musée du Quai Branly (p30)

Getting There

Ⓜ **Metro** Bir Hakeim (line 6) or Champ de Mars–Tour Eiffel (RER C).

Ⓜ **Metro** From Alma Marceau (line 9), it's an easy stroll over the Pont de l'Alma bridge.

⚓ **Boat** In addition to river cruises, the hop-on, hop-off Batobus starts and ends its run near the Eiffel Tower.

Top Sights
Eiffel Tower

No one could imagine Paris today without its signature spire. But Gustave Eiffel constructed this graceful tower – the world's tallest, at 320m, until it was eclipsed by Manhattan's Chrysler Building some four decades later – only as a temporary exhibit for the 1889 Exposition Universelle (World's Fair). Luckily, the tower's popularity (and use as a platform for radiotelegraphy antennas) assured its survival beyond the fair and its elegant art nouveau webbed-metal design has become the defining fixture of the city's skyline.

◎ Map p28, C2

Champ de Mars, 7e

adult/youth/child lift to top €17/14.50/8

⊙ 9am-12.45am mid-Jun–Aug, 9.30am-11.45pm, Sep–mid-Jun

Ⓜ Bir Hakeim or RER Champ de Mars–Tour Eiffel

Eiffel Tower, as seen from the 1st floor

1st Floor

Of the tower's three floors, the 1st (57m) has the most space but the least impressive views. The glass-enclosed **Pavillon Ferrié** – open since summer 2014 – houses an immersion film along with a small cafe and souvenir shop, while the outer walkway features a discovery circuit to help visitors learn more about the tower's ingenious design. Check out the sections of glass flooring that proffer a dizzying view of the antlike people walking on the ground far below.

Not all lifts stop at the 1st floor (check before ascending), but it's an easy walk down from the 2nd floor should you accidentally end up one floor too high.

2nd Floor

Views from the 2nd floor (115m) are the best – impressively high but still close enough to see the details of the city below. Telescopes and panoramic maps placed around the tower pinpoint locations in Paris and beyond. Story windows give an overview of the lifts' mechanics, and the vision well allows you to gaze through glass panels to the ground.

Top Floor

Views from the wind-buffeted top floor (276m) stretch up to 60km on a clear day, though at this height the panoramas are more sweeping than detailed. Celebrate your ascent with a glass of bubbly (€12 to €21) from the Champagne bar (open noon to 10pm). Afterwards peep into Gustave Eiffel's restored top-level office where lifelike wax models of Eiffel and his daughter Claire greet Thomas Edison.

To access the top floor, take a separate lift on the 2nd floor (closed during heavy winds).

☑ Top Tips

▶ Save time by buying lift tickets ahead online (staircase tickets must be bought at the tower). Choose a time slot and preprint tickets or use a smartphone that can be read by the scanner at the entrance.

▶ The top can be breezy, so bring a jacket.

✗ Take a Break

Dine at the tower's 1st-floor brasserie **58 Tour Eiffel** (☏ 01 45 55 20 04; www.restaurants-toureiffel. com; 2-/3-course lunch menu €22.50/27, dinner menu €70/80; ⊙ 11.30am-4.30pm & 6.30-11pm).

Savour cuisine at the Michelin-starred 2nd-floor gastronomic restaurant **Le Jules Verne** (☏ 01 45 55 61 44; www.lejulesverne-paris.com; menus lunch €105, dinner €190-230; ⊙ noon-1.30pm & 7-9.30pm).

Top Sights
Musée Rodin

Sculptor, painter, sketcher, engraver and collector Auguste Rodin donated his entire collection to the French state in 1908 on the proviso that they dedicate his former workshop and showroom, the beautiful Hôtel Biron (1730), to displaying his works. They're now installed not only in the mansion itself but in its rose-filled garden – one of the most peaceful places in central Paris.

◉ Map p28, G3

www.musee-rodin.fr

79 rue de Varenne, 7e

adult/child museum incl garden €10/7, garden only €4/2

⊙10am-5.45pm Tue & Thu-Sun, to 8.45pm Wed

Ⓜ Varenne

Rodin's *The Thinker*

Sculptures

The first large-scale cast of Rodin's famous sculpture **The Thinker** (Le Penseur), made in 1902, resides in the garden – the perfect place to contemplate this heroic naked figure conceived by Rodin to represent intellect and poetry (it was originally titled *The Poet*).

    The Gates of Hell (La Porte de l'Enfer) was commissioned in 1880 as the entrance for a never-built museum, and Rodin worked on his sculptural masterwork up until his death in 1917. Standing 6m high by 4m wide, its 180 figures comprise an intricate scene from Dante's *Inferno*.

    Marble monument to love, **The Kiss** (Le Baiser) was originally part of *The Gates of Hell*. The sculpture's entwined lovers caused controversy on its completion due to Rodin's then radical approach of depicting women as equal partners in ardour.

    The museum also features many sculptures by Camille Claudel, Rodin's protégé.

Collections

In addition to Rodin's own paintings and sketches, don't miss his prized collection of works by artists including Van Gogh and Renoir.

Rodin at the Hôtel Biron

The 'Rodin at the Hôtel Biron' room incorporates original furniture to recreate the space as it was when he lived and worked here.

☑ Top Tips

▶ Prepurchase tickets online to avoid queuing.

▶ Audioguides cost €6.

▶ If you just want to see the outdoor sculptures, cheaper garden-only entry is available.

▶ A combined ticket with the Musée d'Orsay (p148) costs €18; combination tickets are valid for a single visit to each of the museums within three months.

✗ Take a Break

Nearby *boulangeries* (bakeries) include **Besnier** (40 rue de Bourgogne, 7e; ☉7am-8pm Mon-Fri Sep-Jul; Ⓜ Varenne).

For traditional French fare, book a table at Paris' oldest and still excellent restaurant, **À la Petite Chaise** (☎01 42 22 13 35; www.alapetitechaise.fr; 36 rue de Grenelle, 6e; menus lunch/dinner €25/33, mains €21; ☉noon-2pm & 7-11pm; Ⓜ Sèvres-Babylone).

A **B** **C** **D**

Av d'Eylau
Av Georges Mandel
Av Kléber
1 Trocadéro
Av du Président Wilson
Av d'Iéna
Pl d'Iéna
Iéna
Alma Marceau

R Scheffer
Cimetière de Passy
Pl du Trocadéro et du 11 Novembre
Av Albert de Mun
R Fresnel
Av de New York
Passerelle Debilly
Pont de l'Alma

Av Paul Doumer
R Vineuse
Pl de Varsovie
Port de la Bourdonnais
Musée du Quai Branly
R de l'Université

16E
Jardins du Trocadéro
Av des Nations Unies
Av des Nations Unies
Q Branly
Allée Paul Deschanel
Av de la Bourdonnais
R de Monttessuy
Av Rapp

R de la Tour
2
Bd Delessert
Pont d'Iéna
Av Élisée Reclus
Allée Adrienne Lecouvreur

R de Passy
Pl de Costa Rica
Eiffel Tower
Allée Léon Bourgeois
Av Gustave Eiffel
Av Émile Deschanel

R Raynouard
Passy
Champ de Mars–Tour Eiffel
Stade Émile Anthoine
Pl Jacques Rueff
Av Anatole France

3
Av du Président Kennedy
Pont de Bir Hakeim
R Jean Rey
Av de Suffren
Av Joseph Bouvard
Parc du Champ de Mars
Av Pierre Loti

Av de Lamballe
Allée des Cygnes
Pl des Martyrs Juifs du Vélodrome d'Hiver
Bir Hakeim
R de la Fédération
Allée Thomy Thierry
Av Charles Floquet

Île aux Cygnes
4
R R Nélaton
R du Docteur Finlay
15E
R St-Saëns
R Edgar Faure
R Desaix
Pl A Sauvy
R de Presles
R Dupleix

4
Q de Grenelle
Pl de Brazzaville
R Émeriau
R St-Charles
R Viala
Pl Duplex
Dupleix
Bd de Grenelle
Av de Champaubert
14
R du Laos

R Ruelle
R de Lourmel
R Juge
R Tiphaine
La Motte Picquet Grenelle

Q de Grenelle
Pl St-Charles
R de Fondary
R Letellier
Pl Cambronne

For reviews see
◎ Top Sights	p24
◉ Sights	p30
✕ Eating	p32
🍷 Drinking	p35

R Violet
R du Commerce
R Frémicourt
13
R de la Croix Nivert

N 0 ——— 400 m
0 ——— 0.2 miles

◎ Top Sights	p24
◉ Sights	p30
✕ Eating	p32
🍷 Drinking	p35

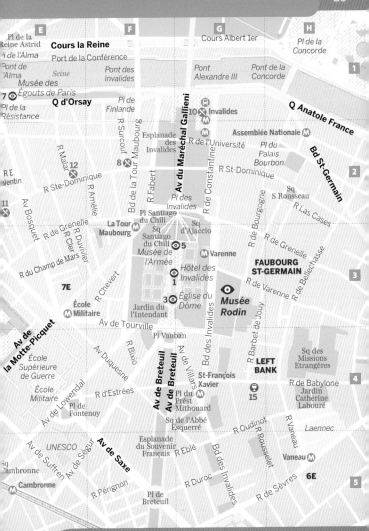

E
Pl de la Reine Astrid
Pl de l'Alma
Pont de l'Alma

Cours la Reine
Port de la Conférence

F

G
Cours Albert 1er

H
Pl de la Concorde

Seine
Pont des Invalides
Pont Alexandre III
Pont de la Concorde

Q Anatole France

Musée des
7 ◉ Égouts de Paris
Q d'Orsay
Pl de Finlande

10 ✕ Invalides

Pl de la Résistance
R Surcouf

Esplanade des Invalides

Assemblée Nationale Ⓜ

R Malar
12 ◉

8 ✕
R Fabert

R de l'Université
Pl du Palais Bourbon

Bd St-Germain

R Ste-Dominique
R Amélie
Bd de la Tour Maubourg

Av du Maréchal Gallieni

R de Constantine
R St-Dominique

Sq S Rousseau
R Las Cases

11 ✕
Av Bosquet

R de Grenelle
R Duvivier
R Cler

Pl des Invalides
Pl Santiago du Chili
Sq d'Ajaccio

R de Bourgogne
R de Grenelle

La Tour Maubourg Ⓜ
Sq Santiago du Chili
Musée de l'Armée ◉ 5

Ⓜ Varenne

R de Bellechasse

R du Champ de Mars
R Chevert

3 ◉
Hôtel des Invalides ◉ 1

FAUBOURG ST-GERMAIN

7E

École Militaire Ⓜ

Jardin du l'Intendant

Église du Dôme ◉

R de Varenne

◉ **Musée Rodin**

R Barbet de Jouy

Av de Tourville

Pl Vauban

Bd des Invalides

R de Jouy

Sq des Missions Etrangères

Av de la Motte-Picquet

École Supérieure de Guerre

Av Duquesne

R Bixio

Av de Breteuil
Av de Breteuil

St-François Xavier

LEFT BANK
◉ 15

R de Babylone
Jardin Catherine Labouré

École Militaire
Av de Lowendal
Pl de Fontenoy

R d'Estrées

Pl du Prêt Mithouard
Sq de l'Abbé Esquerré

R Oudinot

R Rousselet

R Vateau

Laennec

Vaneau Ⓜ

UNESCO
Av de Suffren
Av de Ségur

Av de Saxe

Esplanade du Souvenir Français
R Eblé

Bd des Invalides

6E

Sq Cambronne
Cambronne

R Pérignon

Pl de Breteuil

R Duroc

R de Sèvres

A
1
2
3
4
5

Sights

Hôtel des Invalides
MONUMENT, MUSEUM

1 ◉ Map p28, F3

Flanked by the 500m-long Esplanade des Invalides lawns, the Hôtel des Invalides was built in the 1670s by Louis XIV to house 4000 *invalides* (disabled war veterans). On 14 July 1789, a mob broke into the building and seized 32,000 rifles before heading on to the prison at Bastille and the start of the French Revolution. Admission includes entry to all Hôtel des Invalides sights. Hours for individual sites often vary – check the website for updates. (www.musee-armee.fr; 129 rue de Grenelle, 7e; adult/child €11/free; ⊙10am-6pm Apr-Oct, to 5pm Nov-Mar, hours can vary; Ⓜ Varenne)

Musée du Quai Branly
MUSEUM

2 ◉ Map p28, D2

No other museum in Paris so inspires travellers, armchair anthropologists and those who simply appreciate the beauty of traditional craftsmanship. A tribute to the diversity of human culture, Musée du Quai Branly presents an overview of indigenous and folk art. Its four main sections focus on Oceania, Asia, Africa and the Americas. An impressive array of masks, carvings, weapons, jewellery and more make up the body of the rich collection, displayed in a refreshingly unique interior without

rooms or high walls. (☎01 56 61 70 00; www.quaibranly.fr; 37 quai Branly, 7e; adult/child €9/free; ⊙11am-7pm Tue, Wed & Sun, 11am-9pm Thu-Sat; Ⓜ Alma Marceau or RER Pont de l'Alma)

Église du Dôme
CHURCH

3 ◉ Map p28, F3

With its sparkling golden dome (1677–1735), the landmark church of the Hôtel des Invalides is one of the finest religious edifices erected under Louis XIV and was the inspiration for the United States' Capitol building. It received the remains of Napoléon in 1840; the extravagant **Tombeau de Napoléon 1er** comprises six coffins fitting into one another like a Russian doll. (www.musee-armee.fr; 129 rue de Grenelle, 7e; included in Hôtel des Invalides entry; ⊙10am-6pm Apr-Oct, to 5pm Nov-Mar; Ⓜ Varenne)

Île aux Cygnes
ISLAND

4 ◉ Map p28, A4

Paris' little-known third island, the artificially created Île aux Cygnes, was formed in 1827 to protect the river port and measures just 850m by 11m. On the western side of the Pont de Grenelle is a soaring one-quarter scale **Statue of Liberty replica**, inaugurated in 1889. Walk east along the Allée des Cygnes – the tree-lined walkway that runs the length of the island – for knock-out Eiffel Tower views. (Isle of Swans; btwn Pont de Grenelle & Pont de Bir Hakeim, 15e; Ⓜ Javel–André Citroën or Bir Hakeim)

BRUCE BI/GETTY IMAGES ©

Parc du Champ de Mars

Musée de l'Armée   MUSEUM

5 ⊙ Map p28, G3

North of the Hôtel des Invalides, in the Cour d'Honneur, is the Musée de l'Armée, which holds the nation's largest collection on French military history. Sobering wartime footage screens at this army museum, which also has weaponry, flag and medal displays as well as a multimedia area dedicated to Charles de Gaulle. (Army Museum; www.musee-armee.fr; 129 rue de Grenelle, 7e; included in Hôtel des Invalides entry; ⊙10am-6pm Apr-Oct, to 5pm Nov-Mar; M Varenne)

Parc du Champ de Mars   PARK

6 ⊙ Map p28, D3

Running southeast from the Eiffel Tower, the grassy Champ de Mars – an ideal summer picnic spot – was originally used as a parade ground for the cadets of the 18th-century **École Militaire**, the vast French-classical building at the southeastern end of the park, which counts Napoléon Bonaparte among its graduates. The steel-and-etched-glass **Wall for Peace memorial** (www.wallforpeace.com), erected in 2000, is by Clara Halter. (Champ de Mars, 7e; M École Militaire or RER Champ de Mars–Tour Eiffel)

Musée des Égouts de Paris

MUSEUM

7 Map p28, E1

Raw sewage flows beneath your feet as you walk through 480m of odoriferous tunnels in this working sewer museum. Exhibitions cover the development of Paris' waste-water-disposal system, including its resident rats (there's an estimated one sewer rat for every Parisian above ground). Enter via a rectangular maintenance hole topped with a kiosk across the street from 93 quai d'Orsay, 7e. (http://equipment.paris.fr/musee-des-egouts-5059; place de la Résistance, 7e; adult/child €4.40/3.60; ⏰11am-5pm Tue & Wed May-Sep, 11am-4pm Tue & Wed Oct-Dec & Feb-Apr; Ⓜ Alma Marceau or RER Pont de l'Alma)

Cheese for sale on rue Cler (p34)

OLIVER STREWE/GETTY IMAGES ©

Eating

Restaurant David Toutain

GASTRONOMY $$$

8 Map p28, F2

Prepare to be wowed: David Toutain pushes the envelope at his eponymous Michelin-starred restaurant with some of the most creative high-end cooking in Paris. Mystery degustation courses include unlikely combinations such as smoked eel in green-apple-and-black-sesame mousse; cauliflower, white chocolate and coconut truffles; or candied celery and truffled rice pudding with artichoke praline (stunning wine pairings available). (📞01 45 51 11 10; www.davidtoutain.com; 29 rue Surcouf, 7e; 9-/15-course tasting menus €80/110; ⏰noon-2pm & 8-10pm Mon-Fri; Ⓜ Invalides)

Le Casse Noix

MODERN FRENCH $$

9 Map p28, C4

Proving that a location footsteps from the Eiffel Tower doesn't mean compromising on quality, quantity or authenticity, 'the nutcracker' is a neighbourhood gem with a cosy retro interior, affordable prices, and exceptional cuisine that changes by season and by the inspiration of owner-chef Pierre Olivier Lenormand, who has honed his skills in some of Paris' most fêted kitchens. Book ahead. (📞01 45 66 09 01; www.le-cassenoix.fr; 56 rue de la Fédération, 15e; 2-/3-course lunch menus €21/28, 3-course dinner menu €35; ⏰noon-2.30pm & 7-10.30pm Mon-Fri; Ⓜ Bir Hakeim)

Understand
Charles de Gaulle & WWII

The WWII battle for France began in earnest in May 1940 and by 14 June France had capitulated. Paris was occupied, and almost half the population evacuated. General Charles de Gaulle, France's undersecretary of war, fled to London. In a radio broadcast on 18 June 1940, he appealed to French patriots to continue resisting the Germans. He set up a French government-in-exile and established the Forces Françaises Libres (Free French Forces), fighting alongside the Allies. Paris was liberated on 25 August 1944 by an Allied force spearheaded by Free French units.

De Gaulle returned to Paris and set up a provisional government, but in January 1946 he resigned, wrongly believing that the move would provoke a popular outcry for his return. De Gaulle formed his own party (Rassemblement du Peuple Français) and remained in opposition until 1958, when he was brought back to power to prevent a military coup over the uprising in Algeria. He resigned as president in 1969, succeeded by Gaullist prime minister Georges Pompidou.

Chez Françoise
TRADITIONAL FRENCH $$

10 🍴 Map p28, G1

Buried beneath the enormous Air France building but opening to a retractable-roofed terrace, this old-school 1949-opened restaurant – a favourite with parliamentary workers from the Assemblée Nationale – recalls the early glamour of air travel, the era when it was established at this former off-site terminal for transiting passengers. Specialties include *entrecôte de bœuf* and sublime oysters. (📞 01 47 05 49 03; www.chezfrancoise. com; Aérogare des Invalides, 7e; 2-/3-course menus from €28/33, oysters per half-dozen €15.50-29; 🕑 noon-3pm & 7pm-midnight; Ⓜ Invalides)

Les Fables de la Fontaine
GASTRONOMY $$

11 🍴 Map p28, E2

Prices at this Michelin-starred restaurant are a serious bargain and the lunchtime *menu* (available midweek only) is an absolute steal. Chefs Julia Sedefdjian and David Botteau create true works of art: on-the-shell oysters in vivid green cucumber jelly with green apple and lemon caviar; almond-crusted veal with mashed artichokes and king trumpet mushrooms; and banana soufflé with rum ice cream. (📞 01 44 18 37 55; www.lesfablesdelafontaine.net; 131 rue St-Dominique, 7e; 2-course lunch menu €25, mains €21-29; 🕑 noon-2.30pm & 7-10.30pm; Ⓜ École Militaire or RER Pont de l'Alma)

Local Life
Rue Cler

Pick up fresh bread, sandwich fillings, pastries and wine for a picnic along the typically Parisian commercial street rue Cler, 7e, which buzzes with local shoppers, especially on weekends.

Interspersed between the *boulangeries* (bakeries), *fromageries* (cheese shops), grocers, butchers, delis and other food shops (many with pavement stalls), lively cafe terraces overflow with locals too.

Truffes Folies   MODERN EUROPEAN $$

12 ✕   Map p28, E2

Truffle fans will be in raptures at this restaurant-deli. The prized fungi appears in everything imaginable, from sandwiches to dishes like *œufs en cocotte* (eggs in ramekins), scallop carpaccio, Parmesan and sage ravioli, and wild mushroom risotto, as well as swoon-worthy desserts (crème brûlée; brioche pudding with salted caramel and truffle ice cream). Truffles also appear in every product its deli stocks. (☎01 44 18 05 41; www.truffesfolies.fr; 37 rue Malar, 7e; mains €19-32; ⊙restaurant noon-3pm & 6.30-9.30pm Mon-Fri, noon-3pm Sat, deli 11am-10pm Mon-Fri; Ⓜ La Tour-Maubourg)

La Véraison   MODERN FRENCH $$

13 ✕   Map p28, D5

The elegant simplicity of owner-chef Ulla Bosse's welcoming neighbourhood bistro (bare boards, timber tables, pistachio-coloured walls) belies the outstanding cuisine she creates in her open kitchen. The starters alone – truffled chestnut velouté, foie gras ravioli in Cognac sauce, burrata cheese with orange, crispy 'Peking duck' morsels, Thai crab cakes with mango dip – are reason enough to return. (☎01 45 32 39 39; www.laveraison.com; 64 rue de la Croix Nivert, 15e; mains €18-26; ⊙7.30-10pm Tue-Sat; Ⓜ Commerce)

La Gauloise   TRADITIONAL FRENCH $$

14 ✕   Map p28, D4

With a name like La Gauloise, you wouldn't expect this venerable, terrace-fronted restaurant to serve anything other than traditional fare, which it does, very well. From onion soup to pan-sautéed calf's liver, preserved foie gras with pear and mustard marmalade, and profiteroles or *îles flottantes* for dessert, it refines but doesn't reinvent the classics that make French cuisine iconic. (☎01 47 34 11 64; 59 av de la Motte-Picquet, 15e; 2-/3-course lunch menus €26/31, mains €19-31; ⊙noon-2.30pm & 7-11pm; Ⓜ La Motte Picquet Grenelle)

BERTRAND GARDEL/GETTY IMAGES ©

Musée du Quai Branly (p30)

Drinking

Coutume   COFFEE

15 Map p28, G4

The dramatic improvement in Parisian coffee in recent years is thanks in no small part to Coutume, artisan roaster of premium beans for scores of establishments around town. Its flagship cafe – a bright, light-filled, post-industrial space – is ground zero for innovative preparation methods including cold extraction and siphon brews. Fabulous organic fare and pastries too. (www.coutumecafe.com; 47 rue de Babylone, 7e; 8am-7pm Mon-Fri, 10am-7pm Sat & Sun; M St-François Xavier)

Explore

Arc de Triomphe & Champs-Élysées

Pomp and grandeur reign: Baron Haussmann famously reshaped the Parisian cityscape around the Arc de Triomphe, from which a dozen avenues radiate like the spokes of a wheel. The most celebrated (and the scene of major celebrations) is the luxury-shop-lined av des Champs-Élysées (pictured). The neighbourhood's splendour extends to its *haute cuisine* restaurants and *haute couture* fashion houses.

The Sights in a Day

☼ Climb above the Champs-Élysées to the top of the **Arc de Triomphe** (p38), then stroll – and shop – along this famous avenue named for the Elysian Fields ('heaven' in Greek mythology).

☼ After lunch in the beautiful tea-room of the **Musée Jacquemart-André** (p42), wander among the flagship fashion houses of the **Triangle d'Or**, and admire the ornate Asian artefacts at the **Musée Guimet des Arts Asiatiques** (p42) or catch blockbuster exhibitions at the **Grand Palais** (p42). Visit the resident fish at the **Aquarium de Paris Cinéaqua** (p45), then snap a postcard-perfect photo of the Eiffel Tower from the terrace of the **Palais de Chaillot** (p44) and another from inside its exceptional architectural museum, the **Cité de l'Architecture et du Patrimoine** (p42).

★☽ Options for dinner in the area extend from intimate neighbourhood bistros such as **Le Hide** (p45) to gastronomic heavyweights such as **Lasserre** (p45). Later, hit pumping nightclubs such as **ShowCase** (p46).

 Top Sights

Arc de Triomphe (p38)

💜 **Best of Paris**

Museums
Musée d'Art Moderne de la Ville de Paris (p44)

For Kids
Aquarium de Paris Cinéaqua (p45)

Multicultural Paris
Musée Guimet des Arts Asiatiques (p42)

Panoramas
Arc de Triomphe (p38)

Getting There

Ⓜ **Metro** Charles de Gaulle–Étoile (lines 1, 2, 6 and RER A) is adjacent to the Arc de Triomphe.

Ⓜ **Metro** The Champs-Élysées' other stops are George V (line 1), Franklin D Roosevelt (lines 1 and 9) and Champs-Élysées– Clemenceau (1 and 13).

⚓ **Boat** The hop-on, hop-off Batobus stops near the Champs-Élysées by Pont Alexandre III.

Top Sights
Arc de Triomphe

If anything rivals the Eiffel Tower as the symbol of Paris, it's this magnificent 1836-built monument to Napoléon's 1805 victory at Austerlitz, which he commissioned the following year. The intricately sculpted triumphal arch stands sentinel in the centre of the enormous Étoile ('star') roundabout. At the top, some of the best views of Paris stretch east along the *axe historique* to the Louvre's glass pyramid, and west to the modern Grande Arche in high-rise La Défense.

◎ Map p40, B2

place Charles de Gaulle, 8e

adult/child €12/free

🕙 10am-11pm Apr-Sep, to 10.30pm Oct-Mar

Ⓜ Charles de Gaulle–Étoile

Beneath the Arch

Beneath the arch at ground level lies the **Tomb of the Unknown Soldier**. Honouring the 1.3 million French soldiers who lost their lives in WWI, the Unknown Soldier was laid to rest in 1921, beneath an eternal flame that is rekindled daily at 6.30pm.

Bronze plaques laid into the ground mark significant moments in modern French history, such as the proclamation of the Third French Republic (4 September 1870) and the text from Charles de Gaulle's famous London broadcast on 18 June 1940, which sparked the French Resistance to life.

Sculptures

The arch is adorned with four main sculptures, six panels in relief, and a frieze running beneath the top. The most famous sculpture is the one to the right as you approach from the Champs-Élysées: *La Marseillaise* (Departure of the Volunteers of 1792). Sculpted by François Rude, it depicts soldiers of all ages gathering beneath the wings of victory, en route to drive back the invading armies of Prussia and Austria.

Viewing Platform

Climb the 284 steps to the viewing platform at the top of the 50m-high arch and you'll be suitably rewarded with magnificent panoramas over western Paris. The Arc de Triomphe is the highest point in the line of monuments known as the *axe historique* (historic axis, also called the grand axis); it offers views that swoop east down the Champs-Élysées to the gold-tipped obelisk at place de la Concorde (and beyond to the Louvre's glass pyramid), and west to the skyscraper district of La Défense, where the colossal Grande Arche marks the *axe*'s western terminus.

☑ **Top Tips**

▶ Don't try to cross the traffic-choked roundabout above ground! Stairs on the Champs-Élysées' northeastern side lead beneath the Étoile to pedestrian tunnels that bring you out safely beneath the arch.

▶ Admission to the terrace at the top is free on the first Sunday of the month from November to March.

▶ Don't risk getting skittled by traffic by taking photos while crossing the Champs-Élysées.

▶ There is a lift (elevator) at the arch, but it's only for visitors with limited mobility or those travelling with young children, and there are still some unavoidable steps.

✗ **Take a Break**

▶ Right near the arch, **Publicis Drugstore** (www.publicisdrugstore. com; 133 av des Champs-Élysées, 8e; ⏱ 8am-2am; Ⓜ Charles de Gaulle-Étoile) is handy for a meal, drink or snack.

A **B** **C** **D**

Pl du Gal Patton

R des Acacias

17e

R du Général Lamrezac

R Troyon

13

Av de la Grande Armée

Charles de Gaulle–Étoile

R de Tilsitt

Charles de Gaulle–Étoile

Argentine

R du Faubourg St-Honoré

Av Hoche

R Beaujon

Pl G Guillaumin

Av de Friedland

R Duret

Arc de Triomphe

Av Foch

Pl Charles de Gaulle

Charles de Gaulle–Étoile

R Lord Byron

Av des Champs-Élysées

R de Presbourg

Kléber

R Vernet

George V

R Washington

R Paul Valéry

Av Victor Hugo

Av d'Iéna

12

19

R Galilée

R de Bassano

R Quentin Bauchart

17

Av Kléber

R Copernic

R La Pérouse

R Jean Giraudoux

Av Marceau

TRIANGLE D'OR

R Pierre Charron

R Lauriston

Pl des États-Unis

R de Belloy

R Galilée

Pl Amiral de Grasse

R de Chaillot

Av Pierre 1er de Serbie

R C Marot

R Marbeuf

R de la Trémoille

Boissière

16e

Lycée Assomption

R Boissière

Musée Guimet des Arts Asiatiques

8

Musée de la Mode de la Ville de Paris

Av George V

R du Boccador

Av Raymond Poincaré

R de Longchamp

R de Lübeck

3

Iéna

Pl d'Iéna

Sq Brignole Galliéra

5

9

Musée d'Art Moderne de la Ville de Paris

Alma Marceau

Pl de la Reine Astrid

Pl de l'Alma

Pl du Trocadéro et du 11 Novembre

Av du Président Wilson

Palais de Tokyo

Av d'Iéna

R Fresnel

Av de New York

Pont de l'Alma

Trocadéro

4

Cité de l'Architecture et du Patrimoine

Av Albert de Mun

Pont de l'Alma

Pl de la Résistance

Cimetière de Passy

7

Passerelle Debilly

Q Branly

Av Rapp

Palais de Chaillot

Varsovie

Pl de Varsovie

11

Av des Nations Unies

Port de la Bourdonnais

Aquarium de Paris Cinéaqua

Av Bosquet

E F G H

1

N 0 ———————— 400 m
   0 ———————— 0.2 miles

R de Monceau

R du Docteur Lancereaux

Av de Messine

Sq
M Pagnol

Musée
Jacquemart-
André

2 ⊙ André

R de Miromesnil

R Roy

St-Augustin

Bd Haussmann

Av Percier

R La Boétie

Pl
St-Augustin

Bd Haussmann

Sq
Louis XVI

R de Courcelles

Miromesnil Ⓜ

R Roquépine

R des
Mathurins

R de Berri

R d'Artois

St-Philippe
du Roule

Pl Chassagne-
Goyon

R du Faubourg
St-Honoré

R de Penthièvre

R Cambacérès

Bd Malesherbes

2

Galerie
du Claridge

R de Ponthieu

R la Boétie

8e

Pl Beauvau

R de Surène

R d'Aguesseau

R d'Anjou

Ⓐ 20

R du Colisée

R Jean Mermoz

15
⊗

Av Matignon

Av de Marigny

R de l'Élysée

R du Faubourg St-Honoré

3

Ⓐ 18

Ⓜ Franklin
D Roosevelt

Ⓜ

Rond Point
Champs-Élysées
Marcel Dassault

Av Gabriel

R Boissy
d'Anglas

R Royale

R de Marignan

Champs-Élysées
Clemenceau

10 Ⓐ

R François 1er

Av Montaigne

Av Franklin D Roosevelt

Ⓜ

Av du Général
Eisenhower

Pl
Clemenceau

Av des Champs-Élysées

Musée Maxim's

Ⓜ
Concorde

4

Pl François
1er

14

⊙ 1
Grand
Palais

**Av Winston
Churchill**

⊙ 6
Petit
Palais

Av Dutuit

Pl de la
Concorde

R Jean Goujon

Cours Albert 1er

1er

Cours la Reine

Port de la Conférence

16 Ⓐ

Seine

Pont des
Invalides

Pont
Alexandre III

Pl de
Finlande

Q d'Orsay Ⓜ

For reviews see	
⊙ Top Sights	p38
⊙ Sights	p42
⊗ Eating	p45
Ⓐ Drinking	p46
Ⓐ Shopping	p47

5

Bd de la
Tour Maubourg

**Av du
Maréchal
Gallieni**

Invalides

Ⓜ

Assemblée
Nationale

7e

Esplanade
des Invalides

Ⓜ

R de l'Université

Sights

Grand Palais

ART MUSEUM

1 ⊙ Map p40, F4

Erected for the 1900 Exposition Universelle (World's Fair), the Grand Palais today houses several exhibition spaces beneath its huge 8.5-tonne art nouveau glass roof. Some of Paris' biggest shows (Renoir, Chagall, Turner) are held in the Galeries Nationales, lasting three to four months. Hours, prices and exhibition dates vary significantly for all galleries. Those listed here generally apply to the Galeries Nationales, but always check the website for exact details. Reserving a ticket online for any show is strongly advised. (☎01 44 13 17 17; www.grandpalais.fr; 3 av du Général Eisenhower, 8e; adult/child €15/1; ⊙10am-8pm Sun, Mon & Thu, to 10pm Wed, Fri & Sat; Ⓜ Champs-Élysées–Clemenceau)

Musée Jacquemart-André

ART MUSEUM

2 ⊙ Map p40, F1

If you belonged to the cream of Parisian society in the late 19th century, chances are you would have been invited to one of the dazzling soirées held at this mansion. The home of art collectors Nélie Jacquemart and Édouard André, this opulent residence was designed in the then fashionable eclectic style, which combined elements from different eras – seen here in the presence of Greek and Roman antiquities, Egyptian artefacts, period furnishings and portraits by Dutch masters. (☎01 45 62 11 59; www.musee-jacquemart-andre.com; 158 bd Haussmann, 8e; adult/child €12/10; ⊙10am-6pm, to 8.30pm Mon during temporary exhibitions; Ⓜ Miromesnil)

Musée Guimet des Arts Asiatiques

ART MUSEUM

3 ⊙ Map p40, B4

France's foremost Asian art museum has a superb collection. Observe the gradual transmission of both Buddhism and artistic styles along the Silk Road in pieces ranging from 1st-century Gandhara Buddhas from Afghanistan and Pakistan to later Central Asian, Chinese and Japanese Buddhist sculptures and art. Part of the collection is housed in the nearby **Galeries du Panthéon Bouddhique** (19 av d'Iéna, 16e; admission free; ⊙10am-5.45pm Wed-Mon, garden to 5pm) with a **Japanese garden**. (☎01 56 52 54 33; www.guimet.fr; 6 place d'Iéna, 16e; adult/child €7.50/free; ⊙10am-6pm Wed-Mon; Ⓜ Iéna)

Cité de l'Architecture et du Patrimoine

MUSEUM

4 ⊙ Map p40, A5

This mammoth 23,000-sq-metre space is an ode on three floors to French architecture. The highlight is the light-filled ground floor with a beautiful collection of plaster and wood *moulages* (casts) of cathedral portals, columns and gargoyles; replicas of murals and stained glass originally created for the 1878 Exposition Universelle are on display on the upper

Grand Palais

floors. Views of the Eiffel Tower are equally monumental. (www.citechaillot. fr; 1 place du Trocadéro et du 11 Novembre, 16e; adult/child €8/free; ⊙11am-7pm Wed & Fri-Mon, to 9pm Thu; Ⓜ Trocadéro)

Palais de Tokyo   ART MUSEUM

 Map p40, C4

The Tokyo Palace, created for the 1937 Exposition Universelle, has no permanent collection. Rather its shell-like interior of concrete and steel is a stark backdrop to interactive contemporary art exhibitions and installations. Its bookshop is fabulous for art and design magazines, and its eating and drinking options are magic. (www. palaisdetokyo.com; 13 av du Président Wilson,

16e; adult/child €10/free; ⊙noon-midnight Wed-Mon; Ⓜ Iéna)

Petit Palais   ART MUSEUM

6 ◉ Map p40, G4

This architectural stunner was built for the 1900 Exposition Universelle, and is home to the Musée des Beaux-Arts de la Ville de Paris (City of Paris Museum of Fine Arts). It specialises in medieval and Renaissance objets d'art, such as porcelain and clocks, tapestries, drawings, and 19th-century French painting and sculpture; it also has paintings by such artists as Rembrandt, Colbert, Cézanne, Monet, Gauguin and Delacroix. (☎ 01 53 43 40 00; www.petitpalais.paris.fr; av Winston-Churchill,

8e; permanent collections free; ⊗10am-6pm Tue-Sun; M Champs-Élysées–Clemenceau)

Palais de Chaillot   HISTORIC BUILDING

7 ⊙ Map p40, A5

The two curved, colonnaded wings of this building (built for the 1937 International Expo) and the terrace in between them afford an exceptional panorama of the **Jardins du Trocadéro**, the Seine and the Eiffel Tower. The eastern wing (1 place du Trocadéro, 16e) houses the standout Cité de l'Architecture et du Patrimoine (p42), devoted to French architecture and heritage, as well as the **Théâtre National de Chaillot** (☑01 53 65 30 00; www.theatre-chaillot.fr; M Trocadéro), staging dance and theatre. The western wing (17 place du Trocadéro et du 11 Novembre, 16e) houses the **Musée de la Marine** (Maritime Museum; ☑01 53 65 69 69; www.musee-

---

Local Life

Hidden Oasis

Descending rustic, uneven staircases (by the white-marble Alfred de Musset sculpture on av Franklin D Roosevelt, or the upper garden off cours la Reine) brings you to the tiny 0.7 hectare **Jardin de la Nouvelle France** (cnr av Franklin D Roosevelt & cours la Reine, 8e; ⊗24hr; M Franklin D Roosevelt), an unexpected wonderland of lilacs, lemon, orange, maple and weeping beech trees, with a wildlife-filled pond, waterfall, wooden footbridge and benches to soak up the serenity.

---

marine.fr; adult/child €8.50/free; ⊗11am-6pm Wed-Mon; M Trocadéro) and the **Musée de l'Homme** (Museum of Humankind; ☑01 44 05 72 72; www.museedelhomme.fr; adult/child €10/free; ⊗Thu-Mon 10am-6pm, Wed to 9pm; M Passy, Iéna).

Musée de la Mode de la Ville de Paris   MUSEUM

8 ⊙ Map p40, C4

Housed in 19th-century Palais Galliera, Paris' Fashion Museum warehouses some 100,000 outfits and accessories – from canes and umbrellas to fans and gloves – from the 18th century to the present day. The sumptuous Italianate palace and gardens dating from the mid-19th century are worth a visit in themselves, as are the excellent temporary exhibitions the museum hosts. (☑01 56 52 86 00; www.galliera.paris.fr; 10 av Pierre 1er de Serbie, 16e; adult/child €8/free; ⊗10am-6pm Tue-Sun, to 9pm Thu; M Iéna)

Musée d'Art Moderne de la Ville de Paris   ART MUSEUM

9 ⊙ Map p40, C4

The permanent collection at Paris' modern-art museum displays works representative of just about every major artistic movement of the 20th and (nascent) 21st centuries, with works by Modigliani, Matisse, Braque and Soutine. The real jewel, though, is the room hung with canvases by Dufy and Bonnard. Look out for cutting-edge temporary exhibitions (not free). (www.mam.paris.fr; 11 av du Président Wilson,

16e; admission free; ⊙10am-6pm Tue, Wed,
Fri-Sun, 10am-10pm Thu; Mléna)

Musée Maxim's

MUSEUM

10 Map p40, H4

During the belle époque, Maxim's
bistro was the most glamorous place
to be in the capital. The restaurant
has lost much of its cachet (though
the food is actually excellent), but for
art nouveau buffs, the real treasure
is the upstairs museum. Opened by
Maxim's owner, fashion designer
Pierre Cardin, it's filled with some 550
pieces of art nouveau artworks, objets
d'art and furniture, detailed during
one-hour guided tours. (☑01 42 65
30 47; www.maxims-musee-artnouveau.
com; 3 rue Royale, 8e; adult/child €20/free;
⊙English tours 2pm Wed-Sun, closed Jul &
Aug; MConcorde)

Aquarium de Paris
Cinéaqua

AQUARIUM

11 Map p40, B5

Paris' aquarium, on the eastern side
of the Jardins du Trocadéro, has a
shark tank and 500-odd fish species
to entertain families on rainy days.
Three cinemas screen ocean-related
and other films (dubbed in French,
with subtitles). Budget tip: show
your ticket from the nearby Musée
de la Marine or the Musée Guimet
to get reduced aquarium admission
(adult/child €16.40/10.40). (www.
cineaqua.com; av des Nations Unies, 16e;
adult/child €20.50/13; ⊙10am-7pm;
MTrocadéro)

Eating

Ladurée

PATISSERIE $

12 Map p40, D2

One of the oldest patisseries in Paris,
Ladurée has been around since 1862
and was the original creator of the
lighter-than-air macaron. Its tearoom
is the classiest spot to indulge on the
Champs. Alternatively, pick up some
pastries to go – from croissants to
the trademark macarons, it's all quite
heavenly. (www.laduree.com; 75 av des
Champs-Élysées, 8e; pastries from €1.50;
⊙7.30am-11.30pm Mon-Fri, 8.30am-12.30am
Sat, 8.30am-11.30pm Sun; MGeorge V)

Le Hide

FRENCH $$

13 Map p40, B1

A perpetual favourite, Le Hide is a tiny
neighbourhood bistro serving scrump-
tious traditional French fare: snails,
baked shoulder of lamb with pumpkin
purée, or monkfish in lemon butter.
Unsurprisingly, this place fills up
faster than you can scamper down the
steps of the nearby Arc de Triomphe.
Reserve well in advance. (☑01 45 74 15
81; www.lehide.fr; 10 rue du Général Lanrezac,
17e; 2-/3-course menus €27/35; ⊙6-10.30pm
Mon-Sat; MCharles de Gaulle–Étoile)

Lasserre

GASTRONOMY $$$

14 Map p40, F4

Since 1942, this exceedingly elegant
restaurant in the Triangle d'Or has
hosted style icons like Audrey Hepburn
and is still a superlative choice for a

Local Life
Golden Triangle

A stroll around the legendary **Triangle d'Or** (Golden Triangle; bordered by avs George V, Champs-Élysées and Montaigne, 8e) constitutes the walk of fame of top French fashion. Rubbing shoulders with the world's top international designers are Paris' most influential French fashion houses, such as Chanel, Chloé, Dior, Givenchy, Hermès, Lanvin, Louis Vuitton and Saint Laurent.

Michelin-starred meal to remember. A bellhop-attended lift (elevator), white-and-gold chandeliered decor, extraordinary retractable roof and flawless service set the stage for inspired creations from head chef Adrien Trouilloud and pastry chef Guillaume Bousquet. Dress code required. (☏01 43 59 53 43; www.restaurant-lasserre.com; 17 av Franklin Roosevelt, 8e; lunch menu €90, tasting menu €195, mains €85-120; ⊘noon-2pm Thu & Fri, 7-10pm Tue-Sat; Ⓜ Franklin D Roosevelt)

Framboise
CRÊPERIE $

15 Ⓧ Map p40, F3

Tucked in among a string of Asian takeaways is this delightful, contemporary crêperie. With an emphasis on quality (eg organic buckwheat flour), this is a top pick for an inexpensive meal off the Champs-Élysées. (☏01 74 64 02 79; www.creperieframboise.fr; 7 Rue de Ponthieu, 8e; 2-course lunch €13.50, crêpes from €8.50; ⊘11.45am-2.30pm daily, 7-10pm Mon-Fri; Ⓜ Franklin D Roosevelt)

Drinking

Showcase
CLUB

16 Ⓨ Map p40, F5

This gigantic electro club has solved the neighbour-versus-noise problem that haunts so many Parisian nightlife spots: it's secreted beneath the Pont Alexandre III bridge alongside the Seine. Unlike other exclusive Champs backstreet clubs, the Showcase can pack 'em in (up to 1500 clubbers) and is less stringent about its door policy, though you'll still want to look like a star. (www.showcase. fr; Port des Champs-Élysées, 8e; ⊘11.30pm-6am Thu-Sat; Ⓜ Invalides, Champs-Élysées–Clemenceau)

Blaine
COCKTAIL BAR

17 Ⓨ Map p40, D3

Hidden in plain sight is this underground speakeasy: enter through an unmarked black door, relay the password (hint: research on social media) and enter into a re-created Prohibition-era bar. Good cocktails (from €13) and occasional live jazz and DJ sets. (65 rue Pierre Charron, 8e; ⊘8pm-5am Tue-Sat; Ⓜ Franklin D Roosevelt)

Zig Zag Club
CLUB

18 Ⓨ Map p40, E3

Some of the hippest electro beats in western Paris, with star DJs, a great sound and light system, and a spacious dance floor. It can be pricey, but it still fills up quickly, so don't start

Guerlain

the party too late. (www.zigzagclub.fr; 32 rue Marbeuf, 8e; ⏰11.30pm-7am Fri & Sat; Ⓜ Franklin D Roosevelt)

Queen CLUB

19 Ⓟ Map p40, D3

These days this doyen of a club is as popular with a straight crowd as it is with its namesake clientele, but Monday's disco nights are still prime dancing queen territory. While right on the Champs-Élysées, it's not quite as inaccessible as the other nearby clubs. (📞01 53 89 08 90; www.queen.fr; 79 av des Champs-Élysées, 8e; ⏰11.30pm-6.30am; Ⓜ George V)

Shopping

Guerlain PERFUME

20 🔒 Map p40, E3

Guerlain is Paris' most famous parfumerie, and its shop (dating from 1912) is one of the most beautiful in the city. With its shimmering mirror and marble art deco interior, it's a reminder of the former glory of the Champs-Élysées. For total indulgence, make an appointment at its decadent spa. (📞spa 01 45 62 11 21; www.guerlain.com; 68 av des Champs-Élysées, 8e; ⏰10.30am-8pm Mon-Sat, noon-7pm Sun; Ⓜ Franklin D Roosevelt)

Explore

Louvre, Tuileries & Opéra

Carving its way through the city, Paris' *axe historique* (historic axis) passes through the Tuileries gardens before reaching IM Pei's glass pyramid at the entrance to Paris' mightiest museum, the Louvre. Gourmet shops garland the Église de la Madeleine, while further north are the splendid Palais Garnier opera house and art nouveau department stores of the Grands Boulevards.

The Sights in a Day

☀ Navigating the labyrinthine **Louvre** (p50) takes a while, so it's an ideal place to start your day. Other museums well worth a visit include the **Musée de l'Orangerie** (p60), showcasing Monet's enormous *Water Lilies,* and the **Jeu de Paume** (p60) photography museum, both enveloped by the elegant lawns, fountains and ponds of the **Jardin des Tuileries** (p60).

☀ After visiting the **Église de la Madeleine** (p60), deliberate over the eateries around **place de la Madeleine** (p68). Go behind the scenes of the opulent **Palais Garnier** (p61) opera house. Then shop at the beautiful **Galeries Lafayette** (p68) and **Le Printemps** (p69) department stores and take in the free panoramas from their rooftops.

☾ One of the hottest restaurants in this 'hood, **Frenchie** (p62) offers walk-in wine-bar dining. Afterwards, hit the dance floor of legendary house and techno venue **Le Rex Club** (p66) or catch a jazz session on **rue des Lombards** (p67).

For a local's day in Les Halles, see p56.

👁 Top Sights

Louvre (p50)

◯ Local Life

The Spirit of Les Halles (p56)

💙 Best of Paris

Architecture

Louvre Glass Pyramid (p53)

Forum des Halles (p62)

Museums

Musée de l'Orangerie (p60)

Jeu de Paume (p60)

Eating

Frenchie (p62)

Yam'Tcha (p63)

Getting There

Ⓜ **Metro** The Louvre has two metro stations: Palais Royal–Musée du Louvre (lines 1 and 7), and Louvre–Rivoli (line 1).

Ⓜ **Metro** Châtelet–Les Halles is Paris' main hub, with many metro and RER lines converging here.

⛴ **Boat** The hop-on, hop-off Batobus stops outside the Louvre.

Top Sights
Louvre

Few art galleries are as prized or daunting as the Musée du Louvre, Paris' pièce de résistance that no first-time visitor to the city can resist. This is, after all, one of the world's largest and most diverse museums. Showcasing 35,000 works of art, it would take nine months to glance at every piece, rendering advance planning essential.

◉ Map p58, E5

rue de Rivoli & quai des Tuileries, 1er

adult/child €15/free

⏱9am-6pm Mon, Thu, Sat & Sun, to 9.45pm Wed & Fri

Ⓜ Palais Royal–Musée du Louvre

The Louvre as seen from the Jardin des Tuileries (p60)

Palais du Louvre

The Louvre today rambles over four floors and through three wings: the **Sully Wing** creates the four sides of the Cour Carrée (literally 'Square Courtyard') at the eastern end of the complex; the **Denon Wing** stretches 800m along the Seine to the south; and the northern **Richelieu Wing** skirts rue de Rivoli. The building started life as a fortress built by Philippe-Auguste in the 12th century – medieval remnants are still visible on the Lower Ground Floor (Sully). In the 16th century it became a royal residence and after the Revolution, in 1793, it was turned into a national museum. Its booty was no more than 2500 paintings and objets d'art.

Over the centuries French governments amassed the paintings, sculptures and artefacts displayed today. The 'Grand Louvre' project inaugurated by the late President Mitterrand in 1989 doubled the museum's exhibition space, and both new and renovated galleries have since opened, including the state-of-the-art **Islamic art galleries** (Lower Ground Floor, Denon) in the stunningly restored Cour Visconti.

Priceless Antiquities

Whatever your plans are, don't rush by the Louvre's astonishing cache of treasures from antiquity: both **Mesopotamia** (ground floor, Richelieu) and **Egypt** (ground and 1st floors, Sully) are well represented, as seen in the *Code of Hammurabi* (Room 3, ground floor, Richelieu) and the *Seated Scribe* (Room 22, 1st floor, Sully). Room 12 (ground floor, Sackler Wing) holds impressive friezes and an enormous **two-headed-bull column** from the Darius Palace in ancient Iran, while an enormous seated statue of Pharaoh Ramesses II highlights the temple room (Room 12, Sully).

☑ Top Tips

▸ You need to queue twice to get in: once for security and then again to buy tickets.

▸ The longest queues are outside the Grande Pyramide; use the Carrousel du Louvre entrance (99 rue de Rivoli or direct from the metro) or the Porte de Lions entrance (closed Wednesday and Friday).

▸ A Paris Museum Pass or Paris City Passport gives you priority; buying tickets in advance (on the Louvre website) will also help expedite the process.

✗ Take a Break

▸ Louvre tickets are valid for the whole day, meaning you can nip out for lunch. For a quick and easy meal, grab a sandwich in the Hall Napoléon and picnic like a royal in the Jardin des Tuileries (p60).

▸ Alternatively, stroll five minutes to enjoy fine wine and cuisine at **Racines 2** (39 rue de l'Arbre Sec, 1er; 2-/3-course lunch menu €28/32, mains €24-31; ◷ noon-2.30pm Mon-Fri, 7.30-10.30pm Mon-Sat).

Also worth a look are the mosaics and figurines from the Byzantine empire (lower ground floor, Denon), and the Greek statuary collection, culminating with the world's most famous armless duo, the **Venus de Milo** (Room 16, ground floor, Sully) and the **Winged Victory of Samothrace** (top of Daru staircase, 1st floor, Denon).

Mona Lisa

Easily the Louvre's most admired work (and world's most famous painting) is Leonardo da Vinci's *La Joconde* (in French; *La Gioconda* in Italian), the lady with that enigmatic smile known as *Mona Lisa* (Room 6, 1st floor, Denon).

Mona (*monna* in Italian) is a contraction of *madonna,* and Gioconda is the feminine form of the surname Giocondo. Canadian scientists used infrared technology to peer through paint layers and confirm *Mona Lisa's* identity as Lisa Gherardini (1479–1542?), wife of Florentine merchant Francesco de Giocondo. Scientists also discovered that her dress was covered in a transparent gauze veil typically worn in early 16th-century Italy by pregnant women or new mothers; it's surmised that the work was painted to commemorate the birth of her second son around 1503, when she was aged about 24.

French & Italian Masterpieces

The 1st floor of the Denon Wing, where the *Mona Lisa* is found, is easily the most popular part of the Louvre – and with good reason. Rooms 75 through 77 are hung with monumental French paintings, many iconic: look for the *Consecration of the Emperor Napoleon I* (David), *The Raft of the Medusa* (Géricault) and *Grande Odalisque* (Ingres).

Rooms 1, 3, 5 and 8 are also must-visits. Filled with classic works by **Renaissance masters** – Raphael, Titian, Uccello, Botticini – this area culminates with the crowds around the *Mona Lisa*. But you'll find plenty else to contemplate, from Botticelli's graceful frescoes (Room 1) to the superbly detailed *Wedding Feast at Cana* (Room 6). On the ground floor of the Denon Wing, take time for the Italian sculptures, including Michelangelo's *The Dying Slave* and Canova's *Psyche and Cupid* (Room 4).

Northern European Paintings

The 2nd floor of the Richelieu Wing, directly above the gilt and crystal of the **Napoleon III Apartments** (1st floor), allows for a quieter meander through the Louvre's inspirational collection of Flemish and Dutch paintings spearheaded by works by Peter Paul Rubens and Pieter Bruegel the Elder. Vermeer's *The Lacemaker* can be found in Room 38, while Room 31 is devoted chiefly to works by Rembrandt.

Louis XV's Crown

French kings wore their crowns only once – at their coronation. Lined with

Corridor leading to the *Winged Victory of Samothrace*

embroidered satin and topped with openwork arches and a fleur-de-lis, Louis XV's 1722-crafted crown (Room 66, 1st floor, Denon) was originally adorned with pearls, sapphires, rubies, topazes, emeralds and diamonds.

Louvre Glass Pyramid

Almost as stunning as the masterpieces inside is the 21m-high glass pyramid designed by Chinese-born American architect IM Pei that bedecks the main entrance to the Louvre in a dazzling crown. Beneath Pei's Grande Pyramide is the **Hall Napoléon**, the museum's main entrance area. To revel in another Pei pyramid of equally dramatic dimen-

sions, head towards the **Carrousel du Louvre** (www.carrouseldulouvre.com; 99 rue de Rivoli, 1er; ⊘ 8.30am-11pm, shops 10am-8pm; 🛜; Ⓜ Palais Royal–Musée du Louvre), a busy shopping mall that loops underground from the Grande Pyramide to the **Arc de Triomphe du Carrousel** (place du Carrousel, 1er) – its centrepiece is Pei's **Pyramide Inversée** (inverted glass pyramid).

Trails & Tours

Self-guided thematic trails range from Louvre masterpieces and the art of eating to family-friendly topics. Download trail brochures in advance from the website. Another good option is to rent a Nintendo 3DS multimedia guide (adult/child €5/3; ID required). More formal, English-language **guided tours** (✆01 40 20 51 77; adult/child €12/5; ⏱11.30am & 2pm except 1st Sun of month) depart from the Hall Napoléon. Reserve a spot up to 14 days in advance or sign up on arrival at the museum.

Other Louvre Museums

A trio of privately administered collections – Applied Arts, Advertising and Fashion & Textiles – sit in the Rohan Wing of the vast Palais du Louvre. They are collectively known as the **Musée des Arts Décoratifs** (www.lesartsdecoratifs.fr; 107 rue de Rivoli, 1er; adult/child €11/free; ⏱11am-6pm Tue-Sun, to 9pm Thu; Ⓜ Palais Royal–Musée du Louvre); admission includes entry to all three. For an extra €2, you can scoop up a combo ticket that also includes the Musée Nissim de Camondo in the 8e.

The **Arts Décoratifs (Applied Arts)** section takes up the majority of the space and displays furniture, jewellery and such objets d'art as ceramics and glassware from the Middle Ages and the Renaissance through the art nouveau and art deco periods to modern times. Its collections span from Europe to East Asia.

On the other side of the building is the smaller **Musée de la Publicité** (Advertising Museum), which has some 100,000 posters in its collection dating as far back as the 13th century and innumerable promotional materials. Most of the space is given over to special exhibitions.

Haute couture (high fashion) creations by the likes of Chanel and Jean-Paul Gaultier can be ogled in the **Musée de la Mode et du Textile** (Museum of Fashion & Textiles), home to some 16,000 costumes from the 16th century to the present day. Items are only on display during regularly scheduled themed exhibitions.

Renovating the Louvre

In late 2014, the Louvre embarked on a 30-year renovation plan, with the aim of modernising the museum to make it more accessible. Phase 1 increased the number of main entrances to reduce security wait times (even still, buy tickets online or use the Paris Museum Pass; lines at the underground Carrousel du Louvre entrance are often shorter). It also revamped the central Hall Napoléon to vastly improve what was previously bewildering chaos. Important changes to come include increasing the number of English-language signs and artwork texts to aid navigation.

LOUVRE

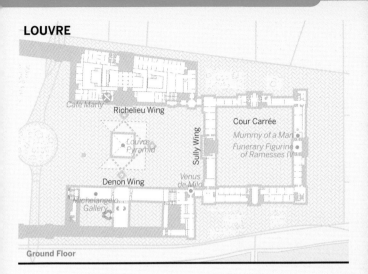

Café Marly

Richelieu Wing

Cour Carrée

Louvre Pyramid

Sully Wing

Mummy of a Man

Funerary Figurine of Ramesses IV

Denon Wing

Venus de Milo

Michelangelo Gallery

Ground Floor

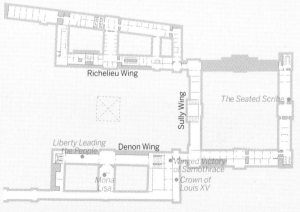

Richelieu Wing

Sully Wing

The Seated Scribe

Liberty Leading the People

Denon Wing

Winged Victory of Samothrace

Mona Lisa

Crown of Louis XV

First Floor

Local Life
The Spirit of Les Halles

In 1137 Louis VI created *halles* (markets) for merchants who converged on the city centre to sell their wares, and for over 800 years they were, in the words of Émile Zola, the 'belly of Paris'. Although the wholesalers moved out to the suburb of Rungis in 1971, the markets' spirit lives on in legacies and local treasures here.

❶ Cookware Shopping
Paris' professional chefs still come to this neighbourhood to stock up on knives, whisks, sieves, slicers, ladles, grinders, pastry moulds, pots, pans, chopping blocks, Champagne buckets, duck presses and more at venerable cookware shops, including the 1820-established **E Dehillerin** (www.e-dehillerin.fr; 18-20 rue Coquillière, 1er; ⏰9am-12.30pm & 2-6pm Mon, 9am-6pm Tue-Sat; Ⓜ Les Halles).

2 Cookbook Shopping

There are more esteemed cookware shops on rue Montmartre, as well as Paris' leading food bookshop **Librairie Gourmande** (www.librairie-gourmande.fr; 92 rue Montmartre, 1er; ⊙11am-7pm Mon-Sat; Ⓜ Sentier) – a perfect place to pick up inspiration. All the classic texts are here, along with cutting-edge collections and cocktail recipe books.

3 Oyster Market Legacy

A splinter of the historic *halles,* pedestrianised rue Montorgueil was its oyster market. The remaining legacy of its original incarnation is the 19th-century timber-lined restaurant **Au Rocher de Cancale** (☑01 42 33 50 29; www.aurocherdecancale.fr; 78 rue Montorgueil, 2e; dozen oysters €19, seafood platter €30; ⊙8am-2am daily; Ⓜ Sentier or Les Halles). At this memorable restaurant, virtually unchanged, you can feast on oysters and seafood from Cancale (Brittany).

4 Picturesque Patisserie

Opened in 1730 the beautiful pastel murals at **Stohrer** (www.stohrer.fr; 51 rue Montorgueil, 2e; ⊙7.30am-8.30pm daily; Ⓜ Étienne Marcel or Sentier) were added in 1864 by Paul Baudry, who also decorated the Palais Garnier's Grand Foyer. Specialities invented here

include *baba au rhum* (rum-drenched brioche) and *puit d'amour* (cream-filled, caramel-topped puff pastry).

5 Gourmet Goods Shopping

If the foie gras, truffles, caviar and other delicacies at the 1894 *épicerie* (specialist grocer) **Comptoir de la Gastronomie** (www.comptoirdelagastronomie.com; 34 rue Montmartre, 1er; ⊙6am-8pm Mon-Sat; Ⓜ Les Halles) tantalise, you can enjoy them at its adjacent restaurant.

6 Apéro at Le Cochon à l'Oreille

A Parisian jewel, the heritage-listed hole-in-the-wall **Le Cochon à l'Oreille** (☑01 42 36 07 56; 15 rue Montmartre, 1er; ⊙10am-2am Tue-Sat; Ⓜ Les Halles) retains laid tiles from the 1890s, depicting vibrant market scenes of the old *halles*. Hours can vary.

7 Late-Night Dinner at Le Tambour

Salvaged street furniture and old metro maps make the good-natured bistro and bar **Le Tambour** (☑01 42 33 06 90; 41 rue Montmartre, 2e; ⊙8.30am-6am; Ⓜ Étienne Marcel or Sentier) a shrine to the soul of Paris and a mecca for Parisian night owls, with food served until 3.30am or 4am.

A

Bd Haussmann

Sq Louis XVI

R des Mathurins

Bd Malesherbes

R de l'Arcade

R d'Anjou

8e

R de Surène

R du Faubourg St-Honoré

Av Gabriel

R Royale

R Tronchet

R Vignon

R de Séze

7 🟡

La Pinacothèque

Église de la Madeleine

4 ⊙

Pl de la Madeleine

Madeleine Ⓜ

R Duphot

R Cambon

B

Havre Caumartin

Ⓜ 🟡 37

R Auber

PI Diaghilev

36 🔴

Palais Garnier

10 ⊙

Nouveau Musée du Parfum

Bd des Capucines

R des Capucines

R de la Paix

C

R de Mogador

R de la Chaussée d'Antin

Auber Ⓜ

R Scribe

R Gluck

PI Ch Garnier

PI de l'Opéra

R Daunou

R Danielle Casanova

PI Vendôme

D

R de Provence

9e

R La Fayette

32 🔴

Chaussée d'Antin

PI J Rouché

6 ⭐
26 ⭐

Opéra
Ⓜ

Bd des Italiens

R du Quatre Septembre

Quatre Septembre

Av de l'Opéra

R du Helder

R Ste-Anne

R Gaillon

1

2

Av Gabriel

Place de la Concorde

Concorde Ⓜ

Ⓜ

3 ⊙
Jeu de Paume

Musée de l'Orangerie

2 ⊙

Pont de la Concorde

3 Av des Champs-Élysées

5 ⊙

4

R du Mont Thabor

R d'Alger

R du Mont Thabor

Pyramides Ⓜ

Paris Convention & Visitors Bureau 🟡

35 🔴

R St-Roch

R du Faubourg St-Honoré

Tuileries Ⓜ

R de Rivoli

1 ⊙
Jardin des Tuileries

R de Richelieu

R Thérèse

R Villedo

28 ⭐

Palais Royal – Musée du Louvre Ⓜ

Jardin du Carrousel

Av du Général Lemonnier

Cour Napoléon

Musée du Louvre

Q des Tuileries

Assemblée Nationale

Pont de la Concorde

5 Musée d'Orsay

7e

Q Anatole France

Musée d'Orsay

R du Bac

Q des Tuileries

Seine

Pont Royal

Q Voltaire

Pont du Carrousel

For reviews see

⊙	Top Sights	p50
⊙	Sights	p60
✖	Eating	p62
🍷	Drinking	p65
★	Entertainment	p66
🔒	Shopping	p68

E

F

G

H

R Laffitte
R le Peletier
R Rossini
R Drouot
R du Faubourg Montmartre
R du Faubourg Poissonnière

R du Faubourg Poissonnière

R Richer

12

10e

1

0   200 m
0   0.1 miles

Bd Haussmann

R de Montyon
R de Trévise
R Bergère

14

Passage des
Panoramas

Cité Bergère

27

R d'Hauteville

R de l'Échiquier

R du Faubourg St-Denis

Richelieu-
Drouot

Grands
Boulevards

18

Bd Poissonnière

Bonne
Nouvelle

30

Bd de Bonne Nouvelle

Strasbourg
St-Denis

2

R Favart

R de Richelieu

R St-Marc

R Feydeau

R Montmartre

R des Jeûneurs

R de la Lune

R Poissonnière

R de Clèry

R St-Augustin

16

La Bourse

Bourse

2e

25

R de Réaumur

22

R du Nil

11

R d'Aboukir

R de Clèry

R d'Aboukir

R du Caire

3

R Vivienne

R de la Banque

Sentier

R du Mail

R d'Aboukir

R Léopold Bellan

R St-Sauveur

Réaumur
Sébastopol

33

Pl des
Petits
Pères

R d'Argout

R Montmartre

R Mandar

R Greneta

R St-Denis

Bd de Sébastopol

R de Turbigo

R des Petits Champs
R de Beaujolais

Pyramides

19

31

9

Jardin du
Palais Royal

Pl des
Victoires

RIGHT
BANK

R Étienne Marcel

Hôtel des
Postes

R Tiquetonne

34

21

Étienne
Marcel

3e

R Beaubourg

Banque
de France

R Coquillière

R du Jour

Église
St-Eustache

R Mondétour

R St-Martin

Palais
Royal

Pl Colette

R de Valois

R du Colonel
Driant

R St-Honoré

Pl des
Deux-Écus

8

Les Halles

17

R Rambuteau

Pl Georges
Pompidou

Rambuteau

Pl du
Palais
Royal

1er

R Croix des
Petits Champs

Pl René
Cassin

29

Châtelet –
Les Halles

R Berger

R Pierre Lescot

Centre
Pompidou

Jardin de
l'Oratoire

Musée du
Louvre

13

23

15

Pl M
Quentin

Pl M de
Navarre

Pl E
Michelet

4e

R du Renard

R du Temple

Cour
Carrée

Pl du
Louvre

R Sauval

R des
Prauvaires

R des
Halles

Châtelet

R des Lombards

Jardin de
l'Infante

Q du Louvre

Pont
Neuf

R de l'Arbre Sec

R du Pont Neuf

R de Rivoli

Châtelet

5

Pont des Arts

Pont
Neuf

Sights

Jardin des Tuileries PARK

1 Map p58, B4

Filled with fountains, ponds and sculptures, the formal, 28-hectare Tuileries Garden, which begins just west of the Jardin du Carrousel, was laid out in its present form in 1664 by André Le Nôtre, who also created the gardens at Vaux-le-Vicomte and Versailles. The Tuileries soon became the most fashionable spot in Paris for parading about in one's finery. It now forms part of the Banks of the Seine Unesco World Heritage Site. (⏰7am-11pm Jun-Aug, shorter hours Sep-May; MTuileries, Concorde)

Musée de l'Orangerie MUSEUM

2 Map p58, A4

Located in the southwestern corner of the Jardin des Tuileries, this museum, with the Jeu de Paume, is all that remains of the former Palais des Tuileries, which was razed during the Paris Commune in 1871. It exhibits important impressionist works, including a series of Monet's *Decorations des Nymphéas* (Water Lilies) in two huge oval rooms purpose-built in 1927 on the artist's instructions, as well as works by Cézanne, Matisse, Picasso, Renoir, Sisley, Soutine and Utrillo. An audioguide costs €5. (☏01 44 77 80 07; www.musee-orangerie.fr; Jardin des Tuileries, 1er; adult/child €9/free; ⏰9am-6pm Wed-Mon; MConcorde)

Jeu de Paume GALLERY

3 Map p58, B3

The Galerie du Jeu de Paume, which stages innovative photography exhibitions, is housed in an erstwhile *jeu de paume* (royal tennis court) in the northwestern corner of the Jardin des Tuileries. (☏01 47 03 12 50; www.jeudepaume.org; 1 place de la Concorde, 8e; adult/child €10/free; ⏰11am-9pm Tue, to 7pm Wed-Sun; MConcorde)

Église de la Madeleine CHURCH

4 Map p58, B2

Place de la Madeleine is named after the 19th-century neoclassical church at its centre, the Église de la Madeleine. Constructed in the style of a massive Greek temple, 'La Madeleine' was consecrated in 1842 after almost a century of design changes and construction delays.The church is a popular venue for classical-music concerts (some free); check the posters outside or the website for dates. (Church of St Mary Magdalene; www.eglise-lamadeleine.com; place de la Madeleine, 8e; ⏰9.30am-7pm; MMadeleine)

Place de la Concorde SQUARE

5 Map p58, A3

Paris spreads around you, with views of the Eiffel Tower, the Seine and along the Champs-Élysées, when you stand in the city's largest square. Its 3300-year-old pink granite obelisk was a gift from Egypt in 1831. The square was first laid out in 1755 and originally named after

King Louis XV, but its royal associations meant that it took centre stage during the Revolution – Louis XVI was the first to be guillotined here in 1793. (8e; M Concorde)

Palais Garnier   OPERA HOUSE

6 ⊙ Map p58, C1

Palais Garnier interior

The fabled 'phantom of the opera' lurked in this opulent opera house designed in 1860 by Charles Garnier (then an unknown 35-year-old architect). Reserve a spot on an English-language guided tour or take an unguided tour of the attached museum, with posters, costumes, backdrops, original scores and other memorabilia, which includes a behind-the-scenes peek (except during matinees and rehearsals). Highlights include the Grand Staircase and horseshoe-shaped, gilded auditorium with red velvet seats, a massive chandelier and Chagall's gorgeous ceiling mural. (☏ 08 25 05 44 05; www.operadeparis.fr; cnr rues Scribe & Auber, 9e; adult/child unguided tour €11/7, guided tour €15.50/11; ⏰ unguided tour 10am-5pm, to 1pm on matinee performance days, guided tour by reservation; M Opéra)

La Pinacothèque   ART MUSEUM

7 ⊙ Map p58, B2

The top private museum in Paris, La Pinacothèque organises three to four major exhibits per year. Its nonlinear approach to art history, with exhibits that range from Mayan masks to retrospectives covering the work of artists such as Edvard Munch, has shaken up the otherwise rigid Paris art world and won over residents used to more formal presentations. (www.pinacotheque.com; 28 place de la Madeleine, 8e; adult/child from €13/free; ⏰ 10.30am-6.30pm Sat-Tue & Thu, to 8.30pm Wed & Fri; M Madeleine)

Église St-Eustache   CHURCH

8 ⊙ Map p58, F4

Just north of the gardens snuggling up to the city's old marketplace, now the bustling Forum des Halles, is one of the most beautiful churches in Paris. Majestic, architecturally magnificent and musically outstanding, St-Eustache has made spirits soar for centuries. (www.st-eustache.org; 2 impasse St-Eustache, 1er; ⏰ 9.30am-7pm Mon-Fri, 9am-7pm Sat & Sun; M Les Halles)

Jardin du Palais Royal

GARDENS

9 Map p58, E3

The Jardin du Palais Royal is a perfect spot to sit, contemplate and picnic between boxed hedges, or shop in the trio of arcades that frame the garden so beautifully: the Galerie de Valois (east), Galerie de Montpensier (west) and Galerie Beaujolais (north). However, it's the southern end of the complex, polka-dotted with sculptor Daniel Buren's 260 black-and-white striped columns, that has become the garden's signature feature. (2 place Colette, 1er; admission free; ⏰7am-10.15pm Apr-May, to 11pm Jun-Aug, shorter hours Sep-Mar; Ⓜ Palais Royal–Musée du Louvre)

Local Life
Forum des Halles

Paris' main wholesale food market stood here for nearly 800 years before being replaced by under-ground shopping mall **Forum des Halles** (www.forumdeshalles. com; 1 rue Pierre Lescot, 1er; ⏰shops 10am-8pm Mon-Sat; Ⓜ Châtelet–Les Halles) in 1971. Its eyesore exterior was demolished to make way for the new golden-hued translucent canopy, unveiled in 2016. Below, four floors of stores, cafes and a cinema extend down to Paris' busiest metro hub.

Nouveau Musée du Parfum

MUSEUM

10 Map p58, C1

If the art of perfume making entices, stop by Fragonard's Perfume Museum. The most recent addition to a trio of Paris locations, it has 30-minute guided tours (in multiple languages) walking visitors through the history of perfume making, the different layers of perfume composition and the ingenious processes of distilling a flower's fragrance. Tours finish in the shop, where you can test your nose on a few different scents. (☎01 40 06 10 09; www.nouveaumuseefragonard.com; 3-5 square de l'Opéra Louis Jouvet, 9e; admission free; ⏰9am-5pm Mon-Sat; Ⓜ Opéra or RER Auber)

Eating

Frenchie

BISTRO $$$

11 Map p58, G3

Tucked down an alley you wouldn't venture down otherwise, this *bijou* bistro with wooden tables and old stone walls is iconic. Frenchie is always packed and for good reason: excellent-value dishes are modern, market-driven and prepared with just the right dose of unpretentious creative flair by French chef Gregory Marchand. (☎01 40 39 96 19; www.frenchie-restaurant.com; 5-6 rue du Nil, 2e; prix-fixe menu €68; ⏰7-11pm Mon-Fri; Ⓜ Sentier)

Richer NEOBISTRO $$

 12 Map p58, G1

Run by the same team as across-the-street neighbour **L'Office**, Richer's pared-back, exposed-brick decor is a smart setting for genius creations like trout tartare with cauliflower and tomato and citrus mousse, and quince and lime cheesecake for dessert. It doesn't take reservations, but it serves up snacks and Chinese tea and has a full bar outside meal times. Fantastic value. (www.lericher.com; 2 rue Richer, 9e; mains €19-20; ☺8am-midnight; ⓜPoissonière, Bonne Nouvelle)

Yam'Tcha FUSION $$$

 13 Map p58, F5

Adeline Grattard's ingeniously fused French and Cantonese flavours (fried squid with sweet-potato noodles) has earned the female chef no shortage of critical praise. Pair dishes on the frequently changing menu with wine or tea, or indulge in the famous steamed buns *(bāozi)* over a pot of oolong at the **Boutique Yam'Tcha**. Reserve up to two months in advance. (☏01 40 26 08 07; www.yamtcha.com; 121 rue St Honoré, 1er; prix-fixe menu lunch/dinner €65/135; ☺noon-2.30pm Wed-Fri, 7.30-10.30pm Tue-Sat; ⓜLouvre Rivoli)

Floquifil TRADITIONAL FRENCH $$

14 Map p58, F1

If you were to envision the ultimate backstreet Parisian wine bar, it would probably look a lot like Floquifil: table-strewn terrace, dark timber furniture, aquamarine-painted walls and bottles galore. But while the by-the-glass wines are superb, you're missing out if you don't dine here (on rosemary-roasted lamb with ratatouille or at the very least a charcuterie platter). (☏01 42 46 11 19; www.floquifil.fr; 17 rue de Montyon, 9e; mains €14-20; ☺11am-midnight Mon-Fri, from 6pm Sat; ⓜGrands Boulevards)

La Tour de Montlhéry – Chez Denise TRADITIONAL FRENCH $$

 15 Map p58, F4

The most traditional eatery near the former Les Halles marketplace, this boisterous old bistro with red-chequered tablecloths has been run by the same team for 30-some years. If you've just arrived and are ready to feast on all the French classics – snails in garlic sauce, veal liver, steak tartare, braised beef cheeks and house-made pâtés – reservations are in order. Open till dawn. (☏01 42 36 21 82; 5 rue des Prouvaires, 1er; mains €23-28; ☺noon-2.30pm & 7.30pm-5am Mon-Fri; ⓜChâtelet)

A Noste REGIONAL FRENCH $$

 16 Map p58, E2

Pull up a stool at one of A Noste's communal tables and feast on original Gascon- and Basque-style tapas: from the airy cornmeal *fougasse* with smoked duck and goat cheese to the deep-fried *panisse* (chickpea flour) and chorizo nuggets. (☏01 47 03 91 91; www.a-noste.com; 6bis rue du Quatre Septembre, 2e; tapas €9-18, taloa sandwich €6.50; ☺noon-11pm; ⓜBourse)

Pirouette

NEOBISTRO $$$

17 ⊗ Map p58, G4

In one of the best restaurants in the vicinity of the old 'belly of Paris', chef Tomy Gousset's kitchen crew works wonders in this cool loftlike space, serving tantalising creations that range from seared duck, asparagus and Buddha's hand fruit to *baba au rhum* (sponge cake soaked in rum-flavoured syrup) with Chantilly and lime. Some unique ingredients and a new spin on French cuisine. (☎01 40 26 47 81; 5 rue Mondétour, 1er; lunch menu €20, 3-/6-course dinner menu €42/62; ⊗noon-2.30pm & 7.30-10.30pm Mon-Sat; ⓂLes Halles)

◯ Local Life
Gluten-Free Dining

Gluten-free kitchens are hard to find in France, but that's only one of the reasons that **Noglu** (☎01 40 26 41 24; www.noglu.fr; 16 Passage des Panoramas, 2e; mains €16-25; ⊗noon-3pm Mon-Sat, 7.30-10.30pm Tue-Sat; ☑; ⓂRichelieu-Drouot, Grands Boulevards) is such a jewel – this chic address builds on French tradition (bœuf bourguignon) while simultaneously drawing on newer culinary trends from across the Atlantic to create some devilishly good pastries, vegetarian plates, and superb pizzas and salads. Don't skip the chocolate-passion tart. Reserve.

Passage 53

MODERN FRENCH $$$

18 ⊗ Map p58, F2

No address inside Passage des Panoramas contrasts more dramatically with the outside hustle and bustle than this elegant restaurant at No 53. An oasis of calm and tranquillity (with window blinds pulled firmly down when closed), this gastronomic address is an ode to the best French produce – worked to perfection in a series of tasting courses by Japanese chef Shinichi Sato. Reserve. (☎01 42 33 04 35; www.passage53.com; 53 Passage des Panoramas, 2e; lunch/dinner menu €70/150; ⊗noon-2.30pm & 8-10.30pm Tue-Sat; ⓂGrands Boulevards, Bourse)

Le Grand Véfour

TRADITIONAL FRENCH $$$

19 ⊗ Map p58, E3

This 18th-century jewel on the northern edge of the Jardin du Palais Royal has been a dining favourite of the Parisian elite since 1784; just look at who gets their names ascribed to each table – from Napoléon and Victor Hugo to Colette (who lived next door). The food is tip-top; expect a voyage of discovery in one of the most beautiful restaurants in the world. (☎01 42 96 56 27; www.grand-vefour.com; 17 rue de Beaujolais, 1er; lunch/dinner menu €115/315; ⊗noon-2.30pm & 7.30-10.30pm Mon-Fri; ⓂPyramides)

Ellsworth

 MODERN AMERICAN $$

20 Map p58, E3

Casual cousin of the sleek **Verjus**, Ellsworth has carved out its own niche in the Parisian ecosystem with a delectable take on American faves: fried buttermilk chicken, braised pork with corn bread, kale salad and possibly the best Brussels sprouts you'll ever taste – roasted with beer, harissa and *buerre noisette* (brown butter). Full lunch menu; small plates for dinner. Reserve. (☎01 42 60 59 66; www.ellsworthparis.com; 34 rue de Richelieu, 1er; 2-/3-course lunch menu €20/26, mains €11-15; ⏱12.30-2.30pm Tue-Sat, 7-10.30pm Mon-Sat, 11.30am-3pm Sun; Ⓜ Pyramides)

Le Grand Véfour

Drinking

Experimental Cocktail Club

COCKTAIL BAR

21 Map p58, G3

Called ECC by trendies, this fabulous speakeasy with a black curtain for a façade and an old-beamed ceiling is effortlessly hip. Oozing spirit and soul, the cocktail bar – with retro-chic decor by American interior designer Cuoco Black and sister bars in London and New York – is a sophisticated flashback to those *années folles* (crazy years) of Prohibition New York. (37 rue St-Saveur, 2e; ⏱7pm-2am; Ⓜ Réaumur-Sébastopol)

Lockwood

CAFE

22 Map p58, G3

A happening address for hip coffee lovers. Savour beans from the Belleville Brûlerie during the day, brunch on weekends and well-mixed cocktails in the subterranean candle-lit *cave* at night. (☎01 77 32 97 21; 73 rue d'Aboukir, 2e; ⏱8am-2am Mon-Sat, 10am-4pm Sun; Ⓜ Sentier)

Le Garde Robe

WINE BAR

23 Map p58, F5

Le Garde Robe is possibly the only bar in the world to serve alcohol alongside a detox menu. While you probably

Local Life

Paris' Best Hot Chocolate

Clink china with lunching ladies, their posturing poodles and half the students from Tokyo University at **Angelina** (226 rue de Rivoli, 1er; ⏱8am-7pm Mon-Fri, 9am-7pm Sat & Sun; Ⓜ Tuileries), a *grande dame* of a tearoom dating to 1903. Delectable pastries are served here, but it's the super-thick, decadently sickening 'African' hot chocolate (€8.20), which comes with a pot of whipped cream and a carafe of water, that prompts the constant queue for a table.

shouldn't come here for the full-on cleansing experience, you can definitely expect excellent, affordable natural wines, a casual atmosphere and a good selection of eats, ranging from the standard cheese and charcuterie plates to more adventurous veg-friendly options. (☏01 49 26 90 60; 41 rue de l'Arbre Sec, 1er; ⏱12.30-2.30pm Mon-Fri, 6.30-midnight Mon-Sat; Ⓜ Louvre Rivoli)

Harry's New York Bar   COCKTAIL BAR

24 🚇 Map p58, C2

One of the most popular American-style bars in the prewar years, Harry's once welcomed writers like F Scott Fitzgerald and Ernest Hemingway, who sampled the bar's unique cocktail and creation: the Bloody Mary. The mahogany interior dates from the mid-19th century and was brought over from a Manhattan bar in 1911. (☏01 42 61 71 14; 5 rue Daunou, 2e; ⏱noon-2am; Ⓜ Opéra)

Social Club   CLUB

25 🚇 Map p58, F2

These subterranean cube-themed rooms presenting electro, hip-hop, funk and live acts are a magnet for young clubbers who take their music seriously. Thursdays showcase local DJs; Fridays are gay nights. (www.parissocialclub.com; 142 rue Montmartre, 2e; ⏱11pm-6am Thu-Sat; Ⓜ Bourse)

Le Rex Club   CLUB

Attached to the art deco Grand Rex cinema (see 30 ⭐ Map p58, G2), this is Paris' premier house and techno venue where some of the world's hottest DJs strut their stuff on a 70-speaker, multi-diffusion sound system. (www.rexclub.com; 5 bd Poissonnière, 2e; ⏱midnight-7am Thu-Sat; Ⓜ Bonne Nouvelle)

Entertainment

Palais Garnier   OPERA, BALLET

26 ⭐ Map p58, C1

The city's original opera house is smaller than its Bastille counterpart, but has perfect acoustics. Due to its odd shape, some seats have limited or no visibility – book carefully. The **box office** (cnr rues Scribe & Auber; ⏱11am-6.30pm Mon-Sat; Ⓜ Opéra) has information about ticket prices and conditions (including last-minute discounts). (☏08 92 89 90 90; www.operadeparis.fr; place de l'Opéra, 9e; Ⓜ Opéra)

Au Limonaire
LIVE MUSIC

27 Map p58, F1

This perfect little wine bar is one of the best places to listen to traditional French *chansons* and local singer-songwriters. Performances begin at 10pm Tuesday to Saturday and 7pm on Sunday. Entry is free; reservations are recommended if you plan on dining. (☎ 01 45 23 33 33; http://limonaire.free.fr; 18 cité Bergère, 9e; ⏱ 6pm-2am Tue-Sat, from 7pm Sun & Mon; M Grands Boulevards)

Comédie Française
THEATRE

28 Map p58, D4

Founded in 1680 under Louis XIV, this state-run theatre bases its repertoire around the works of classic French playwrights. The theatre has its roots in an earlier company directed by Molière at the Palais Royal. (www.comedie-francaise.fr; place Colette, 1er; M Palais Royal–Musée du Louvre)

Forum des Images
CINEMA

29 Map p58, F4

Cinemas showing films set in Paris are the centrepiece of the city's film archive. Created in 1988 to establish 'an audiovisual memory bank of Paris', and renovated in dramatic shades of pink, grey and black, the five-screen centre has a library and research centre with newsreels, documentaries and advertising. (www.forumdesimages.fr; 1 Grande Galerie, Porte St-Eustache, Forum des Halles, 1er; ⏱ 1-9pm Tue-Fri, from 2pm Sat & Sun; M Les Halles)

Le Grand Rex
CINEMA

30 Map p58, G2

A trip to 1932 art deco cinematic icon Le Grand Rex is like no other trip to the flicks. Screenings aside, the cinema runs 50-minute behind-the-scene tours (English soundtracks available) during which visitors – tracked by a sensor slung around their neck – are whisked up (via a lift) behind the giant screen, tour a soundstage and get to have fun in a recording studio. (www.legrandrex.com; 1 bd Poissonnière, 2e; tours adult/child €11/9; ⏱ tours 10am-6pm Tue-Sun, 2-6pm Mon; M Bonne Nouvelle)

○ Local Life
Rue des Lombards

Rue des Lombards is the street to swing by for live jazz.

Le Baiser Salé (☎ 01 42 33 37 71; www.lebaisersale.com; 58 rue des Lombards, 1er; ⏱ daily; M Châtelet) is known for its Afro and Latin jazz, and jazz fusion concerts, the Salty Kiss combines big names and unknown artists. The place has a relaxed vibe, with sets usually starting at 7.30pm or 9.30pm.

You'll find two venues in one at trendy, well-respected **Sunset & Sunside** (☎ 01 40 26 46 60; www.sunset-sunside.com; 60 rue des Lombards, 1er; ⏱ daily; M Châtelet): electric jazz, fusion and the odd salsa session downstairs; acoustics and concerts upstairs.

Shopping

Didier Ludot FASHION & ACCESSORIES

31 Map p58, E3

In the rag trade since 1975, collector Didier Ludot sells the city's finest couture creations of yesteryear in his exclusive twinset of boutiques, hosts exhibitions and has published a book portraying the evolution of the little black dress. (☎ 01 42 96 06 56; www.didierludot.fr; 19-23 & 23-24 Galerie de Montpensier, 1er; ☉ 10.30am-7pm Mon-Sat; M Palais Royal–Musée du Louvre)

Galeries Lafayette DEPARTMENT STORE

32 Map p58, D1

Grande dame department store Galeries Lafayette is spread across the main store (whose magnificent stained-glass dome is over a century old), men's store and homewares store, and includes a gourmet emporium.Catch modern art in the 1st-floor **gallery** (www.galeriedesgaleries.com; admission free; ☉ 11am-7pm Tue-Sat), take in a **fashion show** (☎ bookings 01 42 82 30 25; ☉ 3pm Fri Mar-Jun & Sep-Dec by reservation), ascend to a free, windswept rooftop panorama, or take a break at one of its 24 restaurants and cafes. (http://haussmann.galerieslafayette.com; 40 bd Haussmann, 9e; ☉ 9.30am-8pm Mon-Sat, to 9pm Thu; ☎; M Chaussée d'Antin or RER Auber)

Legrand Filles & Fils FOOD & DRINKS

33 Map p58, E3

Tucked inside Galerie Vivienne since 1880, Legrand sells fine wine and all the accoutrements: corkscrews, tasting glasses, decanters etc. It also has a fancy wine bar, *école du vin* (wine school) and *éspace dégustation* (tasting room) with several tastings a month; check its website for details. (www.caves-legrand.com; 1 rue de la Banque, 2e; ☉ 10am-7.30pm Tue-Sat, 11am-7pm Sun; M Pyramides)

Local Life

Place de la Madeleine

Ultragourmet food shops garland **place de la Madeleine** (place de la Madeleine, 8e; M Madeleine); many have in-house dining options too. Notable names include truffle dealers **La Maison de la Truffe** (☎ 01 42 65 53 22; www.maison-de-la-truffe.com; 19 place de la Madeleine, 8e; ☉ 10am-10pm Mon-Sat; M Madeleine); luxury food shop **Hédiard** (www.hediard.fr; 21 place de la Madeleine, 8e; ☉ 9am-8pm Mon-Sat; M Madeleine); mustard specialist **Boutique Maille** (☎ 01 40 15 06 00; www.maille.com; 6 place de la Madeleine, 8e; ☉ 10am-7pm Mon-Sat; M Madeleine); and Paris' most famous caterer, **Fauchon** (☎ 01 70 39 38 00; www.fauchon.fr; 26 & 30 place de la Madeleine, 8e; ☉ 10am-8.30pm Mon-Sat; M Madeleine), selling incredibly mouth-watering delicacies, from foie gras to jams, chocolates and pastries. Check out the extravagant chocolate sculptures at **Patrick Roger** (www.patrickroger.com; 3 place de la Madeleine; ☉ 10.30am-7.30pm; M Madeleine).

Kiliwatch

FASHION & ACCESSORIES

34 Map p58, F3

A Parisian institution, Kiliwatch gets jam-packed with hip guys and gals rummaging through racks of new and used streetwear. Startling vintage range of hats and boots plus art and photography books, eyewear and the latest sneakers. (01 42 21 17 37; http://espacekiliwatch.fr; 64 rue Tiquetonne, 2e; 10.30am-7pm Mon, to 7.30pm Tue-Sat; Étienne Marcel)

Colette

CONCEPT STORE

35 Map p58, C3

Uber-hip is an understatement. Ogle designer fashion on the 1st floor, and streetwear, limited-edition sneakers, art books, music, gadgets and other high-tech, inventive and/or plain unusual items on the ground floor. End with a drink in the basement 'water bar' and pick up free design magazines and flyers for some of the city's hippest happenings by the door upon leaving. (www.colette.fr; 213 rue St-Honoré, 1er; 11am-7pm Mon-Sat; Tuileries)

La Maison du Miel

FOOD & DRINKS

36 Map p58, B1

In this sticky, very sweet business since 1898, 'the Honey House' stocks more than 50 kinds of honey, with such flavours as Corsican chestnut flower, Turkish pine and Tasmanian leatherwood. (01 47 42 26 70; www.maisondumiel.com; 24 rue Vignon, 9e; 9.30am-7pm Mon-Sat; Madeleine)

Galeries Lafayette

Le Printemps

DEPARTMENT STORE

37 Map p58, C1

Famous department store Le Printemps encompasses Le Printemps de la Mode (women's fashion) and Le Printemps de l'Homme (men's fashion; located on nearby rue de Provence), both with established and up-and-coming designer wear, and Le Printemps de la Beauté et Maison (beauty and homewares), offering a staggering display of perfume, cosmetics and accessories. There's a free panoramic rooftop terrace and luxury eateries, including Ladurée. (www.printemps.com; 64 bd Haussmann, 9e; 9.35am-8pm Mon-Wed & Fri-Sat, to 8.45pm Thu; ; Havre Caumartin)

ROGER COULAM/GETTY IMAGES ©

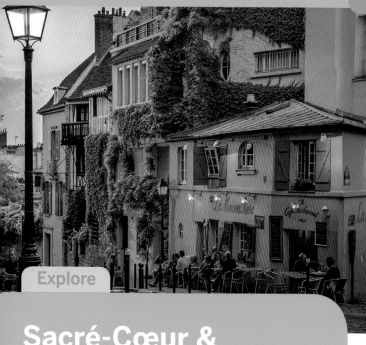

Explore

Sacré-Cœur & Montmartre

Montmartre's slinking streets, lined with crooked ivy-clad buildings, retain a fairy-tale charm, despite the area's popularity. Crowned by the Sacré-Cœur basilica, Montmartre is the city's steepest quarter (*mont* means hill; the martyr was St Denis, beheaded here in about AD 250). The lofty views, wine-producing vines and hidden village squares have lured painters since the 19th century.

The Sights in a Day

☼ Montmartre makes for an enchanting stroll, especially early morning when tourists are few. Start at the top of the Butte de Montmartre at the striking **Sacré-Cœur** (p72) basilica for exceptional views (particularly from inside its dome), then drop by the **Espace Dalí** (p77).

☼ After lunch at **Jeanne B** (p78), wander through the peaceful **Cimetière de Montmartre** (p77), before visiting one of Paris' loveliest small museums, the **Musée de la Vie Romantique** (p77), dedicated to author George Sand. For a romantic museum of an altogether different kind, you might want to check out the **Musée de l'Érotisme** (p78) in Montmartre's southern neighbour, Pigalle – a (tame) red-light district fast becoming better known for its foodie scene. Follow it up with an *apéro* (predinner drink) at **La Fourmi** (p82).

☽ Continue down rue des Martyrs to neighbourhood bistro **Le Miroir** (p80) for dinner, then catch a cabaret at the **Moulin Rouge** (p82) or a concert at **La Cigale** (p82).

For a local's day in Montmartre, see p74.

 Top Sights

Sacré-Cœur (p72)

 Local Life

Art in Montmartre (p74)

 Best of Paris

Museums
Espace Dalí (p77)

Eating
Le Pantruche (p78)

Le Miroir (p80)

Drinking
Le Progrès (p80)

Fashion
Maison Kitsuné (p83)

Nights Out
Moulin Rouge (p82)

Au Lapin Agile (p75)

Getting There

Ⓜ **Metro** Anvers (line 2) is the most convenient for Sacré-Cœur and its funicular.

Ⓜ **Metro** Abbesses and Lamarck-Caulaincourt (line 12) are in Montmartre's heart.

Ⓜ **Metro** Blanche and Pigalle (line 2) are your best bet for the restaurants and nightlife around Pigalle.

Top Sights
Sacré-Cœur

Visible from across the city, the dove-white domes of the Basilique du Sacré-Cœur (Sacred Heart Basilica) crown the 130m-high Butte de Montmartre (Montmartre Hill). The basilica's travertine stone exudes calcite, ensuring that it remains white despite weathering and pollution, while its lofty vantage point offers dizzying Parisian vistas from its steep surrounding streets, steps, and above all, its main dome.

◉ Map p76, D2

place du Parvis du Sacré-Cœur

dome adult/child €6/4, cash only

⊙ 6am-10.30pm, dome 8.30am-8pm May-Sep, to 5pm Oct-Apr

Ⓜ Anvers

History
Initiated in 1873 to atone for the bloodshed and controversy during the Franco-Prussian War (1870–71), designed by architect Paul Abadie and begun in 1875, the Roman-Byzantine basilica was funded largely by private, often small, donations. It was completed in 1914 but wasn't consecrated until after WWI in 1919.

Blessed Sacrament
In a sense atonement here has never stopped: a prayer 'cycle' that began in 1835 continues around the clock, with perpetual adoration of the Blessed Sacrament that's on display above the high altar.

The Dome
The sublime views from Sacré-Cœur get even better when you climb the 234 steps spiralling inside its 83m-high main dome. From here, you can see up to 30km on a clear day.

The Crypt
In conjunction with the dome, for an extra €2 you can visit the enormous chapel-lined crypt.

France's Largest Bell
'La Savoyarde' in the basilica's huge square bell tower is the largest in France, weighing in at 19 tonnes. It can be heard ringing out across the neighbourhood and beyond.

The Christ in Majesty Mosaic
The magnificent apse mosaic *Christ in Majesty*, designed by Luc-Olivier Merson in 1922, is one of the largest of its kind in the world. Its golden hues lighten Sacré-Cœur's otherwise dark interior.

☑ Top Tips
▶ Avoid most of the climb up to the basilica with the short but useful **Funicular de Montmartre** (place St-Pierre, 18e; ⊙6am-12.45am; M Anvers, Abbesses); use a regular metro ticket and watch for pickpockets on board.

▶ For the best views, pick a blue-sky day to visit; don't even consider climbing to the top of the dome in bad weather.

▶ Try to visit early morning or at sunset when seasonal crowds are a little thinner.

✕ Take a Break
In fine weather head to **L'Été en Pente Douce** (☎01 42 64 02 67; 23 rue Muller, 18e; mains €10.30-18.30; ⊙noon-midnight; M Anvers) for classic French fare and jumbo salads on a dreamy pavement terrace with green-lawn view.

Local Life
Art in Montmartre

For centuries Montmartre was a bucolic country village filled with *moulins* (mills) that supplied Paris with flour. Incorporated into the capital in 1860, its picturesque – and affordable – charm attracted painters including Manet, Degas, Renoir, Van Gogh, Toulouse-Lautrec, Dufy, Picasso, Utrillo, Modigliani and Dalí in its late 19th- and early 20th-century heyday. Although much frequented by tourists, its local village atmosphere endures.

1 Amélie's Cafe
Start with a coffee at this arty cafe, where Amélie worked as a waitress in the quirky film of the same name. **Café des Deux Moulins** (15 rue Lepic, 18e; ⏱8am-1am; Ⓜ Blanche) hangs on as a down-to-earth local where you can watch Montmartre go by.

2 Van Gogh's House
Théo Van Gogh owned the house at **54 rue Lepic**; his brother, the artist

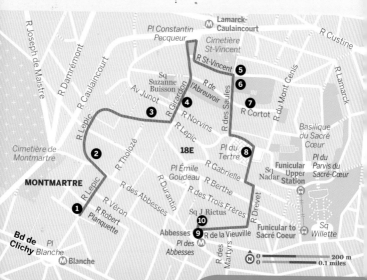

Vincent, stayed with him on the 3rd floor for two years from 1886.

❸ Renoir's Dance Hall

Montmartre's two surviving wind-mills are the **Moulin Blute-Fin** and, 100m east, the **Moulin Radet** (now a restaurant). In the 19th century, the windmills were turned into the open-air dance hall Le Moulin de la Galette, immortalised by Renoir in his 1876 tableau *Le Bal du Moulin de la Galette* (now displayed in the Musée d'Orsay).

❹ Aymé's Walker Through Walls

Crossing place Marcel Aymé you'll see a man emerging from a stone wall. The **Passe-Muraille statue** portrays Dutilleul, the hero of Marcel Aymé's short story *Le Passe-Muraille* (The Walker Through Walls). Aymé lived in the adjacent building from 1902 to 1967.

❺ Gill's Rabbit

Look for caricaturist André Gill's mu-ral *Le Lapin à Gill*. It shows a rabbit jumping out of a cooking pot on the façade of long-running local cabaret **Au Lapin Agile** (📞01 46 06 85 87; www.au-lapin-agile.com; 22 rue des Saules, 18e; adult €28, student except Sat €20; ☺9pm-1am Tue-Sun; Ⓜ Lamarck-Caulaincourt).

❻ Montmartre's Vineyard

The only vineyard in central Paris, **Clos Montmartre** dates from 1933. Its 2000 vines produce on average 800 bottles of wine each October,

celebrated by the five-day Fête des Vendanges de Montmartre, with festivities including a parade.

❼ Local History Lessons

Local history comes to life through paintings and documents at the **Musée de Montmartre** (www.museede montmartre.fr; 12 rue Cortot, 18e; adult/child €9.50/5.50; ☺10am-6pm; Ⓜ Lamarck-Caulaincourt), housed in Montmartre's oldest building – a 17th-century garden-set manor where Renoir, Utrillo and Dufy once lived. The manor also houses Suzanne Valadon's restored studio, open to the public.

❽ Artists at Work

The main square of the original vil-lage, **place du Tertre** (Ⓜ Abbesses) has drawn countless painters in its time. While it's awash with visitors, local, often very talented, artists paint, sketch and sell their creations at stalls here, and the portraitists, buskers and crowds create an unmissable carnival-like atmosphere.

❾ The Art of Travel

With its original glass canopy and twin wrought-iron lamp posts il-luminating the dark-green-on-lemon-yellow *Metropolitain* sign still intact, Abbesses has the finest remaining example of art nouveau designer Hector Guimard's metro entrances.

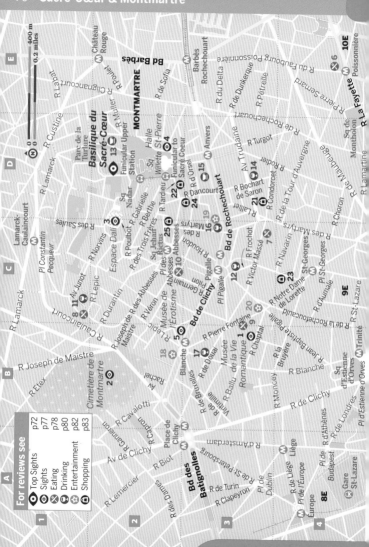

0
400 m
0
0.2 miles

Château Rouge

Bd Barbès

MONTMARTRE

Basilique du Sacré-Cœur

Parc de la Turlure

Lamarck-Caulaincourt

Cimetière de Montmartre

Place de Clichy

Bd des Batignolles

For reviews see
● Top Sights   p72
○ Sights   p77
✕ Eating   p78
✦ Drinking   p80
✿ Entertainment p82
✚ Shopping   p83

Sights

Musée de la Vie Romantique
MUSEUM

1 ⊙ Map p76, B3

This romantic mansion with green shutters and tangled garden sits in a cobbled courtyard at the end of a tree-shaded alley. Writer George Sand and painter Ary Scheffer lived here, and the objects exhibited create a wonderful flashback to Romantic-era Paris when Chopin (Sand's lover), Delacroix et al attended salons in the house. End your literary visit with tea and cake in the museum's enchanting garden cafe, open spring to autumn. (✆01 55 31 95 67; www.vie-romantique.paris.fr; 16 rue Chaptal, 9e; admission free; ⊙10am-6pm Tue-Sun; Ⓜ Blanche, St-Georges)

Cimetière de Montmartre
CEMETERY

2 ⊙ Map p76, B2

This 11-hectare cemetery opened in 1798. It contains the graves of writers Émile Zola (whose ashes are now in the Panthéon), Alexandre Dumas *fils* and Stendhal, composers Jacques Offenbach and Hector Berlioz, artist Edgar Degas, film director François Truffaut and dancer Vaslav Nijinsky, among others. Steps from the rue Caulaincourt road bridge lead down to the entrance on av Rachel, just off bd de Clichy. (2 av Rachel, 18e; ⊙8am-6pm Mon-Fri, 8.30am-6pm Sat, 9am-6pm Sun; Ⓜ Place de Clichy)

Garden cafe, Musée de la Vie Romantique

Espace Dalí
ART MUSEUM

3 ⊙ Map p76, C2

More than 300 works by Salvador Dalí (1904–89), the flamboyant Catalan surrealist printmaker, painter, sculptor and self-promoter, are on display at this surrealist-style basement museum located just west of place du Tertre. The collection includes Dalí's strange sculptures, lithographs, and many of his illustrations and furniture, including the famous Mae West lips sofa. (✆01 42 64 40 10; www.daliparis.com; 11 rue Poulbot, 18e; adult/child €11.50/6.50; ⊙10am-6pm, to 8pm Jul & Aug; Ⓜ Abbesses)

Halle St-Pierre
ART MUSEUM

4 Map p76, D2

Founded in 1986, this museum and gallery is in the lovely old covered St Peter's Market. It focuses on the primitive and Art Brut schools; there is no permanent collection, but the museum stages three temporary exhibitions a year. Auditorium, cafe and bookshop too. (www.hallesaintpierre.org; 2 rue Ronsard, 18e; adult/child €8/6.50; ⏱11am-6pm Mon-Fri, 11am-7pm Sat, noon-6pm Sun; MAnvers)

Musée de l'Érotisme
MUSEUM

5 Map p76, B2

The Museum of Erotic Art attempts to raise around 2000 titillating statuary, stimulating sexual aids and fetishist items to a loftier plane, with antique and modern erotic art from four continents spread out across five floors. (www.musee-erotisme.com; 72 bd de Clichy, 18e; adult/reduced €10/6; ⏱10am-2am; MBlanche)

Eating

Abri
NEOBISTRO $$

6 Map p76, E4

It's no bigger than a shoebox and the decor is borderline non-existent, but that's all part of the charm. Katsuaki Okiyama is a seriously talented chef with an artistic flair, and his surprise tasting menus (three courses at lunch, six at dinner) are exceptional. On Monday and Saturday, a giant gourmet sandwich is all that's served for lunch. Reserve well in advance. (☎01 83 97 00 00; 92 rue du Faubourg Poissonnière, 9e; lunch/dinner menus €26/46; ⏱12.30-2pm Mon, 12.30-2pm & 8-10pm Tue-Sat; MPoissonnière)

Le Pantruche
BISTRO $$

7 Map p76, C3

Named after a nearby 19th-century theatre, classy Pantruche woos foodies in the dining hot spot of south Pigalle with seasonal bistro fare, reasonable prices and an intimate setting. The menu runs from classics (steak with Béarnaise sauce) to more daring creations (scallops served in a Parmesan broth with cauliflower mousseline). Reserve well in advance. (☎01 48 78 55 60; www.lepantruche.com; 3 rue Victor Massé, 9e; menus €19 & €36; ⏱12.30-2.30pm & 7.30-10.30pm Mon-Fri; MPigalle)

Jeanne B
DELI $$

8 Map p76, C1

Choose among the homemade terrines, stuffed veggies, salads, meat pies or roasted lamb and chicken at this gourmet sit-down deli. There's no overwrought buzz about the place, and even if the menu feels pricey, the dishes don't disappoint. House speciality, *croq 'homard de Jeanne,* is a chunky lobster sandwich. Between meals drop in for morning coffee and cakes or an afternoon *goûter* (snack). (☎01 42 51 17 53; www.jeanne-b-comestibles.com; 61 rue Lepic, 18e; 2-/3-course lunch €19/24, dinner €25/29; ⏱9.30am-10.30pm; 🛜🚻; MAbbesses, Lamarck-Caulaincourt)

Understand
Belle Époque Paris

La Belle Époque saw creativity flourish from the advent of France's Third Republic in 1870.

This 'Beautiful Era' launched art nouveau architecture, a whole field of artistic 'isms' from impressionism onwards, and advances in science and engineering, including the first metro line (1900). World Exhibitions were held in the capital in 1889 (showcased by the Eiffel Tower) and again in 1900 (by the Grand Palais and Petit Palais).

The Paris of nightclubs and artistic cafes made its first appearance around this time, and Montmartre became a magnet for artists, writers, pimps and prostitutes, with artists such as Toulouse-Lautrec creating cabaret posters of the Moulin Rouge's cancan dancers.

Other glamorous hot spots still operating include the restaurant Maxim's, now with an art nouveau museum upstairs, and the newly renovated Ritz Paris. The Musée d'Orsay contains a wealth of artistic expression from this era, from paintings through to exquisite furniture.

This inspired time lasted until the onset of WWI in 1914 – it was named in retrospect, recalling a peaceful 'golden age'.

Le Garde Temps   MODERN FRENCH $$

9 Map p76, B3

The chalkboard menus at this contemporary bistro are framed and hung on the walls, and thankfully the promise of gastronomic art doesn't disappoint. Old bistro standards are swept away in favour of more imaginative creations (fondant of red cabbage with quail confit) and – here's where Le Garde Temps scores big points – dinner prices aren't much more than that ho-hum cafe down the street. (☑09 77 40 34 13; www.restaurant-legardetemps.fr; 19bis rue Pierre Fontaine, 9e; 2-/3-course menu €29/35; ⊙noon-2pm & 7-10.30pm Mon-Fri, 7-10.30pm Sat; Ⓜ Pigalle)

Chez Toinette   TRADITIONAL FRENCH $$

10 Map p76, C2

The atmosphere of this convivial restaurant is rivalled only by its fine cuisine (seared duck with honey, venison with foie gras). In the heart of one of the capital's most touristy neighbourhoods, Chez Toinette has kept alive the tradition of old Montmartre with its simplicity and culinary expertise. An excellent if touristy choice for a traditional French meal. (☑01 42 54 44 36; 20 rue Germain Pilon, 18e; mains €19-24; ⊙7-11.30pm Mon-Sat; Ⓜ Abbesses)

Drinking

Le Progrès
BAR

A real live *café du quartier* perched in the heart of Abbesses (see 24 Map p76, D3), the 'Progress' occupies a corner site with huge windows and simple seating and attracts a relaxed mix of local artists, shop staff, writers and hangers-on. It's great for convivial evenings, but it's also a good place to come for meals (mains €17.90

Local Life
Rue des Martyrs
Gourmet shops along foodie strip rue des Martyrs include *boulangerie* **Arnaud Delmontel** (www.arnaud-delmontel.com; 39 rue des Martyrs, 9e; baguette €1.15; ⏰7am-8.30pm Wed-Mon; MPigalle), known for its award-winning baguettes. For a sit-down meal, unassuming bistro **Le Miroir** (📞01 46 06 50 73; www.restaurantmiroir.com; 94 rue des Martyrs, 18e; lunch menu €19.50, dinner menus €35-46; ⏰noon-2pm & 7.30-10pm; MAbbesses) serves delightful pâtés and rillettes and well-prepared standards, and has its own wine shop across the street. Also here is the excellent cross-cultural venue **Le Divan du Monde** (📞01 40 05 06 99; www.divandumonde.com; 75 rue des Martyrs, 18e; ⏰variable; MPigalle), with cinematographic events, *nouvelles chansons françaises* (new French songs), soul/funk fiestas, air-guitar face-offs, rock parties and more.

to €20.50), coffee and well-priced cocktails (€9). (7 rue des Trois Frères, 18e; ⏰9am-2am; MAbbesses)

Le Très Particulier
COCKTAIL BAR

11 Map p76, C1

There is possibly no more enchanting spot for a summertime alfresco cocktail than Le Très Particulier, the utterly unique and clandestine cocktail bar of Hôtel Particulier Montmartre. Ring the buzzer at the unmarked black gated entrance to get in and make a beeline for the 1871 mansion's flowery walled garden bar with conservatory-style interior. DJs spin tunes from 10pm every Friday and Saturday. (📞01 53 41 81 40; www.hotel-particulier-montmartre.com; 23 av Junot, 18e, Pavillon D; ⏰6pm-2am Tue-Sun; MLamarck-Caulaincourt)

Lulu White
COCKTAIL BAR

12 Map p76, C3

Sip absinthe-based cocktails in Prohibition-era New Orleans surrounds at this elegant, serious and supremely busy cocktail bar on rue Frochot; several more line the same street making for a fabulous evening out. Should you be wondering, Lulu White was an infamous African American brothel owner in early 20th-century New Orleans. (www.luluwhite.bar; 12 rue Frochot, 9e; ⏰7pm-3am Mon-Sat; MPigalle)

Hardware Société
COFFEE

13 Map p76, D2

With its black-and-white floor, Christian Lacroix butterflies fluttering

Cimetière de Montmartre (p77)

across one wall and perfect love-heart-embossed cappuccinos, there's no finer spot around the Sacré-Cœur to linger over superb barista-crafted coffee (yes, that is a Slayer espresso machine). This is the Paris outpost of Melbourne's Hardware Société, with feisty breakfasts and brunches cooked up by Di and Will complementing the coffee. (☎01 42 51 69 03; 10 rue Lamarck, 18e; ☺9am-4.30pm Thu-Mon, kitchen 9am-3.30pm Thu-Mon; 🛜; ⓜChâteau Rouge, Lamarck-Caulaincourt)

Artisan   COCKTAIL BAR

14 📍 Map p76, D3

For a sophisticated drink in trendy SoPi (South Pigalle), white-walled Artisan fits the bill with delicious small plates, wines by the glass, well-mixed

shaken or stirred cocktails (€13), and formidable Hot Gin and Philadelphia Fish House punches to share. (☎01 48 74 65 38; www.artisan-bar.fr; 14 rue Bochart de Saron, 9e; ☺7pm-2am Tue-Sat; ⓜAnvers)

La Machine du Moulin Rouge   CLUB

Part of the original Moulin Rouge (well, the boiler room, anyway; see 18 ⚙ Map p76, B2), this club (admission €9 to €15) packs 'em in on weekends with a dance floor, concert hall, Champagne bar and outdoor terrace. Check the agenda online for weekday soirées and happenings. (www.lamachinedumoulinrouge. com; 90 bd de Clichy, 18e; ☺11pm-6am Fri & Sat, variable Sun-Thu; ⓜBlanche)

Le Petit Trianon

CAFE

15 Map p76, D3

With its large windows and a few carefully chosen antiques, this belle époque cafe at the foot of Montmartre seems as timeless as the Butte itself. Dating back to 1894 and attached to the century-old Le Trianon theatre, it's no stretch to imagine artists like Toulouse-Lautrec and crowds of show-goers once filling the place in the evening. Food all day too. (☑ 01 44 92 78 08; 80 bd de Rochechouart, 18e; ⏰ 8am-midnight; Ⓜ Anvers)

La Fourmi

BAR

16 Map p76, C3

A Pigalle institution, La Fourmi hits the mark with its high ceilings, long zinc bar and unpretentious vibe. Get up to speed on live music and club nights or sit down for a reasonably priced meal and drinks. (74 rue des Martyrs, 18e; ⏰ 8am-1am Mon-Thu, to 3am Fri & Sat, 10am-1am Sun; Ⓜ Pigalle)

Au P'tit Douai

BAR

17 Map p76, B3

This quirky cafe is just down the street from the Moulin Rouge. Trade in the tourist mayhem for a mellow moment over a coffee and newspaper, an excellent-value lunch (€10.50), cocktails or wine by the glass, while taking in the eclectic array of bric-a-brac decorating the place. Kids generally love the welly boots of felt-tip pens adorning some tables. (92 rue Blanche, 9e; ⏰ 8am-2am Sat, 11am-8pm Sun; ☎; Ⓜ Blanche)

Entertainment

Moulin Rouge

CABARET

18 Map p76, B2

Immortalised in the posters of Toulouse-Lautrec and later on screen by Baz Luhrmann, Paris' mythical cabaret club twinkles beneath a 1925 replica of its original red windmill. Yes, it's rife with bus-tour crowds. But from the opening bars of music to the last high cancan-girl kick, it's a whirl of fantastical costumes, sets, choreography and Champagne. (☑ 01 53 09 82 82; www.moulinrouge.fr; 82 bd de Clichy, 18e; show €105-130, dinner show from €190; ⏰ shows 9pm & 11pm summer, 9pm Sun-Thu, 9pm & 11pm Fri & Sat winter; Ⓜ Blanche)

La Cigale

LIVE MUSIC

19 Map p76, D3

Now classed as a historical monument, this music hall dates from 1887 but was redecorated 100 years later by Philippe Starck. Artists who have performed here recently include Rufus Wainwright, Ryan Adams and Ibrahim Maalouf. (☑ 01 49 25 89 99; www.lacigale.fr; 120 bd de Rochechouart, 18e; admission €25-75; Ⓜ Anvers, Pigalle)

Bus Palladium

LIVE MUSIC

20 Map p76, C3

Once the place to be in the 1960s, the Bus is now back in business 50 years later, with funky DJs and a mixed bag of performances by indie and pop groups. (www.lebuspalladium.com; 6 rue Pierre Fontaine, 9e; ⊘hours vary; Ⓜ Blanche)

Shopping

Maison Kitsuné FASHION & ACCESSORIES

21 🔒 Map p76, D3

Paris fashion label Kitsuné is the secret to looking effortlessly French. Shop here for ready-to-wear fashion, accessories and must-have everyday items for men and women. (www.shop.kitsune.fr; 68 rue Condorcet, 9e; ⊘1.30-7pm Mon-Sat, noon-6.30pm Sun; Ⓜ Pigalle)

Belle du Jour FASHION & ACCESSORIES

22 🔒 Map p76, D2

Be whisked back in time to the elegance of belle époque Paris with this sweet-smelling Montmartre shop specialising in perfume bottles. Gorgeous 19th-century atomisers, smelling salts and powder boxes in engraved or enamelled Bohemian, Baccarat and St-Louis crystal jostle for the limelight with more contemporary designs. Art deco or art nouveau, pink-frosted or painted glass, it's here. (www.belle-de-jour.fr; 7 rue Tardieu, 18e; ⊘10.30am-1pm & 2-7pm Tue-Fri, 10.30am-1pm & 2-6pm Sat; Ⓜ Anvers)

Pigalle FASHION & ACCESSORIES

23 🔒 Map p76, C4

Blend in with local hipsters with a hoodie emblazoned with the B&W

Pigalle logo from this leading Parisian menswear brand, created by wild-child designer and amateur basketball player Stéphane Ashpool, who grew up in the 'hood. (www.pigalle-paris.com; 7 rue Henry Monnier, 9e; ⊘noon-8pm Mon-Sat, 2-8pm Sun; Ⓜ Pigalle)

Jeremie Barthod JEWELLERY

24 🔒 Map p76, D3

Fantasy necklaces, bracelets and other jewellery pieces are crafted from metal springs dipped in antique silver, bronze or copper at this hybrid boutique-*atelier* (workshop) in Montmartre. (www.jeremiebarthod.com; 7 rue des Trois Frères, 18e; ⊘11.15am-7.15pm; Ⓜ Abbesses)

Spree FASHION & ACCESSORIES

25 🔒 Map p76, C2

Sift through Montmartre's tourist shops to find this super-stylish boutique-gallery, with a carefully curated collection of vintage fashion (1950s to 1980s) put together by Paris stylist Roberta Oprandi. What makes shopping here fun is that all the furniture – several lovely 1950s and 1960s pieces by Eames et al – is also for sale, as is the contemporary artwork on the walls. (☎01 42 23 41 40; www.spree.fr; 16 rue de la Vieuville, 18e; ⊘11am-7.30pm Tue-Sat, 3-7pm Mon & Sun; Ⓜ Abbesses)

Local Life
Exploring the Canal St-Martin

Getting There

Canal St-Martin is about 4km north of Notre Dame.

Ⓜ **Metro** République (lines 3, 5, 8, 9 and 11) is centrally located.

Ⓜ **Metro** Château d'Eau, Jacques Bonsergent, Gare de l'Est and Parmentier are useful stations.

Bordered by shaded towpaths and criss-crossed with iron footbridges, Canal St-Martin wends through the city's northern *quartiers* (quarters). You can float past them on a canal cruise, but strolling among this rejuvenated neighbourhood's cool cafes, offbeat boutiques and hip bars and clubs lets you see why it's beloved by Parisian *bobos* (bourgeois bohemians).

❶ Coffee with the Locals

Kick off with coffee at **52 Faubourg St-Denis** (52 rue du Faubourg St-Denis, 10e; ⏱8am-midnight, kitchen noon-2.30pm & 7-11pm; MChâteau d'Eau), a thoroughly contemporary neighbourhood restaurant-cafe that is also a brilliant space to hang out in at any time of day.

❷ Retro Clothes Shopping

Flip through colour-coded racks of vintage cast-offs at **Frivoli** (26 rue Beaurepaire, 10e; ⏱11am-7pm Mon-Fri, 2-7pm Sat & Sun; MJacques Bonsergent), on boutique-lined rue Beaurepaire.

❸ Pizza Picnic

Order a Poulidor (duck, apple and goats cheese) or Basquiat (gorgonzola, figs and cured ham) pizza from **Pink Flamingo** (📞01 42 02 31 70; www.pinkflamingopizza.com; 67 rue Bichat, 10e; pizzas €11.50-17; ⏱7-11.30pm Mon-Thu, noon-3pm & 7-11.30pm Fri-Sun; 🍴; MJacques Bonsergent) and receive a pink helium balloon; it's used to locate you and your perfect canal-side picnic spot when the pizza is delivered.

❹ Cultural Cool

Within a converted warehouse, alternative cultural centre **Point Éphémère** (www.pointephemere.org; 200 quai de Valmy, 10e; ⏱12.30pm-2am Mon-Sat, 12.30-11pm Sun; 🛜; MLouis Blanc) has resident artists and musicians, exhibitions and a chilled bar-restaurant. Pop back at night for live music, DJs and clubbing events.

❺ Cafe Culture

Watch the boats from spirited **L'Atmosphère** (49 rue Lucien Sampaix, 10e; ⏱9.30am-1.45am Mon-Sat, to midnight Sun; MJacques Bonsergent or Gare de l'Est), hit barista-run **Holybelly** (www.holybel.ly; 19 rue Lucien Sampaix, 10e; ⏱9am-6pm Thu-Mon, from 10am Sat & Sun; MJacques Bonsergent) or head to original *bobo* hang-out **Chez Prune** (71 quai de Valmy, 10e; ⏱8am-2am Mon-Sat, 10am-2am Sun; MRépublique).

❻ Hilltop Haven

A far cry from its former incarnation as a rubbish tip and quarry for Baron Haussmann's 19th-century reformation, hilly, forested **Parc des Buttes Chaumont** (rue Manin & rue Botzaris, 19e; ⏱7am-10pm May-Sep, to 8pm Oct-Apr; MButtes-Chaumont or Botzaris) conceals grottoes, artificial waterfalls and a temple-topped island reached by footbridges, as well as the **Rosa Bonheur** dance hall and cafe.

❼ Post-Industrial Dining

Book ahead to dine on contemporary bistro fare at white-walled shop turned restaurant **Chatomat** (📞01 47 97 25 77; 6 rue Victor Letalle, 20e; mains €15-20; ⏱7.30-10.30pm Tue-Sat & 1st Sun of month; MMénilmontant, Couronnes or Père Lachaise).

❽ Nightcap, Nightlife

Finish with a drink at the belle époque **Café Charbon** (109 rue Oberkampf, 11e; ⏱9am-2am Mon-Wed & Sun, 9am-4am Thu-Sat; 🛜; MParmentier) or kick on at its live music and DJ venue, **Le Nouveau Casino** (109 rue Oberkampf, 11e; ⏱Tue-Sun; MParmentier).

Explore

Centre Pompidou & Le Marais

Paris' *marais* (marsh) was cleared in the 12th century but Hauss-mann's reformations left its tangle of medieval laneways largely intact. Hip bars and restaurants, emerging designers' boutiques and the city's thriving gay and Jewish communities all squeeze into this vibrant neighbourhood and its equally buzzing eastern neighbour, Bastille.

The Sights in a Day

The twice-weekly **Marché Bastille** (p99) is one of the largest, liveliest street markets in Paris – catch it if you can before visiting the **Musée National Picasso** (p94) and the **Maison de Victor Hugo** (p96), the author's former home on elegant **place des Vosges** (p96).

Join the locals queuing at the takeaway window of **L'As du Fallafel** (p97). After lunch, stroll along the leafy **Promenade Plantée** (p95) walkway above an old railway viaduct, or simply spend the afternoon browsing the Marais' trove of colourful and quirky shops, stopping for a fresh juice fix at **Wild & the Moon** (p101).

The **Centre Pompidou** (p88) stays open until 9pm, so head here in the late afternoon to see its amazing collection of modern and contemporary art and the awesome views from its roof. After dinner at **Le Bistrot Paul Bert** (p97), begin a bar-hop at **Le Cap Horn** (p102).

For a local's day in the Haut Marais, see p90.

 Top Sights

Centre Pompidou (p88)

 Local Life

A Heads-Up on the Haut Marais (p90)

 Best of Paris

Eating
Le Bistrot Paul Bert (p97)
Chambelland (p99)

Drinking
Le Pure Café (p102)
La Fée Verte (p101)
La Caféothèque (p101)

Architecture
Bofinger (p100)
Centre Pompidou (p88)
Opéra Bastille (p102)

Getting There

Ⓜ **Metro** Rambuteau (line 11) is the most convenient for the Centre Pompidou.

Ⓜ **Metro** Other central metro stations include Hôtel de Ville (lines 1 and 11), St-Paul (line 1) and Bastille (lines 1, 5 and 8).

🚣 **Boat** The hop-on, hop-off Batobus stops outside the Hôtel de Ville.

Top Sights
Centre Pompidou

The building housing Paris' premier cultural centre is so iconic that you could spend hours looking at it without ever going inside. But you should! As well as containing France's national modern and contemporary art museum, the Musée National d'Art Moderne, the centre's cutting-edge cultural offerings include temporary exhibition spaces, a public library, cinemas and entertainment venues.

◉ Map p92, A2

www.centrepompidou.fr

place Georges Pompidou, 4e

museum, exhibitions & panorama adult/child €14/free

⏱ 11am-10pm Wed-Mon

Ⓜ Rambuteau

The Architecture

Former French president Georges Pompidou wanted an ultra-contemporary artistic hub and he got it: competition-winning architects Renzo Piano and Richard Rogers effectively designed the building inside out, with utilitarian features such as plumbing, pipes, air vents and electrical cables forming part of the external façade, freeing up the interior space for exhibitions and events.

The then controversial, now much-loved centre opened in 1977. Viewed from a distance (such as from Sacré-Cœur) its primary-coloured, box-like form amid a sea of muted-grey Parisian rooftops makes it look like a child's Meccano set abandoned on someone's elegant living-room rug.

Musée National d'Art Moderne

Europe's largest collection of modern art fills the airy, well-lit galleries of the National Museum of Modern Art. On a par with the permanent collection are the two temporary exhibition halls (on the ground floor/basement and the top floor) which host memorable blockbuster exhibits. There's a wonderful children's gallery on the 1st floor.

The permanent collection changes every two years, but incorporates artists such as Picasso, Matisse, Chagall, Kandinsky, Kahlo, Warhol, Pollock and many more. The 5th floor showcases artists active between 1905 and 1970 (give or take a decade); the 4th floor focuses on more contemporary creations, roughly from the 1980s onward.

The Rooftop

Although the Centre Pompidou is just six storeys high, Paris' low-rise cityscape means sweeping views extend from its rooftop, reached by external escalators enclosed in tubes.

☑ Top Tips

▶ The Centre Pompidou opens late every night (except Tuesday, when it's closed), so head here around 5pm to avoid the daytime crowds.

▶ You'll still have to queue to get through security, but the entry process will go faster if you buy museum and events tickets online.

▶ Rooftop entry is included in museum and exhibition admission; alternatively, buy a panorama ticket (€3) just for the roof.

✕ Take a Break

▶ Georges' outdoor terrace on the 6th floor is a fabulous spot for a drink with a view, though it's not so great for dining.

▶ For a meal or a casual drink, head to nearby **Café La Fusée** (☎01 42 76 93 99; 168 rue St-Martin, 3e; ⊙8am-2am; Ⓜ Rambuteau, Étienne Marcel) or **Dame Tartine** (☎01 42 77 32 22; 2 rue Brisemiche, 4e; tartines €9.90-13.50; ⊙9am-11.30pm; ☎; Ⓜ Hôtel de Ville).

Local Life
A Heads-Up on the Haut Marais

The lower Marais has long been fashionable but the real buzz these days is in the *haut* Marais (upper, ie northern Marais). Its warren of narrow streets is a hub for up-and-coming fashion designers, art galleries, and vintage, accessories and homewares boutiques, all sitting alongside long-established enterprises enjoying a renaissance. Look out for new openings, exhibitions, events and pop-up shops.

❶ Charitable Fashion
Fronted by a Fiat Cinquecento, unique concept store **Merci** (www.merci-merci.com; 111 bd Beaumarchais, 3e; ⊙10am-7pm Mon-Sat; Ⓜ St-Sébastien Froissart) donates all profits from its cutting-edge fashions, homewares, gifts, cafe and canteen to a children's charity in Madagascar.

2 Coffee Fix

Reboot with a Parisian-roasted coffee at **Boot Café** (19 rue du Pont aux Choux, 3e; ⊙10am-6pm; Ⓜ Filles du Calvaire). Set inside an old cobbler's shop, whose original washed-blue façade and 'Cordonnerie' lettering have been beautifully preserved.

3 Discounted Fashion

Savvy Parisians grab last season's designer wear (for both men and women) at up to 70% off original prices at **L'Habilleur** (www.lhabilleur.fr; 44 rue de Poitou, 4e; ⊙noon-7.30pm Mon-Sat; Ⓜ St-Sébastien Froissart).

4 Market Lunch

Hidden behind an inconspicuous green metal gate, **Marché des Enfants Rouges** (39 rue de Bretagne, 3e; ⊙8.30am-1pm & 4-7.30pm Tue-Fri, 4-8pm Sat, 8.30am-2pm Sun; Ⓜ Filles du Calvaire) has produce stalls and dishes that range from bento boxes to crêpes, which you can eat at communal tables.

5 Handbag Heaven

Super-soft, super-stylish **Pauline Pin** (www.paulinepin.com; 51 rue Charlot, 3e; ⊙11am-7.30pm Tue-Sat; Ⓜ Filles du Calvaire) handbags are made here at founder-designer Clarisse's flagship store and workshop.

6 Fibre Fashion

Clothing and textile artworks crafted from natural and rare animal fibres are exhibited and sold at **La Boutique Extraordinaire** (67 rue Charlot, 3e; ⊙11am-8pm Tue-Sat, 3-7pm Sun; Ⓜ Filles du Calvaire).

7 Cultural Happenings

The quarter's old covered market with magnificent art nouveau ironwork, **Le Carreau du Temple** (☎01 83 81 93 30; www.carreaudutemple.eu; 4 rue Eugène Spuller, 3e; ⊙ticket office 2-6pm Mon-Sat; Ⓜ Temple) is now a vast stage for exhibitions, concerts, sports classes and theatre.

8 Cocktail Hour

Snag a stool at the central circular bar of ubercool **Le Mary Céleste** (www.lemaryceleste.com; 1 rue Commines, 3e; cocktails €12-13, tapas €8-12; ⊙6pm-2am; Ⓜ Filles du Calvaire) for creative cocktails and tapas-style 'small plates'.

Oberkampf Ⓜ

R Oberkampf

Passage St-
Pierre Amelot

Passage St-
Sébastien
R St-Sébastien

R Pelée

R Amelot

Chemin
Vert Ⓜ

Bd Beaumarchais

R de la
Bastille

Place
de la
Bastille

Ⓜ Bastille

Ⓜ Bastille

R de la Folie
Méricourt

Ⓜ St-
Ambroise

Richard
Lenoir

R Mouffe

R Froment

R Daval

R St-Sabin

Sq
Bréguet
Sabin

Bréguet
Sabin

Ⓜ R Ternaux Ⓧ 13

Av Parmentier

St-Maur Ⓜ

For reviews see

◉ Top Sights   p88
◉ Sights   p94
Ⓧ Eating   p97
Ⓓ Drinking   p100
Ⓔ Entertainment   p102
Ⓐ Shopping   p103

R St-Ambroise

R St-Maur

Sq
Maurice
Gardette

Ⓝ 0 _____ 400 m
0 _____ 0.2 miles

Bd Voltaire

R du Chemin Vert

R Bréguet

R Sedaine

Cadet Lamy

R du
Taillandiers

R des
Taillandiers

Passage Thiéré

R de Lappe

Ⓐ 29

R de Charenton

Ⓧ 15

Ⓧ 19

Ⓔ 27

Ⓧ 12

Av Parmentier

11E

R Duranti

Sq
de la
Roquette

R de la Roquette

R Popincourt

R de la Roquette

Sq
Denis
Poulot

Pl Léon
Blum

Ⓜ
Voltaire

Passage Charles Dallery

R Basfroi

R Keller

Ⓟ 23

R de Charonne

Ⓧ 16

R Godefroy Cavaignac

R de Belfort

R Léon Frot

Charonne Ⓜ

Ⓧ 25

R Jean Macé

R Charles Delescluze

R Faidherbe

R Chanzy

R Paul Bert

Ⓧ 11

R Jules Vallès

R Titon

Ⓔ 26

Bd de la Bastille

Bd de Lyon

R de Lyon

R de Charenton

Ledru-Rollin Ⓜ

Ⓜ Ledru-Rollin

12E

Av Ledru-Rollin

Av Daumesnil

R Jules César

R Émilio Castelar

R Traversière

R de Prague

Sq
Trousseau

R de Cotte

R d'Aligre

Pl
d'Aligre

R de Charenton

R Crozatier

R de Cîteaux

Pl
Dr Antoine
Béclère

Faidherbe
Chaligny Ⓜ

R de
Montreuil

St-Antoine

R de Chaligny

R de Reuilly

Ⓐ 30 Ⓟ 5

Promenade
Plantée

Sights

Musée National Picasso

ART MUSEUM

1 ⊙ Map p92, C2

One of Paris' most beloved collections is showcased inside the mid-17th-century Hôtel Salé, an exquisite private mansion owned by the city since 1964. Inside is the Musée National Picasso, a staggering art museum devoted to the Spanish artist, Pablo Picasso (1881–1973), who spent much of his life in Paris. The collection includes more than 5000 drawings, engravings, paintings, ceramic works and sculptures by the *grand maître* (great master), although they're not all displayed at the same time. (☑ 01 85 56 00 36; www.museepicasso paris.fr; 5 rue de Thorigny, 3e; adult/child €12.50/free; ⊙ 11.30am-6pm Tue-Fri, 9.30am-6pm Sat & Sun; M St-Paul, Chemin Vert)

Mémorial de la Shoah

MUSEUM

2 ⊙ Map p92, B3

Established in 1956, the Memorial to the Unknown Jewish Martyr has metamorphosed into the Memorial of the Shoah – 'Shoah' a Hebrew word meaning 'catastrophe' and synonymous in France with the Holocaust. Exhibitions relate to the Holocaust and German occupation of parts of France and Paris during WWII. The actual memorial to the victims of the Shoah stands at the entrance. The wall is inscribed with the names of 76,000 men, women and children deported from France to Nazi extermination camps. (www.memo rialdelashoah.org; 17 rue Geoffroy l'Asnier, 4e; admission free; ⊙ 10am-6pm Sun-Wed & Fri, to 10pm Thu; M St-Paul)

Musée des Arts et Métiers

MUSEUM

3 ⊙ Map p92, C1

The Arts & Crafts Museum, dating to 1794 and Europe's oldest science and technology museum, is a must for anyone with kids – or an interest in how things tick or work. Housed inside the sublime 18th-century priory of St-Martin des Champs, some 3000 instruments, machines and working models from the 18th to 20th centuries are displayed across three floors. In the attached church of St-Martin des Champs is Foucault's original pendulum, introduced to the world at the Universal Exhibition in Paris 1855. (www.arts-et-metiers.net; 60 rue de Réaumur, 3e; adult/child €8/free; ⊙ 10am-6pm Tue, Wed & Fri-Sun, to 9.30pm Thu; M Arts et Métiers)

Place de la Bastille

SQUARE

4 ⊙ Map p92, E4

The Bastille, a 14th-century fortress built to protect the city gates, is the most famous Parisian monument that no longer exists. Nothing remains of the prison it became under Cardinal Richelieu, which was mobbed on 14 July 1789, igniting the French Revolution. Today it's a skirmishly busy roundabout, with traffic flying around the 52m-high **Colonne de Juillet** in its centre. The unmissable green-

PHILIPPE RENAULT/GETTY IMAGES ©

Promenade Plantée

bronze column is topped by a gilded, winged Liberty, and revolutionaries from the uprising of 1830 are buried beneath. (place de la Bastille, 12e; Ⓜ Bastille)

Promenade Plantée PARK

5 ◉ Map p92, F5

The disused 19th-century Vincennes railway viaduct has been reborn as the world's first elevated park, planted with a fragrant profusion of cherry trees, maples, rose trellises, bamboo corridors and lavender. Three storeys above ground, it provides a unique aerial vantage point on the city. Access is via staircase and it starts just south of place de la Bastille on rue de Lyon. Along the first section, above av

Daumesnil, chic art-gallery-workshops squat gracefully beneath the arches to form the Viaduc des Arts (p103). (La Coulée Verte René-Dumont; cnr rue de Lyon & av Daumesnil, 12e; ⊗ 8am-9.30pm May-Aug, to 5.30pm Sep-Apr; Ⓜ Bastille, Gare de Lyon)

Tour St-Jacques TOWER

6 ◉ Map p92, A3

Just north of place du Châtelet, the Flamboyant Gothic, 54m-high St James Tower is all that remains of the Église St-Jacques la Boucherie, built by the powerful butchers guild in 1523 as a starting point for pilgrims setting out for the shrine of St James at Santiago de Compostela in Spain. Guided 50-minute tours (in French) of the

Local Life

Place des Vosges

Inaugurated in 1612 as place Royale and thus Paris' oldest square, **place des Vosges** (place des Vosges, 4e; Ⓜ St-Paul, Bastille) is a strikingly elegant ensemble of 36 symmetrical houses with ground-floor arcades, steep slate roofs and large dormer windows arranged around a leafy square with four symmetrical fountains and an 1829 copy of a mounted statue of Louis XIII. The square received its present name in 1800 to honour the Vosges *département* (administrative division) for being the first in France to pay its taxes.

recently restored tower take visitors up 300 stairs to an expansive panorama. Children must be 10 years or older. (📞 01 83 96 15 05; 39 rue de Rivoli, 4e; adult/child €10/8; ⏰ 10am-5pm Fri-Sun Jun-Sep; Ⓜ Châtelet)

Maison de Victor Hugo   MUSEUM

7 ◉ Map p92, D3

Between 1832 and 1848 the writer Victor Hugo lived in an apartment in Hôtel de Rohan-Guéménée, a townhouse overlooking one of Paris' most elegant squares. He moved here a year after the publication of *Notre Dame de Paris* (The Hunchback of Notre Dame), completing *Ruy Blas* during his stay. His house is now a museum devoted to the life of this celebrated novelist and poet, with an impressive collection of his personal drawings and portraits.

Temporary exhibitions command an admission fee. (www.musee-hugo.paris.fr; 6 place des Vosges, 4e; admission free; ⏰ 10am-6pm Tue-Sun; Ⓜ St-Paul, Bastille)

Hôtel de Ville   ARCHITECTURE

8 ◉ Map p92, A3

Paris' beautiful town hall was gutted during the Paris Commune of 1871 and rebuilt in luxurious neo-Renaissance style between 1874 and 1882. The ornate façade is decorated with 108 statues of illustrious Parisians, and the outstanding temporary exhibitions (admission free) held inside in its **Salle St-Jean** almost always have a Parisian theme. During most winters from December to early March, an ice-skating rink is set up outside this beautiful building, creating a real picture-book experience. (www.paris.fr; place de l'Hôtel de Ville, 4e; admission free; Ⓜ Hôtel de Ville)

Musée Cognacq-Jay   MUSEUM

9 ◉ Map p92, C2

This museum inside Hôtel de Donon displays oil paintings, pastels, sculpture, objets d'art, jewellery, porcelain and furniture from the 18th century assembled by Ernest Cognacq (1839–1928), founder of La Samaritaine department store, and his wife Louise Jay. Although Cognacq appreciated little of his collection, boasting that he had never visited the Louvre and was only acquiring collections for the status, the artwork and objets d'art give a good idea of upper-class tastes during the Age of Enlightenment. (www.cognacq-jay.paris.fr; 8 rue Elzévir, 3e; admission free; ⏱10am-6pm Tue-Sun; Ⓜ St-Paul, Chemin Vert)

Musée d'Art et d'Histoire du Judaïsme   MUSEUM

10 Map p92, B2

To delve into the historic heart of the Marais' long-established Jewish community in Pletzl (from the Yiddish for 'little square'), visit this fascinating museum inside Hôtel de St-Aignan, dating from 1650. The museum traces the evolution of Jewish communities from the Middle Ages to the present, with particular emphasis on French Jewish history. Highlights include documents relating to the Dreyfus Affair, and works by Chagall, Modigliani and Soutine. Creative workshops for children, adults and families complement excellent temporary exhibitions. (📞 01 53 01 86 62; www.mahj.org; 71 rue du Temple, 4e; adult/child €8/free; ⏱11am-6pm Mon-Fri, 10am-6pm Sun; Ⓜ Rambuteau)

Eating

Le Bistrot Paul Bert   BISTRO $$

11 Map p92, H4

When food writers list Paris' best bistros, one name that consistently pops up is Paul Bert. The timeless vintage decor and perfectly executed classic dishes like *steak-frites* (steak and chips) and hazelnut-cream Paris-Brest pastry merit booking ahead. Look out for its siblings **L'Écailler du Bistrot** (seafood), **La Cave Paul Bert** (wine bar with small plates) and **Le 6 Paul Bert** (modern cuisine) in the same street. (📞 01 43 72 24 01; 18 rue Paul Bert, 11e; 2-/3-course lunch/dinner menu €19/41; ⏱noon-2pm & 7.30-11pm Tue-Sat; Ⓜ Faidherbe-Chaligny)

Dersou   NEOBISTRO $$$

12 Map p92, F5

Leave any preconceptions you might have at the door, ignore or enjoy the brutishly understated decor, and be wooed by the creative fusion cuisine of Taku Sekine. Much of the seating is at the counter, meaning first-class views of the Japanese chef at work, and options are limited to tasting menus, with each course exquisitely

---

Local Life
Pletzl

The Jewish area around Le Marais' rue des Rosiers and rue des Écouffes was traditionally known as the Pletzl, and it's still filled with kosher delis and takeaway falafel windows such as Parisian favourite **L'As du Fallafel** (34 rue des Rosiers, 4e; takeaway €6-8.50; ⏱noon-midnight Sun-Thu, to 5pm Fri; Ⓜ St-Paul) – the inevitable queue is worth the wait. For a sit-down meal, try **Chez Marianne** (2 rue des Hospitalières St-Gervais, 4e; mains €18-25; ⏱noon-midnight; Ⓜ St-Paul). The Pletzl's **art nouveau synagogue** (10 rue Pavée, 4e; Ⓜ St-Paul) was designed in 1913 by Hector Guimard (who also designed Paris' iconic metro entrances).

Understand
Village Life

Within the Walls

Paris is defined by its walls (that is, the Périphérique or ring road). *Intra-muros* (Latin for 'within the walls'), the 105-sq-km interior has a population of just under 2.2 million, while the greater metropolitan area (the Île de France *région*, encircled by rivers) has some 12 million inhabitants, about 19% of France's total population. This makes Paris – the capital of both the *région* and the highly centralised nation – in effect an 'island within an island' (or, as residents elsewhere might say, a bubble).

Communal Living

Paris isn't merely a commuter destination, however – its dense inner-city population defines city life. Paris' shops, street markets, parks and other facets of day-to-day living evoke a village atmosphere, and its almost total absence of high-rises gives it a human scale. Single-occupant dwellings make up around half of central Paris' households. And space shortages mean residential apartments are often minuscule. As a result, communal areas are the living and dining rooms and backyards of many Parisians, while neighbourhood shops are cornerstones of community life. This high concentration of city dwellers is why there are few late-night bars and cafes or inner-city nightclubs, due to noise restrictions. It's also why so many pet dogs live in Paris. But hefty fines have meant the pavements (which are washed every day) are the cleanest they've ever been.

Beyond the Walls

The *Grand Paris* (Greater Paris) redevelopment project connects the outer suburbs with the city proper. This is a significant break in the physical and conceptual barrier that the Périphérique has imposed. Its crux is a massive decentralised metro expansion, with 68 new stations and six suburban lines, with a target completion date of 2030. The principal goal is to connect the suburbs with one another, instead of relying on a central inner-city hub from which all lines radiate outwards (the current model). Progress is swift: tunnelling, which began in 2015, continues at a rate of some 12.5m per day.

Ultimately, the surrounding suburbs – Vincennes, Neuilly, Issy, St-Denis etc – will lose their autonomy and become part of a much larger *Grand Paris* governed by the Hôtel de Ville.

paired with a bespoke cocktail. Reservations essential. (☎09 81 01 12 73; www.dersouparis.com; 21 rue St-Nicolas, 12e; 5-/6-/7-course tasting menu incl drinks €95/115/135; ☉7.30pm-midnight Tue-Fri, noon-3.30pm & 7.30pm-midnight Sat, noon-3.30pm Sun; Ⓜ Ledru-Rollin)

Chambelland BOULANGERIE $

13 Map p92, F1

In a city known for its bakeries, it's only right there's Chambelland – a 100% gluten-free bakery with serious breads to die for. Using rice and buckwheat flour milled at the bakery's very own mill in southern France, this pioneering bakery creates exquisite cakes and pastries as well as sourdough loaves and brioches (sweet breads) peppered with nuts, seeds, chocolate and fruit. (☎01 43 55 07 30; www.chambelland.com; 14 rue Ternaux, 11e; lunch menu €12; ☉9am-8pm Tue-Sun; Ⓜ Parmentier)

Breizh Café CRÊPERIE $

14 Map p92, C2

It is a well-known fact among Parisians: everything at the Breton Café (*breizh* is 'Breton' in Breton) is 100% authentic, rendering it the top spot in the city for crêpes. Be it the Cancale oysters, 20 types of cider or the buttery organic-flour crêpes, everything here is cooked to perfection. If you fail to snag a table, try **L'Épicerie** next door. (www.breizhcafe.com; 109 rue Vieille du Temple, 3e; crêpes & galettes €6.50-18; ☉11.30am-11pm Wed-Sat, to 10pm Sun; Ⓜ St-Sébastien–Froissart)

Olive stall at Marché Bastille

Marché Bastille MARKET $

15 Map p92, E3

If you only get to one open-air street market in Paris, this one – stretching between the Bastille and Richard Lenoir metro stations – is among the city's very best. (http://equipement.paris.fr/marche-bastille-5477; bd Richard Lenoir, 11e; ☉7am-2.30pm Thu, 7am-3pm Sun; Ⓜ Bastille, Richard Lenoir)

Septime MODERN FRENCH $$$

16 Map p92, G4

The alchemists in Bertrand Grébaut's Michelin-starred kitchen produce truly beautiful creations, while blue-smocked waitstaff ensure culinary surprises are all pleasant ones: each dish on the menu is a mere listing of three ingredients, while the mystery *carte blanche* menu puts your taste buds in the hands of the innovative chef. Snagging a table requires planning and perseverance – book three weeks in advance. (☎01 43 67 38 29; www.septime-charonne.fr; 80 rue de Charonne, 11e; lunch menus €28 & €55, dinner menu €58; ⏱7.30-10pm Mon, 12.15-2pm & 7.30-10pm Tue-Fri; MCharonne)

Candelaria   MEXICAN $

 17 Map p92, D1

You need to know about this terribly cool *taquería* to find it. Made of pure, unadulterated hipness in that brazenly nonchalant manner Paris does so well, clandestine Candelaria serves delicious homemade tacos, quesadillas and tostadas in a laid-back setting – squat at the bar in the front or lounge out back around a shared table with bar stools or at low coffee tables. (☎01 42 74 41 28; www.candelariaparis.com; 52 rue de Saintonge, 3e; tacos €3-5; ⏱12.30pm-11pm Sun-Wed, 12.30pm-midnight Thu-Sat, bar 6pm-2am; MFilles du Calvaire)

Brasserie Bofinger   BRASSERIE $$

 18 Map p92, E4

Founded in 1864, Bofinger is reputedly Paris' oldest brasserie, though its polished art nouveau brass, glass and mirrors indicates redecoration a few decades later. Specialities include Alsatian-inspired dishes like *choucroute* (sauerkraut), oysters (from €27.90 for a dozen) and magnificent seafood platters (€29.90 to €122). Ask for a seat downstairs beneath the *coupole* (stained-glass dome). Kids are catered for with a €14.50 children's *menu*. (☎01 42 72 87 82; www.bofingerparis.com; 5-7 rue de la Bastille, 4e; menus €31 & €56; ⏱noon-2pm & 6.30pm-midnight Mon-Sat, noon-11pm Sun; 🚻; MBastille)

Drinking

Café des Anges   CAFE

19 Map p92, F3

With its aqua-blue paintwork and locals sipping coffee beneath terracotta awning on its busy pavement terrace, Angels Cafe lives up to the 'quintessential Paris cafe' dream. In winter wrap up beneath a ginger blanket outside, or push your way through the crowds at the zinc bar to snag a coveted table inside – for breakfast, a burger lunch, steak dinner (mains €10 to €17) and everything in between. (☏01 73 20 21 10; www.cafedesangesparis.com; 66 rue de la Roquette, 11e; ⏱7.30am-2am; Ⓜ Bastille)

Wild & the Moon JUICE BAR

20 Map p92, D1

A beautiful crowd hobnobs over nut milks, vitality shots, smoothies, cold-pressed juices and raw food in this sleek new juice bar in the fashionable Haut Marais. Ingredients are fresh, seasonal and organic, and it is one of the few places in town where you can have moon porridge or avocado slices on almond and rosemary crackers for breakfast. (www.wildandthemoon.com; 55 rue Charlot, 3e; ⏱8am-7pm Mon-Fri, 10am-7pm Sat, 11am-5pm Sun; Ⓜ Filles du Calvaire)

PasDeLoup COCKTAIL BAR

21 Map p92, E1

This trendy cocktail bar next to the Cirque d'Hiver in Le Marais is a small place with a simple wood bar and copper-tube shelving evoking Scandinavia in its design. But what makes it stand out for the city's increasingly discerning cocktail crowd is its interesting and superbly gourmet food pairings (from €10). (☏09 54 74 16 36; www.facebook.com/pasdelouparis; 108 rue Amelot, 11e; ⏱6pm-2am Tue-Sun; Ⓜ Filles du Calvaire)

La Caféothèque COFFEE

22 Map p92, B4

From the industrial grinder to elaborate tasting notes, this coffee house is

serious. Grab a seat, pick your bean, and get it served just the way you like it (espresso, ristretto, latte etc). The coffee of the day keeps well-travelled taste buds on their toes and there are tastings of different *crus*. Two-hour Saturday-morning tasting initiations cost €60. (☏01 53 01 83 84; www.lacafeotheque.com; 52 rue de l'Hôtel de Ville, 4e; ⏱8.30am-7.30pm Mon-Fri, 10am-7.30pm Sat & Sun; 🛜; Ⓜ St-Paul, Hôtel de Ville)

La Fée Verte BAR

23 Map p92, G3

Absinthe, predictably, is the speciality of the Green Fairy, a thronging neighbourhood bar that serves good food (burgers, salads) as well as 20-odd types of the devilish drink (traditionally,

Local Life
Gay & Lesbian Marais

Guys' favourite venues in Le Marais include sociable **Open Café** (www.opencafe.fr; 17 rue des Archives, 4e; ⏱11am-2am; Ⓜ Hôtel de Ville) and cruisy **Quetzal** (10 rue de la Verrerie, 4e; ⏱5pm-2am; Ⓜ Hôtel de Ville).

Girls will want to head to **3w Kafé** (8 rue des Écouffes, 4e; ⏱7pm-3am Wed & Sun, to 4am Thu, to 6.30am Fri & Sat; Ⓜ St-Paul), which stands for 'women with women'.

A mixed gay and lesbian crowd loves **Le Tango** (www.boiteafrissons.fr; 13 rue au Maire, 3e; ⏱10.30pm-5am Fri & Sat, 6-11pm Sun; Ⓜ Arts et Métiers), especially during Sunday's legendary gay tea dance.

Marché d'Aligre

All the staples of French cuisine can be found in the chaotic **Marché d'Aligre** (http://marchedaligre.free. fr; rue d'Aligre, 12e; ⊙8am-1pm Tue-Sun; M Ledru-Rollin): cheese, coffee, chocolate, wine and charcuterie included. It adjoins the historic covered market hall **Marché Beau-vau** (place d'Aligre, 12e; ⊙9am-1pm & 4-7.30pm Tue-Fri, 9am-1pm & 3.30-7.30pm Sat, 9am-1.30pm Sun). The **Marché aux Puces d'Aligre** (place d'Aligre, 12e; ⊙8am-1pm Tue-Sun) flea market takes place here. Food shops, wine bars – such as the wonderful, barrel-lined **Le Baron Rouge** (☎01 43 43 14 32; 1 rue Théophile Roussel, 12e; ⊙10am-2pm & 5-10pm Tue-Fri, 10am-10pm Sat, 10am-4pm Sun) – and a rapidly increasing number of restaurants fan out into the surrounding streets.

with spoons and sugar cubes). Sunday brunch too. (☎01 43 72 31 24; 108 rue de la Roquette, 11e; ⊙7am-2am; 🛜; M Voltaire)

Le Cap Horn
BAR

24 🚇 Map p92, D4

On summer evenings the ambience at this laid-back, Chilean bar is electric. The crowd spills onto the pavement, parked cars doubling as table tops for well-shaken pina coladas, punch cocos and cocktails made with *pisco*, a fiery Chilean grape *eau-de-vie*. Find it steps from place des Vosges. (8 rue de Birague, 4e; ⊙10am-1am; M St-Paul, Chemin Vert)

Le Pure Café
CAFE

25 🚇 Map p92, H4

With vintage wood and zinc bar, this cherry-red Parisian corner cafe is an easy spot to drop in for a morning coffee, aperitif, meal (mains €13 to €16) or copious Sunday brunch (€19). Its selection of natural and organic wines by the glass is particularly good. Film buffs: spot its quaint cinematic façade and traditional interior used in the film *Before Sunset*. (www.lepurecafe.fr; 14 rue Jean Macé, 11e; ⊙7am-1am Mon-Fri, 8am-1am Sat, 9am-midnight Sun; M Charonne)

Entertainment

Opéra Bastille
OPERA, CLASSICAL MUSIC

26 ⭐ Map p92, E4

This 3400-seat venue is the city's main opera hall; it also stages ballet and classical concerts. Tickets go on sale online up to two weeks before they're available by telephone or at the box office. Standing-only tickets (*places débouts;* €5) are available 90 minutes before performances begin. By day, explore the eyesore opera house with a 90-minute guided tour backstage; check hours online. (☎08 92 89 90 90, 01 40 01 19 70; www.operadeparis.fr; 2-6 place de la Bastille, 12e; guided tour €15; ⊙box office 2.30-6.30pm Mon-Sat; M Bastille)

Badaboum
LIVE MUSIC

27 ⭐ Map p92, F4

Formerly La Scène Bastille and freshly refitted, the onomatopoeically named

Badaboum hosts a mixed bag of concerts on its up-close-and-personal stage, but focuses on electro, funk and hip-hop. Great atmosphere, super cocktails and a secret room upstairs. (www.badaboum-paris.com; 2bis rue des Taillandiers, 11e; ⏲cocktail bar 7pm-2am Wed-Sat, club & concerts vary; Ⓜ Bastille, Ledru-Rollin)

Shopping

Paris Rendez-Vous   CONCEPT STORE

28 🔒 Map p92, A3

Only the city of Paris could be so chic as to have its own designer line of souvenirs, sold in its own ubercool concept store inside Hôtel de Ville (city hall). Shop here for everything from clothing and homewares to Paris-themed books, toy sailing boats and signature Jardin du Luxembourg's Fermob chairs. *Quel style!* (www.rendezvous.paris.fr; 29 rue de Rivoli, 4e; ⏲10am-7pm Mon-Sat; Ⓜ Hôtel de Ville)

La Manufacture
de Chocolat   FOOD

29 🔒 Map p92, E4

If you dine at chef Alain Ducasse's restaurants, the chocolate will have been made here at Ducasse's own factory (the first in Paris to produce 'bean-to-bar' chocolate), which he set up with his former executive pastry chef Nicolas Berger. Deliberate over ganaches, pralines, truffles and more than 44 flavours of chocolate bar. (www.lechocolat-

Creation from La Manufacture de Chocolat

alainducasse.com; 40 rue de la Roquette, 11e; ⏲10.30am-7pm Tue-Sat; Ⓜ Bastille)

Viaduc des Arts   ARTS & CRAFTS

30 🔒 Map p92, F5

Located beneath the red-brick arches of the Promenade Plantée (p95) is the Viaduc des Arts, a line-up of craft shops where traditional artisans and contemporary designers carry out antique renovations and create new items using traditional methods. Artisans include furniture and tapestry restorers, interior designers, cabinetmakers, violin- and flute-makers, embroiderers and jewellers. (www.leviaducdesarts.com; 1-129 av Daumesnil, 12e; ⏲variable; Ⓜ Bastille, Gare de Lyon)

Top Sights
Père Lachaise

Getting There

Père Lachaise is about 4.5km northeast of Notre Dame.

M Metro Philippe Auguste (line 2), Gambetta (lines 3 and 3b) and Père Lachaise (lines 2 and 3).

The world's most visited cemetery opened in 1804. Its 44 hectares hold more than 70,000 ornate tombs – a stroll here is akin to exploring a verdant sculpture garden. Père Lachaise was intended for Parisians, a response to local neighbourhood graveyards being full. It was groundbreaking for Parisians to be buried outside the *quartier* in which they'd lived.

Bronze statues adorn a tomb

A Perfect City Stroll

For those visiting Paris for its exceptional art and architecture, this vast cemetery – the city's largest – is not a bad starting point. It's one of central Paris' biggest green spaces, with 5300 trees and a treasure trove of magnificent 19th-century sculptures by artists such as David d'Angers, Hector Guimard, Visconti and Chapu. Consider the walking tour detailed in the photographic book *Meet Me At Père Lachaise* by Anna Erikssön and Mason Bendewald, or simply start with architect Étienne-Hippolyte Godde's neoclassical chapel and portal at the main entrance and get beautifully lost.

Famous Occupants

Paris residency was the only criterion needed to be buried in Père Lachaise, hence the cemetery's cosmopolitan population. Among the 800,000-odd buried here are the composer Chopin; the playwright Molière; the poet Apollinaire; writers Balzac, Proust, Gertrude Stein and Colette; the actors Simone Signoret, Sarah Bernhardt and Yves Montand; the painters Pissarro, Seurat, Modigliani and Delacroix; the *chanteuse* Édith Piaf alongside her two-year-old daughter; and the dancer Isadora Duncan.

Oscar Wilde

The grave of Irish playwright and humorist Oscar Wilde (1854–1900), division 89, is among the most visited (as the unfortunate glass barrier erected around his sculpted tomb, designed to prevent fans impregnating the stone with red lipstick imprints, attests).

📞 01 55 25 82 10

www.pere-lachaise.com

16 rue du Repos & 8 bd de Ménilmontant, 20e

🕐 8am-6pm Mon-Fri, 8.30am-6pm Sat, 9am-6pm Sun, shorter hours winter

Ⓜ Père Lachaise, Gambetta

☑ Top Tips

▶ The cemetery has five entrances, two of which are on bd de Ménilmontant.

▶ Get a free map of the graves from the Conservation Office (16 rue du Repos) in the cemetery's southwestern corner.

▶ Book a themed guided tour led by entertaining cemetery historian Thierry Le Roi (www.necro-romantiques.com).

✕ Take a Break

Head to **Yard** (6 rue de Mont Louis, 11e 🕐 noon-2.30pm & 8-10.30pm Mon-Fri, tapas 6pm-midnight Mon-Fri; Ⓜ Philippe Auguste), a short walk from the cemetery, to lunch on modern French fare in a trendy neobistro.

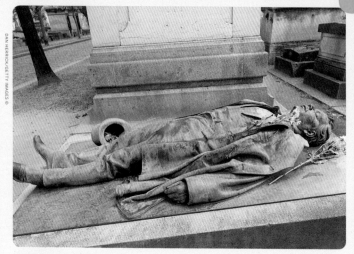

The legendary grave of Monsieur Noir

Jim Morrison

The other big hitter, also barricaded from over-zealous fans, is 1960s rock star Jim Morrison (1943–71; he died in Le Marais), division 6.

Monsieur Noir

Up in division 92, protests saw the removal of a fence around the grave of Monsieur Noir, aka journalist Yvan Salman (1848–70), shot aged 22 by Pierre Bonaparte, great-nephew of Napoléon. Legend says women who stroke the amply filled crotch of Monsieur Noir's prostrate bronze effigy will enjoy a better sex life and fertility.

Mur des Fédérés

Commemorative memorials to victims of almost every war in modern history form a poignant alley alongside the Mur des Fédérés, an unmemorable plain brick wall against which Communard insurgents were lined up, shot and buried in a mass grave in 1871.

Explore

Notre Dame & the Islands

Paris' geographic and spiritual heart is situated here in the Seine. The city's watery beginnings took place on the Île de la Cité (pictured on the left of the Seine, above), the larger of the two inner-city islands. To its east, the serene Île St-Louis is graced with elegant, exclusive apartments, along with a handful of intimate hotels and charming eateries and boutiques.

The Sights in a Day

☀️ The city's landmark cathedral, **Notre Dame** (p110), dominates the Île de la Cité, so where better to start your explorations? (Heading here first also means you'll beat the crowds.) In addition to viewing its stained-glass interior, allow around an hour to visit the top and another to explore the archaeological crypt. For even more beautiful stained-glass, don't miss nearby **Sainte-Chapelle** (p118). From here it's a few footsteps to the intriguing French Revolution prison, the **Conciergerie** (p118).

☀️ Cross the **Pont St-Louis** (p122) to the enchanting little Île St-Louis. After lunch at deliciously Parisian hang-out **Café Saint Régis** (p121), browse the island's boutiques and buy a **Berthillon** (p119) ice cream.

🌙 After a traditional French meal at **Mon Vieil Ami** (p121), stroll back over the Pont St-Louis (where you're likely to catch buskers) for a nightcap at the Île de la Cité's venerable wine bar **Taverne Henri IV** (p123). If you're still going strong, cross the **Pont Neuf** (p118) for entertainment options on either side of the Seine.

👁️ **Top Sights**

Notre Dame (p110)

💜 **Best of Paris**

History
Notre Dame (p110)

Sainte-Chapelle (p118)

Conciergerie (p118)

Drinking
Taverne Henri IV (p123)

Churches
Notre Dame (p110)

Sainte-Chapelle (p118)

Getting There

Ⓜ **Metro** Cité (line 4) on the Île de la Cité is the islands' only metro station, and the most convenient for Notre Dame.

Ⓜ **Metro** Pont Marie (line 7), on the Right Bank, is the Île St-Louis' closest station.

⛴ **Boat** The hop-on, hop-off Batobus stops opposite Notre Dame on the Left Bank.

Top Sights
Notre Dame

Paris' most visited unticketed site, with upwards of 14 million crossing its threshold each year, is a masterpiece of French Gothic architecture. Highlights of the mighty cathedral include its three spectacular rose windows, treasury and bell towers. From the North Tower, 400-odd steps spiral to the top of the western façade, with frightening gargoyles and a spectacular view of Paris.

◉ Map p116, D3

www.cathedraledeparis.com

6 place du Parvis Notre Dame, 4e

cathedral free, towers adult/child €8.50/free

🕑 cathedral 8am-6.45pm Mon-Fri, to 7.15pm Sat-Sun

Ⓜ Cité

Don't Miss

Architecture

Built on a site occupied by earlier churches and, a millennium prior, a Gallo-Roman temple, Notre Dame was begun in 1163 and largely completed by the early 14th century. The cathedral was badly damaged during the Revolution, prompting architect Eugène Emmanuel Viollet-le-Duc to oversee extensive renovations between 1845 and 1864. Enter the magnificent forest of ornate **flying buttresses** that encircle the cathedral chancel and support its walls and roof.

Notre Dame is known for its sublime balance, though if you look closely you'll see all sorts of minor asymmetrical elements introduced to avoid monotony, in accordance with standard Gothic practice. These include the slightly different shapes of each of the three main **portals**, whose statues were once brightly coloured to make them more effective as a *Biblia pauperum* – a 'Bible of the poor' to help the illiterate faithful understand Old Testament stories, the Passion of the Christ and the lives of the saints.

Rose Windows

When you enter the cathedral its grand dimensions are immediately evident: the interior alone is 127m long, 48m wide and 35m high and can accommodate some 6000 worshippers.

The most spectacular interior features are three rose windows, particularly the 10m-wide window over the western façade above the organ – one of the largest in the world, with 7800 pipes (900 of which have historical classification), 111 stops, five 56-key manuals and a 32-key pedalboard – and the window on the northern side of the transept (virtually unchanged since the 13th century).

☑ Top Tips

▶ Opening hours for the towers and treasury differ to those for the cathedral. Check the website for details.

▶ Queues can be huge and get longer throughout the day, especially during the summer months – arrive as early as possible.

▶ Pick up an audioguide (€5) from Notre Dame's information desk, just inside the entrance.

▶ Audioguide rental includes admission to the treasury.

▶ Free 45-minute English-language tours take place at 2pm Wednesday and Thursday and 2.30pm Saturday.

▶ Remember that Notre Dame is an active place of worship.

✖ Take a Break

Head to hidden place Dauphine for contemporary French fare at Le Caveau du Palais (p121).

Pop across to the adjacent Île St-Louis for a drink, snack or meal at Café Saint Régis (p121).

Towers

A constant queue marks the entrance to the **Tours de Notre Dame**, the cathedral's bell towers. Climb the 400-odd spiralling steps to the top of the western façade of the North Tower, where you'll find yourself on the rooftop **Galerie des Chimères** (Gargoyles Gallery), face-to-face with frightening and fantastic gargoyles. These grotesque statues divert rainwater from the roof to prevent masonry damage, with the water exiting through the elongated, open mouth – and, purportedly, ward off evil spirits. Although they appear medieval, they were installed by Eugène Emmanuel Viollet-le-Duc in the 19th century. From the rooftop there's a spectacular view over Paris.

In the South Tower hangs Emmanuel, the cathedral's original 13-tonne bourdon bell (all of the cathedral's bells are named). During the night of 24 August 1944, when the Île de la Cité was retaken by French, Allied and Resistance troops, the tolling of the Emmanuel announced Paris' approaching liberation. Emmanuel's peal purity comes from precious gems and jewels Parisian women threw into the pot when it was recast from copper and bronze in 1631.

As part of 2013's celebrations for Notre Dame's 850th anniversary since construction began, nine new bells were installed, replicating the original medieval chimes.

Treasury

In the southeastern transept, the *trésor* (treasury) contains artwork, liturgical objects and relics; pay a small fee to enter. Among its religious jewels and gems is the **Ste-Couronne** (Holy Crown), purportedly the wreath of thorns placed on Jesus' head before he was crucified. It is exhibited from 3pm to 4pm on the first Friday of each month, 3pm to 4pm every Friday during Lent, and 10am to 5pm on Good Friday.

Easier to admire is the treasury's wonderful collection, **Les Camées des Papes** (Papal cameos). Sculpted with incredible finesse in shell and framed in silver, the 268-piece collection depicts every pope in miniature from St Pierre to the present day, ending with Pope Benoit XVI. Note the different posture, hand gestures and clothes of each pope.

The Hunchback of Notre Dame

The damage inflicted on Notre Dame during the French Revolution saw it fall into ruin, and it was destined for demolition. Salvation came with the widespread popularity of Victor Hugo's 1831 novel, *The Hunchback of Notre Dame,* which sparked a petition to save it. Subsequently, in 1845, architect Eugène Emmanuel Viollet-le-Duc began the cathedral's grand-scale renovations.

The Mays

Walk past the **choir**, with its carved wooden stalls and statues representing the Passion of the Christ, to admire the cathedral's wonderful collection of paintings in its nave side chapels. From 1449 onwards, city goldsmiths offered to the cathedral each

NOTRE DAME

High Altar

Choir

Treasury

North Rose Window

South Rose Window

Transept

Nave

Towers Entrance

Towers Exit

Organ

West Rose Window

Portal of the Virgin

Portal of the Last Judgement

Portal of Saint Anne

Western Façade

Rose window on Notre Dame's western façade

year on 1 May a tree strung with devotional ribbons and banners to honour the Virgin Mary – to whom Notre Dame (Our Lady) is dedicated. Fifty years later the goldsmiths' annual gift, known as a May, had become a tabernacle decorated with scenes from the Old Testament, and, from 1630, a large canvas – 3m tall – commemorating one of the Acts of the Apostles, accompanied by a poem or literary explanation. By the early 18th century, when the brotherhood of goldsmiths was dissolved, the cathedral had received 76 such monumental paintings – just 13 can be admired today.

Music at Notre Dame

Music has been a sacred part of Notre Dame's soul since birth. The best day to appreciate its musical heritage is on Sunday at a Gregorian or polyphonic Mass (10am and 6.30pm respectively) or a free organ recital (4.30pm).

From October to June the cathedral stages evening concerts; find the program online at www.musique-sacree-notredamedeparis.fr.

If you can't make it in person, you can listen to Sunday's 6.30pm Mass on Radio Notre Dame 1 (100.7 FM), or streamed on the cathedral's website.

Landmark Occasions

Historic events that have taken place at Notre Dame include Henry VI of England's 1431 coronation as King of France; the 1558 marriage of Mary, Queen of Scots, to the Dauphin Francis (later Francis II of France); the 1804 coronation of Napoléon I by Pope Pius VII; and the 1909 beatification and 1920 canonisation of Joan of Arc.

The Heart of Paris

Notre Dame is very much the heart of Paris – so much so that distances from Paris to every part of metropolitan France are measured from place du Parvis Notre Dame, the vast square in front of the Cathedral of Our Lady of Paris where crowds gather in the afternoon sun to admire the cathedral façade. A bronze star across the street from the cathedral's main entrance marks the exact location of **Point Zéro des Routes de France**.

Crypt

Under the square in front of Notre Dame lies the **Crypte Archéologique**

Understand
Notre Dame Timeline

▶ **1160** The Bishop of Paris, Maurice de Sully, orders the demolition of the original cathedral, the 4th-century St-Étienne (St Stephen's).

▶ **1163** Notre Dame's cornerstone is laid and construction begins on the new cathedral.

▶ **1182** The apse and choir are completed.

▶ **Early 1200s** Work commences on the western façade.

▶ **1225** The western façade is completed.

▶ **1250** Work is finished on the western towers and north rose window.

▶ **Mid-1200s** To 'modernise' the cathedral, the transepts are remodelled in the Rayonnant style.

▶ **1345** The cathedral reaches completion.

▶ **1548** Huguenots storm and damage the cathedral following the Council of Trent.

▶ **1793** Damage during the most radical phase of the French Revolution sees many of Notre Dame's treasures plundered or destroyed.

▶ **1845–64** Following petitions to save the by-then-derelict cathedral from demolition, architect Eugène Emmanuel Viollet-le-Duc carries out extensive repairs and architectural additions.

▶ **1991** A lengthy maintenance and restoration program is initiated.

▶ **2013** Notre Dame celebrates 850 years since construction began.

(Archaeological Crypt; www.crypte.paris.fr; 1 place du Parvis Notre Dame, 4e; adult/child €7/5; ⊘10am-6pm Tue-Sun; ⓂCité), a 117m-long and 28m-wide area displaying in situ the remains of structures built on this site during the Gallo-Roman period, a 4th-century enclosure wall, the foundations of the medieval foundlings hospice and a few of the original sewers sunk by Haussmann. Audioguides cost €5.

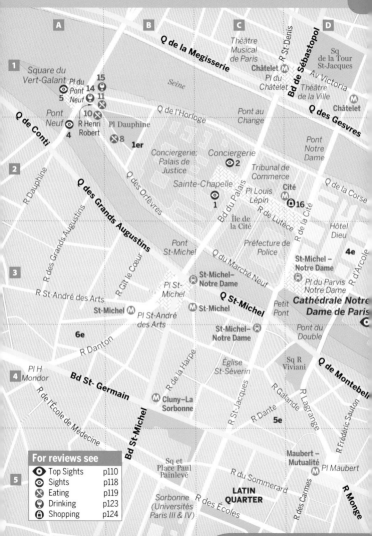

A

B

C

D

1

Square du
Vert-Galant

Pl du **15**
Pont **14**
Neuf **5** **11**

Q de Conti

Pont
Neuf **4**

10

R Henri
Robert

8 Pl Dauphine

1er

Q de la Megisserie

Seine

Q de l'Horloge

Théâtre
Musical
de Paris

Châtelet

Pl du
Châtelet

Pont au
Change

R St-Denis

Bd de Sébastopol

Sq
de la Tour
St-Jacques

Av Victoria

Théâtre
de la Ville

Q des Gesvres

Châtelet

2

Q des Grands Augustins

R Dauphine

Q des Orfèvres

Conciergerie;
Palais de
Justice

Sainte-Chapelle

1

Conciergerie

2

Bd du Palais

Tribunal de
Commerce

Pl Louis
Lépin

Île de
la Cité

Pont
Notre
Dame

Q de la Corse

Cité

16

R de la Cité

R de Lutèce

Hôtel
Dieu

3

R des Grands Augustins

R Gît le Cœur

Pont
St-Michel

Pl St-
Michel

St-Michel (M)

Pl St-André
des Arts

R St-André des Arts

6e

R Danton

St-Michel–
Notre Dame

St-Michel (M)

Q du Marché Neuf

Q St-Michel

Préfecture de
Police

Petit
Pont

St-Michel–
Notre Dame

St-Michel –
Notre Dame

Pl du Parvis
Notre Dame

Cathédrale Notre
Dame de Paris

Pont du
Double

d'Arcole

4e

4

Pl H
Mondor

R de l'École de Médecine

Bd St- Germain

Bd St-Michel

R de la Harpe

Cluny–La
Sorbonne

Église
St-Séverin

R St-Jacques

R Dante

Sq R
Viviani

R Galande

R Lagrange

Q de Montebell

R Frédéric Sauton

5e

Maubert –
Mutualité

Pl Maubert

R Monge

5

Sq et
Place Paul
Painlevé

Sorbonne
(Universités
Paris III & IV)

R des Écoles

R du Sommerard

LATIN
QUARTER

R des Carmes

For reviews see

◉	Top Sights	p110
◎	Sights	p118
✖	Eating	p119
●	Drinking	p123
⬟	Shopping	p124

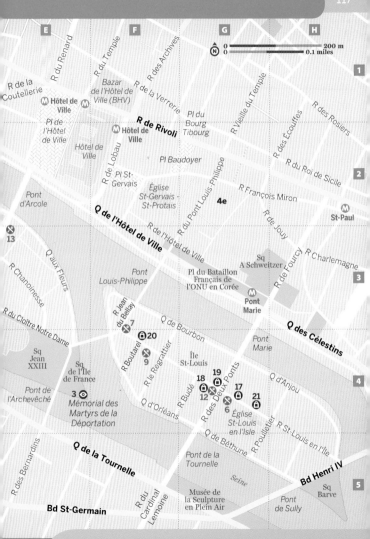

E

F

G

H

R du Renard

R de la Coutellerie

R du Temple

R des Archives

Bazar de l'Hôtel de Ville (BHV)

R de la Verrerie

R Vieille du Temple

R des Écouffes

R des Rosiers

1

M Hôtel de Ville

Pl de l'Hôtel de Ville

M Hôtel de Ville

R de Rivoli

Pl du Bourg Tibourg

N 0 ——— 200 m
0 ——— 0.1 miles

Hôtel de Ville

R de Lobau

Pl Baudoyer

R du Roi de Sicile

2

Pl St-Gervais

Église St-Gervais - St-Protais

R du Pont Louis-Philippe

4e

R François Miron

R de Jouy

M St-Paul

Pont d'Arcole

Q de l'Hôtel de Ville

R de l'Hôtel de Ville

Sq A Schweitzer

R de Fourcy

R Charlemagne

13

Q aux Fleurs

R Chanoinesse

Pont Louis-Philippe

Pl du Bataillon Français de l'ONU en Corée

M Pont Marie

3

R du Cloître Notre Dame

R Jean du Bellay

7

Q de Bourbon

Pont Marie

Q des Célestins

Sq Jean XXIII

Sq de l'Île de France

R Boutarel

20

9

R le Regrattier

Île St-Louis

18 19

R Budé

17

Q d'Anjou

4

Pont de l'Archevêché

3 Mémorial des Martyrs de la Déportation

12

R des Deux Ponts

6

21

Église St-Louis en l'Isle

R Poulletier

R St-Louis en l'Île

Q d'Orléans

Q de Béthune

R des Bernardins

Q de la Tournelle

Pont de la Tournelle

Seine

Bd Henri IV

Sq Barye

5

Bd St-Germain

R du Cardinal Lemoine

Musée de la Sculpture en Plein Air

Pont de Sully

Sights

Sainte-Chapelle CHAPEL

1 Map p116, C2

Try to save Sainte-Chapelle for a sunny day, when Paris' oldest, finest stained glass is at its dazzling best. Enshrined within the **Palais de Justice** (Law Courts), this gemlike Holy Chapel is Paris' most exquisite Gothic monument. Sainte-Chapelle was built in just six years (compared with nearly 200 years for Notre Dame) and consecrated in 1248. The chapel was conceived by Louis IX to house his personal collection of holy relics, including the famous Holy Crown (now in Notre Dame). (☎01 53 40 60 80, concerts 01 42 77 65 65; www. monuments-nationaux.fr; 4 bd du Palais, 1er; adult/child €8.50/free, joint ticket with Conciergerie €15; ⏰9.30am-6pm Thu-Tue, to 9pm Wed mid-May–mid-Sep, 9.30am-6pm Mar–mid-May & mid-Sep–Oct, 9am-5pm Nov–Feb; MCité)

Conciergerie MONUMENT

2 Map p116, C2

A royal palace in the 14th century, the Conciergerie later became a prison. During the Reign of Terror (1793–94) alleged enemies of the Revolution were incarcerated here before being brought before the Revolutionary Tribunal next door in the Palais de Justice. Top-billing exhibitions take place in the beautiful, Rayonnant Gothic **Salle des Gens d'Armes**, Europe's largest surviving medieval hall. (www.monuments-nationaux.fr; 2 bd du Palais, 1er; adult/child €8.50/free, joint ticket with Sainte-Chapelle €15; ⏰9.30am-6pm; MCité)

Mémorial des Martyrs de la Déportation MONUMENT

3 Map p116, E4

The Memorial to the Victims of the Deportation, erected in 1962, remembers the 200,000 French residents (including 76,000 Jews, of whom 11,000 were children) who were deported to and murdered in Nazi concentration camps during WWII. A single barred 'window' separates the bleak, rough-concrete courtyard from the waters of the Seine. Inside lies the **Tomb of the Unknown Deportee**. (www.cheminsdememoire.gouv.fr; square de l'Île de France, 1er; admission free; ⏰10am-7pm Apr-Sep, to 5pm Tue-Sun Oct-Mar; MCité, ℝRER St-Michel–Notre Dame)

Pont Neuf BRIDGE

4 Map p116, A2

Paris' oldest bridge, ironically named 'New Bridge', has linked the western end of Île de la Cité with both river banks since 1607, when the king, Henri IV, inaugurated it by crossing the bridge on a white stallion. View the bridge's arches (seven on the northern stretch and five on the southern span), decorated with 381 *mascarons* (grotesque figures) depicting barbers, dentists, pickpockets, loiterers etc, from a spot along the river or afloat. (MPont Neuf)

Mascarons on the Point Neuf

Square du Vert-Galant

PARK

5 ⊙ Map p116, A1

Chestnut, yew, black walnut and weeping willow trees grace this picturesque park at the westernmost tip of the Île de la Cité, along with migratory birds including mute swans, pochard and tufted ducks, black-headed gulls and wagtails. Sitting at the islands' original level, 7m below their current height, the waterside park is reached by stairs leading down from the Pont Neuf. It's romantic at any time of day but especially in the evening watching the sun set over the river. (place du Pont Neuf; ⊙24hr; MPont Neuf)

Eating

Berthillon

ICE CREAM **$**

6 ✗ Map p116, G4

Founded here in 1954, this esteemed *glacier* (ice-cream maker) is still run by the same family today. Its 70 all-natural, chemical-free flavours include fruit sorbets such as blackcurrant or pink grapefruit, and richer ice creams made from fresh milk and eggs, such as salted caramel, *marrons glacés* (candied chestnuts) and Agenaise (Armagnac and prunes). (www.berthillon.fr; 31 rue St-Louis en l'Île, 4e; 1/2/3 scoops take away €3/4/6.50, eat-in €4.50/7.50/10.50; ⊙10am-8pm Wed-Sun, closed Aug; MPont Marie)

Understand

The French Revolution

Beginnings

By the late 1780s, the extravagance of Louis XVI and his queen, Marie Antoinette, had alienated virtually every segment of society and the king became increasingly isolated as unrest and dissatisfaction reached boiling point. When he tried to neutralise the power of the more reform-minded delegates at a meeting of the États-Généraux (States-General), the masses took to the streets. On 14 July 1789, a mob raided the Hôtel des Invalides for rifles, seizing 32,000 muskets, and then stormed the prison at Bastille. The French Revolution had begun.

Girondins vs Jacobins

At first the Revolution was in the hands of moderate republicans called the Girondins. France was declared a constitutional monarchy and re-forms were introduced, including the adoption of the Déclaration des Droits de l'Homme and du Citoyen (Declaration of the Rights of Man and of the Citizen). But as the masses armed themselves against the external threat to the new government by Austria, Prussia and the exiled French nobles, patriotism and nationalism combined with extreme fervour to both popularise and radicalise the Revolution. It was not long before the Girondins lost out to the extremist Jacobins, who abolished the monarchy and declared the First Republic in 1792. The Assemblée Nationale (National Assembly) was replaced by an elected Revolutionary Convention.

End of the Monarchy

Louis XVI, who had unsuccessfully tried to flee the country, was convicted of 'conspiring against the liberty of the nation' and guillotined at today's place de la Concorde in January 1793. Marie Antoinette was later executed in October 1793.

The Jacobins set up the notorious Committee of Public Safety to deal with national defence and to apprehend and try 'traitors'. This body had dictatorial control over the city and the country during the Reign of Terror (from September 1793 to July 1794), which saw thousands beheaded, most religious freedoms revoked and churches closed to worship and desecrated.

After the Reign of Terror faded, moderate republicans set themselves up to rule the republic. A group of royalists bent on overthrowing them were led by Napoléon, whose victories would soon turn him into an independent political force.

Café Saint Régis
CAFE $

7 Map p116, F3

Waiters in long white aprons, a white ceramic-tiled interior, and retro vintage decor make hip Le Saint Régis (as regulars call it) a deliciously Parisian hang-out any time of day – from breakfast pastries to mid-morning pancakes, lunchtime salads and burgers, and early-evening oyster platters. Come midnight it morphs into a late-night hot spot. (www.cafesaintregisparis.com; 6 rue Jean du Bellay, 4e; breakfast & snacks €3.50-14.50, mains €18-32; ⏰8am-2am; 📶; Ⓜ Pont Marie)

Le Caveau du Palais
MODERN FRENCH $$

8 Map p116, B2

Even when the western Île de la Cité shows few other signs of life, the Caveau's half-timbered dining areas and (weather permitting) alfresco terrace are packed with diners tucking into bountiful fresh fare: steak tartare with quail's egg, artichoke and mushroom risotto with braised spinach, turbot with sweet potato and sea salt mash, and deconstructed lemon tart. (📞01 43 26 04 28; www.caveaudupalais.fr; 19 place Dauphine, 1er; mains €21-27; ⏰noon-2.30pm & 7-10pm Mon-Sat; Ⓜ Pont Neuf)

Mon Vieil Ami
TRADITIONAL FRENCH $$$

9 Map p116, F4

Alsatian chef Antoine Westermann is the creative talent behind this sleek black neobistro where guests are treated like old friends (hence the name) and vegetables get star billing. From Wednesday to Sunday only, the good-value lunchtime *plat du jour* (dish of the day), such as wintertime kale with smoked bacon and roast chicken, is a perfect reflection of the season. (📞01 40 46 01 35; www.mon-vieil-ami.com; 69 rue St-Louis en l'Île, 4e; menu €48, mains €14-25; ⏰noon-2.30pm & 7-11pm; 📶; Ⓜ Pont Marie)

Les Voyelles

MODERN FRENCH $$

10 Map p116, A1

Worth the short walk from Notre Dame, the Vowels – spot the letters scattered between books and beautiful objects on the shelves lining the intimate 'library' dining room – is thoroughly contemporary, with fare ranging from finger food (including a daily burger) to full-blown *menus,* which might feature *onglet de bœuf* (hanger steak) with béarnaise sauce. Its pavement terrace is Paris gold. (☑ 01 46 33 69 75; www.les-voyelles.com; 74 quai des Orfèvres, 4e; 2-/3-course menus €17/22.50; ⏱ noon-3pm & 7-10.30pm Tue-Sat; Ⓜ Pont Neuf)

Ma Salle à Manger

BISTRO $$

11 Map p116, A1

Framed by a pretty-as-a-picture blue-and-white striped awning and pavement tables, on tucked-away place Dauphine, convivial little bistro-wine bar 'My Dining Room' chalks its changing menu on the blackboard. Simple yet inspired dishes might include French onion soup, Camembert baked with wine, confit of duck with baked apple, filet Mignon with potato dauphinoise (grated baked potatoes) and a feather-light crème brûlée. (☑ 01 43 29 52 34; www.masalleamanger.fr; 26 place Dauphine, 1er; 2-/3-course lunch menus €20.50/25.50, dinner menus €23.50/28.50; ⏱ 9am-10.30pm; Ⓜ Pont Neuf)

L'Îlot Vache

TRADITIONAL FRENCH $$

12 Map p116, G4

Named for one of the Île St-Louis' previous two islands and decorated with cow statuettes, this former butcher shop flickers with candles that give its exposed stone and wooden beams a romantic glow. Traditional French classics span Burgundy snails with parsley butter to bœuf bourguignon, duck breast with raspberry jus, and roast seasonal fruits with blackcurrant sorbet. (☑ 01 73 20 21 64; www.lilotvache.fr; 35 rue St-Louis en l'Île, 4e; 3-course menu €39, mains €24.50-35; ⏱ 7-11.30pm; 🛜; Ⓜ Pont Marie)

◯ Local Life

Buskers

Paris' eclectic gaggle of clowns, mime artists, living statues, acrobats, roller-bladers, buskers and other street entertainers cost substantially less than a theatre ticket (a few coins in the hat is appreciated). Some excellent musicians audition to perform aboard the metro and in the corridors. Outside, you can be sure of a good show at countless spots around the city. Two of the best are **Pont St-Louis** (Ⓜ Pont Marie), the bridge between the Île de la Cité and Île St-Louis, and **Pont au Double**, the pedestrian bridge linking the Île de la Cité near Notre Dame with the Left Bank.

Parisian al fresco dining

Huré

BOULANGERIE $

13  Map p116, E3

Feisty savoury tarts and quiches, jumbo salads bursting with fresh veggies, mountains of giant meringues piled high on the counter, giant cookies and cakes every colour of the rainbow: if you're after a light alfresco lunch, you'll be hard-pushed to find a better *boulangerie* near Notre Dame. (www.hure-createur.fr; 1 rue d'Arcole, 4e; takeaway lunch menus €8.50-9.50, sandwiches €3-6; ☺6.30am-8pm Mon-Sat; MSt-Michel Notre Dame, Châtelet)

Drinking

Taverne Henri IV

WINE BAR

14 Map p116, A1

Dating from 1885, this venerable wine bar lures legal types from the nearby Palais de Justice (not to mention celeb writers and actors, as the autographed snaps testify). A choice of *tartines* (open-faced sandwiches), charcuterie and aromatic cheese platters complement its extensive wine list. (13 place du Pont Neuf, 1er, ☺noon-11pm Mon-Sat, closed Aug; MPont Neuf)

KIM ROGERSON/GETTY IMAGES ©

Marché aux Fleurs Reine Elizabeth II

Les Jardins du Pont-Neuf

COCKTAIL BAR

15 Map p116, A1

Island life became more glamorous with the opening of this ultra-chic floating cocktail bar aboard a barge moored by the Pont Neuf. Decked out with art-nouveau-inspired decor including rattan furniture and hanging plants, its two vast terraces overlook the Seine. There's also a dance floor; check the website for upcoming soirées. (www.jdp9.com; quai de l'Horloge, 1er; ⊘7pm-2am Tue-Sat; 🛜; Ⓜ Pont Neuf)

Shopping

Marché aux Fleurs Reine Elizabeth II

MARKET

16 🔒 Map p116, D2

Blooms have been sold at this flower market since 1808, making it the oldest market of any kind in Paris. On Sunday, between 8am and 7pm, it transforms into a cacophonous bird market, the **Marché aux Oiseaux**. (place Louis Lépin, 4e; ⊘8am-7.30pm Mon-Sat; Ⓜ Cité)

38 Saint Louis

FOOD & DRINKS

17 🔒 Map p116, G4

Not only does this contemporary, creamy white-fronted *fromagerie* run by a young, dynamic, food-driven duo have an absolutely superb selection of first-class French *fromage* (cheese), it also offers Saturday wine tastings, artisan fruit juices and prepared dishes to go such as sheep's-cheese salad with truffle oil, and wooden boxes filled with vacuum-packed cheese to take home. (38 rue St-Louis en l'Île, 4e; ⊘8.30am-10pm Tue-Sat, 9.30am-4pm Sun; Ⓜ Pont Marie)

Clair de Rêve

TOYS

18 🔒 Map p116, G4

Stringed marionettes made of papier mâché, leather and porcelain bob from the ceiling of this endearing little shop. It also sells wind-up toys and music boxes. (www.clairdereve.com; 35 rue St-Louis en l'Île, 4e; ⊘11am-1pm & 1.30-7.15pm Mon-Sat; Ⓜ Pont Marie)

L'Îles aux Images ART

19 Map p116, G4

Original and rare vintage posters, photographs and lithographs dating from 1850 onwards from artists including Man Ray, Salvador Dalí, Paul Gauguin and Pablo Picasso are stocked at this gallery-boutique. Many depict Parisian scenes and make evocative home decorations. Framing can be arranged. (01 56 24 15 22; www.lileauximages.com; 51 rue Saint-Louis en l'Île, 4e; 2-7pm Mon-Sat & by appointment; M Pont Marie)

Il Campiello ARTS & CRAFTS

20 Map p116, F4

Venetian carnival masks – intricately crafted from papier mâché, ceramics and leather – are the speciality of this exquisite shop, which also sells jewellery made from Murano glass beads. It was established by a native of Venice, to which the Île St-Louis bears more than a passing resemblance. (www.ilcampiello.com; 88 rue St-Louis en l'Île, 4e; noon-7pm; M Pont Marie)

Librairie Ulysse BOOKS

21 Map p116, G4

You can barely move in between this shop's antiquarian and new travel guides, *National Geographic* back editions and maps. Opened in 1971 by the intrepid Catherine Domaine, this was the world's first travel bookshop. Hours vary, but ring the bell and Catherine will open up if she's around. (www.ulysse.fr; 26 rue St-Louis en l'Île, 4e; 2-8pm Tue-Fri; M Pont Marie)

Explore

The Latin Quarter

So named because international students communicated in Latin here until the French Revolution, the Latin Quarter remains the hub of academic life in Paris. Centred on the Sorbonne's main university campus (pictured above), graced by fountains and lime trees, this lively area is also home to some outstanding museums and churches, along with Paris' beautiful art deco mosque and botanic gardens.

The Sights in a Day

☼ The Batobus stops at Paris' botanic gardens, the **Jardin des Plantes** (p134), so consider cruising here first and exploring its **natural history museums** (p136) and small **zoo** (p134). Then make your way to the **Mosquée de Paris** (p134) for a *hammam* (Turkish steambath). Enjoy sweet mint tea in its courtyard and delicious *tajines* for lunch.

☼ Check out amazing Arab art and ingenious architecture at the **Institut du Monde Arabe** (p134) and pay your respects to some of France's most illustrious thinkers and innovators at the **Panthéon** (p134) mausoleum. For the ultimate medieval history lesson, visit the **Musée National du Moyen Âge** (p128).

☾ After fusion cuisine at **Sola** (p137), browse late-night bookshops like the charming, cluttered **Shakespeare & Company** (p142), then catch jazz at the **Caveau de la Huchette** (p141) or head to lively bars like **Le Crocodile** (p141).

For a local's day in the Latin Quarter, see p130.

◉ Top Sights

Musée National du Moyen Âge (p128)

◯ Local Life

A Stroll along Rue Mouffetard (p130)

♥ Best of Paris

Architecture
Institut du Monde Arabe (p134)

History
Musée National du Moyen Âge (p128)

Arènes de Lutèce (p135)

Sorbonne (p136)

Panthéon (p134)

Getting There

Ⓜ **Metro** St-Michel (line 4) and the connected St-Michel–Notre Dame (RER B and C) is the neighbourhood's gateway.

Ⓜ **Metro** Other handy metro stations include Cluny–La Sorbonne (line 10) and Place Monge (line 7).

⚓ **Boat** The hop-on, hop-off Batobus stops in the Latin Quarter opposite Notre Dame and near the Jardin des Plantes.

Top Sights
Musée National du Moyen Âge

Sublime treasures at the National Museum of the Middle Ages span medieval statuary, stained glass and objets d'art to its celebrated series of tapestries, *The Lady with the Unicorn*. Evocatively housed in an ornate 15th-century mansion (the Hôtel de Cluny) and the much older *frigidarium* (cold room) of an enormous Roman-era bathhouse, this is one of Paris' top small museums.

◉ Map p132, A2

www.musee-moyenage.fr

6 place Paul Painlevé, 5e

adult/child €8/free, during temporary exhibitions €9/free

◷ 9.15am-5.45pm Wed-Mon

Ⓜ Cluny–La Sorbonne

'À Mon Seul Désir', part of *The Lady with the Unicorn* series of tapestries

Don't Miss

The Hôtel de Cluny

Initially the residential quarters of the Cluny Abbots, the Hôtel de Cluny was later occupied by Alexandre du Sommerard, who moved here in 1833 with his collection of medieval and Renaissance objects. Bought by the state after his death, the museum opened a decade later, retaining the Hôtel de Cluny's original layout and features.

An entire room (No 8) is dedicated to statuary from Notre Dame's façade that was removed during the Revolution.

Gallo-Roman Bathhouse

The museum's northwestern corner is where you'll find the remains of the Gallo-Roman bathhouse, built around AD 200. Look for the display of the fragment of mosaic *Love Riding a Dolphin,* as well as a gorgeous marble bathtub from Rome. Outside the museum, remnants of the other rooms – a *palestra* (exercise room), *tepidarium* (warm bath) and *calidarium* (hot bath) – are visible.

Tapestries

Upstairs on the 1st floor (room 13) are the unicorn tapestries, representing the five senses and an enigmatic sixth, perhaps the heart. It's believed that they were originally commissioned around 1500 by the Le Viste family in Paris. Discovered in 1814 in the Château de Boussac, they were acquired by the museum in 1882.

Gardens

Small gardens to the museum's northeast, including the Jardin Céleste (Celestial Garden) and the Jardin d'Amour (Garden of Love), are planted with flowers, herbs and shrubs that appear in works hanging throughout the museum.

☑ **Top Tips**

▶ Admission includes an audioguide.

▶ Guided tours in French costing €4.50 for one hour or €6.50 for 1½ hours are available by reservation.

▶ School visits of the museum generally take place on Mondays, Thursdays and Fridays, so if you're planning to visit on those days, you're best aiming for noon to 2pm or after 3.30pm when it's quieter.

▶ Check the schedule for daytime concerts (adult/child €6/4) lasting 45 minutes and evening concerts (€16/13) lasting 1½ hours.

✕ Take a Break

Local bistro **Le Pré Verre** (☏ 01 43 54 59 47; www.lepreverre.com; 8 rue Thénard, 5e; lunch menu €14.50, mains €20; ☺ noon-2pm & 7.30-10.30pm Tue-Sat; 🛜 🚻; Ⓜ Maubert-Mutualité) offers lively, great-value dining.

Local Life
A Stroll along Rue Mouffetard

Originally a Roman road, rue Mouffetard acquired its name in the 18th century, when the now-underground River Bievre became the communal waste disposal for local tanners and wood-pulpers. The odours gave rise to the name Mouffettes ('skunks'), which evolved into Mouffetard. Today the aromas on 'La Mouffe', as it's nicknamed, are infinitely more enticing, particularly at its market stalls.

1 Market Shopping
Grocers, butchers, fish-mongers and other food purveyors set their goods out on street stalls along this sloping, cobbled street during the **Marché Mouffetard** (🕑8am-7.30pm Tue-Sat, to noon Sun; **M**Censier Daubenton).

2 Fine Cheeses

You won't even have to worry about aromas if you're taking home something scrumptious from the *fromagerie* (cheese shop) **Androuet** (www.androuet.com; 134 rue Mouffetard, 5e; ⊙9.30am-1pm & 4-7.30pm Tue-Fri, 9.30am-7.30pm Sat, to 1.30pm Sun; MCensier Daubenton); all of its cheeses can be vacuum-packed for free. (Be sure to look up to see the beautiful murals on the building's façade!)

3 Delicious Deli

Stuffed olives and capsicums, and marinated eggplant are among the picnic goodies at gourmet Italian deli **Delizius** (134 rue Mouffetard, 5e; ⊙9.30am-8pm Tue-Sat, 9am-2pm Sun; MCensier Daubenton), which also sells ready-to-eat hot meals, and fresh and dried pasta.

4 Movie Time

Even locals find it easy to miss the small doorway leading to cinema **L'Epée de Bois** (100 rue Mouffetard, 5e; MCensier Daubenton), which screens both art-house flicks and big-budget blockbusters.

5 Sweet Treats

Light, luscious macarons in flavours such as jasmine, raspberry and blackcurrant, and a mouth-watering range of chocolates are laid out like jewels at **Chocolats Mococha** (www.chocolats-mococha.com; 89 rue Mouffetard, 5e; ⊙11am-8pm; MCensier Daubenton). They are the creations of three *maîtres chocolatiers* (master chocolate-makers) – Fabrice Gillotte, Jacques Bellanger and Patrice Chapoare.

6 Apéro at Le Vieux Chêne

Hosting revolutionary meetings in 1848 and believed to be Paris' oldest bar, **Le Vieux Chêne** (69 rue Mouffetard, 5e; ⊙4pm-2am Sun-Thu, to 5am Fri & Sat; MPlace Monge) is a student favourite these days, especially during happy hour (4pm to 9pm Tuesday to Sunday, and from 4pm until closing on Monday).

7 Ice Cream

All that walking and peering in at gourmet food shops will no doubt leave you hungry, which means it's time for a stop at **Gelati d'Alberto** (45 rue Mouffetard, 5e; ⊙noon-midnight; MPlace Monge), where Italian ice-cream wizards shape your coned treat into a multiflavour flower.

8 Crêpes at Chez Nicos

The signboard outside crêpe artist Nicos' unassuming little shop, **Chez Nicos** (44 rue Mouffetard, 5e; crêpes €3-6; ⊙noon-2am; ; MPlace Monge), lists dozens of fillings. Ask by name for his masterpiece 'La Crêpe du Chef', stuffed with eggplant, feta, mozzarella, lettuce, tomatoes and onions. There's a handful of tables; otherwise, head to a nearby park.

For reviews see

● Top Sights	p128	
◎ Sights	p134	
⊗ Eating	p136	
⊗ Drinking	p140	
⊕ Entertainment	p141	
⊕ Shopping	p142	

Sq Marie Curie

Hôpital de la Pitié-Salpêtrière

R Jenner

R Jeanne d'Arc

R Esquirol

Ⓜ St-Marcel

R Buffon

R Poliveau

Museum National d'Histoire Naturelle

Mosquée de l'Ermite de Paris

Pl du Puits 3 ◎

R Larrey

Ⓜ R Monge

R Daubenton

R Mirbel

Ⓜ Censier Daubenton

Pl B Halpern

R Censier

Sq St-Médard

R Mouffetard

R Brossolette

R de l'Arbalète

R Vauquelin

R Rataud

R Claude Bernard

R des Feuillantines

R St-Jacques

24

Val de Grâce

R Broca

Sq Broca

R Pascal

Bd de Port Royal

R St-Hippolyte

19 ⊗

R de la Glacière

R Berbier du Mets

Sq René Le Gall

R de la Colladière

R Pascal

R Corvisart

R Vulpian

R Léon Maurice Nordmann

Bd Arago

R de la Santé

Cochin

Bd Auguste Blanqui

Ⓜ Glacière

R de Croulebarbe

R Abel Hovelacque

◎7

R Geoffroy-St-Hilaire

R des Wallons

Bd de l'Hôpital

R Duméril

R Pirandello

LATIN QUARTER

R du Fer à Moulin

R Scipion

Bd St-Marcel

R Lebrun

R du Banquier

Les Gobelins Ⓜ

Av des Gobelins

R Pinel

Campo Formio Ⓜ

R Rubens

R Coypel

13e

Ⓜ Place d'Italie

Pl d'Italie

Bd Vincent Auriol

14e

400 m

0.2 miles

Sights

Panthéon
MAUSOLEUM

1 ⊙ Map p132, A3

Overlooking the city from its Left Bank perch, the Panthéon's stately neoclassical dome stands out as one of the most recognisable icons on the Parisian skyline. An architectural masterpiece, the interior is impressively vast. Originally a church and now a mausoleum, it has served since 1791 as the resting place of some of France's greatest thinkers, including Voltaire, Rousseau, Braille and Hugo. Its four newest 'residents' are Resistance fighters Germaine Tillion, Genèvieve de Gaulle-Anthonioz, Pierre Brossolette and Jean Zay. (www.monum.fr; place du Panthéon, 5e; adult/child €8.50/free; ⊘10am-6.30pm Apr-Sep, to 6pm Oct-Mar; M Maubert-Mutualité or RER Luxembourg)

Institut du Monde Arabe
ARCHITECTURE, MUSEUM

2 ⊙ Map p132, D3

The Arab World Institute was jointly founded by France and 18 Middle Eastern and North African nations in 1980, with the aim of promoting cross-cultural dialogue. In addition to hosting concerts, film screenings and a research centre, the stunning landmark is also home to a museum and temporary exhibition space. (Arab World Institute; www.imarabe.org; 1 place Mohammed V, 5e; adult/child €8/4; ⊘10am-6pm Tue-Thu, to 9.30pm Fri, to 7pm Sat & Sun; M Jussieu)

Mosquée de Paris
MOSQUE

3 ⊙ Map p132, C5

Paris' central mosque, with a striking 26m-high minaret, was completed in 1926 in an ornate art deco Moorish style. You can visit the interior to admire the intricate tile work and calligraphy. A separate entrance at 39 rue Geoffray-St-Hilaire leads to the wonderful North African–style **hammam** (admission €18; spa package from €43; ⊘10am-9pm Mon, Wed, Thu & Sat, 2-9pm Fri), **restaurant** (mains €15-26; ⊘kitchen noon-2.30pm & 7.30-10.30pm) and **tearoom** (⊘9am-11.30pm), and a small *souk* (actually more of a gift shop). Visitors must be modestly dressed. (☏01 43 31 14 32; www.la-mosquee.com; 2bis place du Puits de l'Ermite, 5e; adult/child €3/2; ⊘9am-noon & 2-7pm Sat-Thu Apr-Sep, 9am-noon & 2-6pm Sat-Thu Oct-Mar; M Place Monge)

Jardin des Plantes
GARDENS

4 ⊙ Map p132, E4

Founded in 1626 as a medicinal herb garden for Louis XIII, Paris' 24-hectare botanic gardens – visually defined by the double alley of plane trees that run the length of the park – are an idyllic spot to stroll around, break for a picnic (watch out for the automatic sprinklers!) and escape the city concrete for a spell. Three museums from the Muséum National d'Histoire Naturelle (p136) and a small **zoo** (www.mnhn.fr; 57 rue Cuvier, 5e; adult/child €13/9; ⊘9am-6pm Mon-Fri, to 6.30pm Sat & Sun Easter-Oct, to 5pm Nov-Easter;

Panthéon

Ⓜ Gare d'Austerlitz) increase its appeal. (www.jardindesplantes.net; place Valhubert & 36 rue Geoffroy-St-Hilaire, 5e; admission free; ⊙ 7.30am-8pm Apr-Oct, 8am-5.30pm Nov-Mar; Ⓜ Gare d'Austerlitz, Censier Daubenton, Jussieu)

Musée de la Sculpture en Plein Air
MUSEUM

5 ◉ Map p132, D2

Along quai St-Bernard, this open-air sculpture museum (also known as the Jardin Tino Rossi) has more than 50 late 20th-century unfenced sculptures, and makes a great picnic spot. A salad beneath a César or a baguette beside a Brancusi is a pretty classy way to see the Seine up close. (quai St-Bernard, 5e; admission free; Ⓜ Gare d'Austerlitz)

Arènes de Lutèce
RUINS

6 ◉ Map p132, C4

The 2nd-century Roman amphitheatre Lutetia Arena once seated 10,000 people for gladiatorial combats and other events. Found by accident in 1869 when rue Monge was under construction, it's now used by locals playing football and, especially, boules (similar to lawn bowls). Hours can vary. (www.arenesdelutece.com; 49 rue Monge, 5e; admission free; ⊙ 8am-9.30pm Apr-Oct, to 5.30pm Nov-Mar; Ⓜ Place Monge)

Muséum National d'Histoire Naturelle
MUSEUM

7 Map p132, D5

Despite the name, the Natural History Museum is not a single building, but a collection of sites throughout France. Its historic home is in the Jardin des Plantes (p134), and it's here you'll find the greatest number of branches: taxidermied animals in the excellent **Grande Galerie de l'Évolution** (36 rue Geoffroy-St-Hilaire, 5e; adult/child €9/free; ⏰10am-6pm Wed-Mon; Ⓜ Censier Daubenton), and fossils and dinosaur skeletons in the **Galeries d'Anatomie Comparée et de Paléontologie** (2 rue Buffon, 5e; adult/child €7/free; ⏰10am-5pm Mon & Wed-Fri, to 6pm Sat & Sun Apr-Sep, 10am-5pm Wed-Mon Oct-Mar; Ⓜ Gare d'Austerlitz). The **Galerie de Minéralogie et de Géologie** (36 rue Geoffroy-St-Hilaire, 5e; adult/child €6/free; ⏰10am-5pm Mon & Wed-Fri, to 6pm Sat & Sun Apr-Sep, 10am-5pm Wed-Mon Oct-Mar; Ⓜ Censier Daubenton) is home to meteorites and crystals. (www.mnhn.fr)

Sorbonne
UNIVERSITY

8 Map p132, A2

The crème de la crème of academia flock to this distinguished university, one of the world's most famous. Today 'La Sorbonne' embraces most of the 13 autonomous universities – some 45,215 students in all – created when the University of Paris was reorganised after the student protests of 1968. Visitors are not permitted to enter. (www.sorbonne.fr; 12 rue de la Sorbonne, 5e; Ⓜ Cluny–La Sorbonne or RER Luxembourg)

Square René Viviani
PARK

9 Map p132, B1

Opened in 1928 on the site of the former graveyard of adjoining church Église St-Julien-le-Pauvre, this picturesque park is home to the oldest tree in Paris. The black locust *(Robinia pseudoacacia)* was planted here in 1602 by Henri III, Henri IV and Louis XII's gardener, Jean Robin, and is now supported by concrete pillars disguised as branches and trunks. A 1995-installed bronze fountain by Georges Jeanclos depicts the legend of Saint Julien. (quai de Montebello, 5e; ⏰24hr; Ⓜ St-Michel)

Eating

Shakespeare & Company Café
CAFE $

10 Map p132, B1

Instant history was made when this light-filled, literary-inspired cafe opened in 2015 adjacent to magical bookshop Shakespeare & Company (p142), designed from long-lost sketches to fulfil a dream of late bookshop founder George Whitman from the 1960s. Its primarily vegetarian menu (with vegan and gluten-free dishes available) includes homemade bagels, rye bread, soups, salads and pastries, plus Parisian-roasted Café Lomi coffee. (www.shakespeareandcompany.com; 2 rue St-Julien le Pauvre, 5e; dishes €4-9.50; ⏰10am-6.30pm Mon-Fri, to 7.30pm Sat & Sun; 🛜🖊🚻; Ⓜ St-Michel)

Understand
A Pivotal Year: 1968

The year 1968 was a watershed. In March a large demonstration in Paris against the Vietnam War gave impetus to protests by students of the University of Paris. In May police broke up yet another demonstration, prompting angry students to occupy the Sorbonne and erect barricades in the Latin Quarter. Workers quickly joined in, with six million people across France participating in a general strike that virtually paralysed the country.

But while workers wanted to reap greater benefits from the consumer market, the students supposedly wanted to destroy it. De Gaulle took advantage of this division and appealed to people's fear of anarchy. A 100,000-strong crowd of Gaullists marched in support for the government, quashing any idea of revolution.

Once stability was restored the re-elected government immediately decentralised the higher education system, and implemented a series of reforms (including lowering the voting age to 18 and enacting an abortion law) throughout the 1970s to create the modern society France is today.

Restaurant AT
GASTRONOMY $$$

12 Map p132, C2

Trained by some of the biggest names in gastronomy (Pierre Gagnaire included), chef Atsushi Tanaka showcases abstract artlike masterpieces incorporating rare ingredients (charred bamboo, kohlrabi turnip cabbage, juniper berry powder, wild purple fennel, Nepalese Timut pepper) in a blank-canvas-style dining space on stunning outsized plates. Just off the entrance, steps lead to **Bar à Vins AT** (dishes €12-16; ⊙7pm-2am Tue-Sun), his cellar wine bar. (☏01 56 81 94 08; www.atsushitanaka.com; 4 rue du Cardinal Lemoine, 5e; 4-/6-course lunch menus €35/55, 12-course dinner tasting menu €95; ⊙12.15-2pm & 8-9.30pm Tue-Sat; Ⓜ Cardinal Lemoine)

Sola
FUSION $$$

13 Map p132, B1

Pedigreed chef Hiroki Yoshitake combines French technique with Japanese sensibility, resulting in gorgeous signature creations (such as miso-marinated foie gras on *feuille de brick* served on sliced tree trunk). The artful presentations and attentive service make this a perfect choice for a romantic meal – go for the full experience and reserve a table in the Japanese dining room downstairs. (☏dinner 01 43 29 59 04, lunch 09 65 01 73 68; www.restaurant-sola.com; 12 rue de l'Hôtel Colbert, 5e; menus lunch €48-78, dinner €98; ⊙noon-1.30pm & 7.30-9pm Tue-Sat; Ⓜ St-Michel)

Local Life

Café de la Nouvelle Mairie

Hidden away in a small, fountained square just around the corner from the Panthéon, the narrow wine bar **Café de la Nouvelle Mairie** (☑01 44 07 04 41; 19 rue des Fossés St-Jacques, 5e; mains €12-32; ☺kitchen 8am-midnight Mon-Fri; Ⓜ Cardinal Lemoine) is a neighbourhood secret, serving blackboard-chalked natural wines by the glass and delicious seasonal bistro fare.

Le Coupe-Chou   FRENCH $$

14 🍴 Map p132, B3

This maze of candlelit rooms inside a vine-clad 17th-century townhouse is overwhelmingly romantic. Ceilings are beamed, furnishings are antique, open fireplaces crackle and background classical music mingles with the intimate chatter of diners. As in the days when Marlene Dietrich dined here, advance reservations are essential. Timeless French dishes include Burgundy snails, steak tartare and bœuf bourguignon. (☑01 46 33 68 69; www.lecoupechou.com; 9 & 11 rue de Lanneau, 5e; 2-/3-course menus €27/33; ☺noon-2pm & 7-10.45pm Sep-Jul, 7-10.45pm Aug; Ⓜ Maubert-Mutualité)

L'AOC   TRADITIONAL FRENCH $$

15 🍴 Map p132, C2

'Bistrot carnivore' is the strapline of this ingenious restaurant concocted around France's most respected culinary products. The concept is Appellation d'Origine Contrôlée (AOC), the French precursor to Europe-wide AOP, meaning everything has been reared or produced according to strict guidelines. The results are outstanding. Choose between favourites (steak tartare) or the rotisserie menu, ranging from roast chicken to suckling pig. (☑01 43 54 22 52; www.restoaoc.com; 14 rue des Fossés St-Bernard, 5e; 2-/3-course lunch menus €21/29, mains €19-34; ☺noon-2pm & 7.30-11pm Tue-Sat; Ⓜ Cardinal Lemoine)

Les Pipos   TRADITIONAL FRENCH $$

16 🍴 Map p132, B3

Natural wines are the speciality of this *bar à vins*, which it keeps in its vaulted stone cellar. First-rate food includes a fish of the day and oysters from Brittany, along with standards like confit of duck and a mouthwatering cheese board, which includes all the gourmet names (bleu d'Auvergne, brie de Meaux, Rocamadour and St-Marcellin). No credit cards. (☑01 43 54 11 40; www.les-pipos.com; 2 rue de l'École Polytechnique, 5e; mains €11-30; ☺8am-2am Mon-Sat; Ⓜ Maubert-Mutualité)

La Tour d'Argent   GASTRONOMY $$$

17 🍴 Map p132, D2

The venerable Michelin-starred 'Silver Tower' is famous for its *caneton* (duckling), rooftop garden with glimmering Notre Dame views and fabulous history harking back to 1582 – from Henry III's inauguration of the first fork in France to inspiration for the winsome animated film *Ratatouille*. Its wine cellar is one of Paris' best; dining is dressy and exceedingly fine. (☎01 43 54 23 31; www.latourdargent.com; 15 quai de la Tournelle, 5e; menus lunch €85, dinner €180-200, mains €75-100; ⊗12.30-2pm & 7-10.30pm Tue-Sat Sep-Jul; ⓂCardinal Lemoine)

Le Comptoir du Panthéon

CAFE $

18 Map p132, A3

Enormous, creative meal-size salads are the reason to choose this as a dining spot. Magnificently placed across from the domed Panthéon on the shady side of the street, its pavement terrace is big, busy and quintessentially Parisian – turn your head away from Voltaire's burial place and the Eiffel Tower pops into view. The bar closes at 1.45am every day. (☎01 43 54 75 36; 5 rue Soufflot, 5e; salads €11-13, mains €12.40-15.40; ⊗kitchen 7am-11pm Mon-Sat, 8am-11pm Sun; 🛜; ⓂCardinal Lemoine or RER Luxembourg)

Odette

PATISSERIE $

19 Map p132, B1

Odette's ground-floor space sells *choux* (pastry puffs) with seasonal flavoured cream fillings (nine at any one time), such as coffee, lemon, green tea, salted caramel, pistachio and forest berries. Upstairs, its art deco tearoom plays 1920s music and serves *choux* along with tea, coffee and Champagne. The black-painted timber façade, fronted by tables, and geranium-filled 1st-floor window box are charming. (www.odette-

Odette

paris.com; 77 rue Galande, 5e; 1/6/12 pastry puffs €1.90/9.90/19.80; ⊗10.30am-7.30pm; ⓂSt-Michel)

Prosper et Fortunée

MODERN FRENCH $$

20 Map p132, B6

Chef Eric Lévy's 12-seat premises is effectively a clandestine supper club. Dining at this tucked-away little restaurant is an intimate experience, from watching Lévy prepare daily changing dishes (raw mackerel with yuzu and lemon confit; prime fillet with black radish) using mostly organic premium produce in his open kitchen then personally delivering each course (and bill). Prior reservations are essential.

BRIAN JANNSEN/ALAMY STOCK PHOTO ©

> ### Understand
> #### Local Lingo
> --
>
> Parisians have long had a reputation for being unable or unwilling to speak English, but this has changed dramatically, particularly in the digital age. Signposts, menus, establishment names and buzzwords increasingly incorporate English.
>
> Addressing people in French makes a huge difference, even simply *'Bonjour/bonsoir, parlez-vous anglais?'* (Good day/evening, do you speak English?). Often what is mistaken for Parisian arrogance is the equivalent of someone addressing you in a foreign language in your home country. On detecting an accent, many Parisians will switch to English to facilitate conversation (feel free to say if you prefer to converse in French).
>
> Another potential cause for misunderstanding is the cut-to-the-chase directness of French communication. Whereas in English it's common to say, for example, 'Can I have a coffee, please?', the French *'Un café, s'il vous plaît.'* (A coffee, please.) can sound abrupt to an anglophone ear. Likewise, the French tendency to frame a question 'You would like a coffee?' rather than 'Would you like a coffee?' may seem forward, though it's unintentional.

(☎ 01 43 37 70 39; 50 rue Broca, 5e; lunch/dinner menus €23/45; ⊗ noon-3pm & 7-10.30pm Tue-Fri, 7-10.30pm Sat Sep-Jul; Ⓜ Les Gobelins)

(2 rue Valette, 5e; ⊗ 3pm-2am Mon-Thu, 4pm-5am Fri & Sat; Ⓜ Maubert-Mutualité)

Drinking

Le Pub St-Hilaire PUB

21 Map p132, B3

'Buzzing' fails to do justice to the pulsating vibe inside this student-loved pub. Generous happy hours last from 5pm to 9pm and the place is kept packed with a trio of pool tables, board games, music on two floors, hearty bar food and various gimmicks to rev up the party crowd (a metre of cocktails, 'be your own barman' etc).

Little Bastards COCKTAIL BAR

22 Map p132, B4

Only house-creation cocktails are listed on the menu at uberhip Little Bastards – among them Fal' in Love (Beefeater gin, cranberry juice, lime, mint, guava purée and Falernun clove-, ginger- and almond-syrup), Be a Beet Smooth (Jameson, coriander, sherry, egg white and pepper) and Deep Throat (Absolut vodka, watermelon syrup and Pernod) – but they'll also mix up classics if you ask. (5 rue Blainville, 5e; ⊗ 6pm-2am Mon-Thu, to 4am Fri & Sat; Ⓜ Place Monge)

Le Crocodile
BAR

23 Map p132, A3

This green-shuttered bar has been dispensing affordable cocktails (363 at last count, with gummy-'bear' crocodiles in the glass) since 1966. Arrive late for a truly eclectic crowd, including lots of students, and raucous revelry. Hours can vary (dawn closings are common). Happy hour runs from 6pm to 11pm Monday to Thursday and 6pm to 10pm Friday and Saturday. (6 rue Royer-Collard, 5e; ⏰6pm-2am Mon-Sat; MOdéon or RER Luxembourg)

Strada Café
COFFEE

24 Map p132, C3

Beans from Parisian roastery l'Arbre à Café (Brazilian, Ethiopian and Costa Rican espresso blend, and Ethiopian filter blend), Lyon roastery Mokxa (Honduran bio single-origin espresso) and hot new Amsterdam roastery White Label (Rwandan filter) underpin the success of sunlit corner cafe Strada. Electrical sockets are plentiful and the international baristas are passionate about their brews. (www.stradacafe.fr; 24 rue Monge, 5e; ⏰8am-6.30pm Mon-Fri, 10am-6.30pm Sat & Sun; 📶; MCardinal Lemoine)

Entertainment

Café Universel
JAZZ, BLUES

25 Map p132, A5

Café Universel hosts a brilliant array of live concerts with everything from bebop and Latin sounds to vocal jazz sessions. Plenty of freedom is given to young producers and artists, and its convivial relaxed atmosphere attracts a mix of students and jazz lovers. Concerts are free, but tip the artists when they pass the hat around. (📞01 43 25 74 20; www.cafeuniversel.com; 267 rue St-Jacques, 5e; ⏰9pm-2am Mon-Sat; 📶; MCensier Daubenton or RER Port Royal)

Le Champo
CINEMA

26 Map p132, A2

This is one of the most popular of the many Latin Quarter cinemas, featuring classics and retrospectives looking at the films of such actors and directors as Alfred Hitchcock, Jacques Tati, Alain Resnais, Frank Capra, Tim Burton and Woody Allen. One of the two *salles* (cinemas) has wheelchair access. (www.lechampo.com; 51 rue des Écoles, 5e; tickets adult/child €9/4; MCluny–La Sorbonne)

Caveau de la Huchette
JAZZ, BLUES

27 Map p132, B1

Housed in a medieval *caveau* (cellar) used as a courtroom and torture chamber during the Revolution, this club is where virtually all the jazz greats (Georges Brassens, Thibault...) have played since the end of WWII. It attracts its fair share of tourists, but the atmosphere can be more electric than at the more serious jazz clubs. Sessions start at 10pm. (📞01 43 26 65 05; www.caveaudelahuchette.fr; 5 rue de la Huchette, 5e; Sun-Thu €13, Fri & Sat €15; ⏰9.30pm-2.30am Sun-Wed, to 4am Thu-Sat; MSt-Michel)

Shopping

Shakespeare & Company   BOOKS

28 🔒 Map p132, B1

Shakespeare's enchanting nooks and crannies overflow with new and secondhand English-language books. The original shop (12 rue l'Odéon, 6e; closed by the Nazis in 1941) was run by Sylvia Beach and became the meeting point for Hemingway's 'Lost Generation'. Readings by emerging and illustrious authors take place at 7pm most Mondays. There's a wonderful cafe (p136) and various workshops and festivals. (📞01 43 25 40 93; www.shakespeareandcompany.com; 37 rue de la Bûcherie, 5e; ⏰10am-11pm; Ⓜ️St-Michel)

Le Bonbon au Palais   SWEETS

29 🔒 Map p132, C3

Kids and kids-at-heart will adore this sugar-fuelled *tour de France*. The school-geography-themed boutique stocks rainbows of artisan sweets from around the country. Old-fashioned glass jars brim with treats like *calissons* (diamond-shaped, icing-sugar-topped ground fruit and almonds from Aix-en-Provence), *rigolettes* (fruit-filled pillows from Nantes), *berlingots* (striped, triangular boiled sweets from Carpentras and elsewhere) and *papalines* (herbal liqueur-filled pink-chocolate balls from Avignon). (www.bonbonsaupalais.fr; 19 rue Monge, 5e; ⏰10.30am-7.30pm Tue-Sat; Ⓜ️Cardinal Lemoine)

Bières Cultes   DRINKS

30 🔒 Map p132, C3

At any one time this beer-lovers' fantasyland stocks over 400 different craft and/or international brews and also has two on tap to taste on the spot. Its wares when you visit might include US-brewed Alaskan Smoked Porter, German smoked Aecht Schlenkerla Rauchbier from Bamberg, and New Zealand Monteith's. Check its website for events and seasonal releases. (www.bierescultes.fr; 44 rue des Boulangers, 5e; ⏰3-8pm Mon, 11am-2pm & 3-9pm Tue-Thu, 11am-9pm Fri & Sat; Ⓜ️Cardinal Lemoine)

Abbey Bookshop   BOOKS

31 🔒 Map p132, A1

In a heritage-listed townhouse, this welcoming Canadian-run bookshop serves free coffee (sweetened with maple syrup) to sip while you browse tens of thousands of new and used books, and organises literary events and countryside hikes. (📞01 46 33 16 24; 29 rue de la Parcheminerie, 5e; ⏰10am-7pm Mon-Sat, 2-7pm Sun; Ⓜ️Cluny–La Sorbonne)

Crocodisc   MUSIC

32 🔒 Map p132, B2

Music might be more accessible than ever before in the digital age, but for many it will never replace rummaging through racks for treasures. New and secondhand CDs and vinyl discs at 40 rue des Écoles span world music, rap, reggae, salsa, soul and disco, while No 42 has pop, rock, punk, new wave, elec-

Shakespeare & Company

tro and soundtracks. (www.crocodisc.com; 40 & 42 rue des Écoles, 5e; ⊙11am-7pm Tue-Sat mid-Aug–late Jul; MMaubert-Mutualité)

Au Vieux Campeur
SPORTS & OUTDOORS

33 🔒 Map p132, B2

This outdoor store has colonised the Latin Quarter, with 30-and-counting different outlets scattered about. Each is devoted to your favourite sport: climbing, skiing, diving, camping, biking and so on. While it's a great resource if you need any gear, the many boutiques make shopping something of a treasure hunt – especially as many outlets change what they sell with the seasons. (www.auvieuxcampeur.fr;

48 rue des Écoles, 5e; ⊙11am-7.30pm Mon-Wed & Fri, 11am-9pm Thu, 10am-7.30pm Sat; MMaubert-Mutualité)

Album
COMICS

34 🔒 Map p132, B2

Album specialises in *bandes dessinées* (comics and graphic novels), which have an enormous following in France, with everything from Tintin and Babar to erotic comics and Japanese manga. Serious comic collectors – anyone excited by Harry Potter wands, Star Wars, Superman and other superhero figurines and T-shirts (you know who you are!) – shouldn't miss it. (www.album.fr; 67 bd St-Germain, 5e; ⊙10am-8pm Mon-Sat, noon-7pm Sun; MCluny–La Sorbonne)

Local Life
Southeastern Discovery

Getting There

Southeastern Paris is about 3km southeast of Notre Dame.

M Metro Gare de Lyon (lines 1 and 14) and Place d'Italie (lines 5, 6 and 7) are convenient start/end points.

Spanning both banks of the Seine, Paris' southeast is an eclectic mix of *quartiers* (quarters) that makes for a fascinating stroll if you've stood in one tourist queue too many. But while it's an authentic slice of local life, there are plenty of big-hitting attractions here too, including France's national cinema institute and national library.

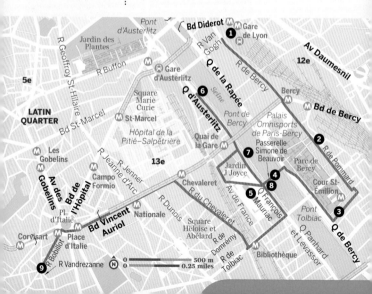

❶ Railway Station Splendour

Start your journey in style with a drink or classical fare like beef tartare prepared at your table at belle époque showpiece **Le Train Bleu** (☑01 43 43 09 06; www.le-train-bleu.com; 1st fl, Gare de Lyon, 26 place Louis Armand, 12e; menu €60-105, mains €25-45; ☺restaurant 11.30am-2.45pm & 7-10.45pm, bar 7.30am-10.30pm Mon-Sat, 9am-10.30pm Sun; 🛜♿; Ⓜ Gare de Lyon).

❷ Cinematic History

Cinephiles shouldn't miss **Cinémathèque Française** (www.cinematheque.fr; 51 rue de Bercy, 12e; adult/child €5/2.50, with film €8; ☺noon-7pm Mon & Wed-Sat, to 8pm Sun; Ⓜ Bercy), showcasing the history of French cinema at its museum, as well as screening classics and edgy new films.

❸ Village Spirit

There are more cinemas at **Bercy Village** (www.bercyvillage.com; cour St-Émilion, 12e; ☺shops 11am-9pm Mon-Sat, restaurants & bars 11am-2am daily; Ⓜ Cour St-Émilion), but its main draw is its strip of former wine warehouses, sheltering shops, eateries and bars.

❹ Crossing the Bridge

Opened in 2006, Paris' 37th bridge, the oak-and-steel foot and cycle bridge, **Passerelle Simone de Beauvoir**, links the Right and Left Banks.

❺ Hitting the Books

Topped by four sunlit glass towers shaped like open books, a rainforest wraps around the reading rooms of the **Bibliothèque Nationale de France** (☑01 53 79 59 59; www.bnf.fr; 11 quai François Mauriac, 13e; temporary exhibitions adult/child from €3/free; ☺exhibitions 10am-7pm Tue-Sat, 1-7pm Sun, closed early-late Sep; Ⓜ Bibliothèque), which mounts exhibitions revolving around 'the word'.

❻ Dockside Fashion

Transformed warehouse **Docks en Seine** (Cité de la Mode et du Design; www.citemodedesign.fr; 34 quai d'Austerlitz, 13e; ☺10am-midnight; Ⓜ Gare d'Austerlitz), aka the Cité de la Mode et du Design, is the French fashion institute's HQ, with exhibitions and events as well as hip restaurants, bars and clubs.

❼ Swimming on the Seine

Splash on (not in!) the Seine at the floating swimming pool **Piscine Joséphine Baker** (☑01 56 61 96 50; quai François Mauriac, 13e; adult/child pool €3/1.70, sauna €10/5; ☺7-8.30am & 1-9pm Mon, Wed & Fri, 1-11pm Tue & Thu, 11am-8pm Sat, 10am-8pm Sun; Ⓜ Bibliothèque or Quai de la Gare).

❽ Drinking, Dining & Dancing on the Seine

Board floating bar-restaurant-clubs like the red tugboat **Le Batofar** (www.batofar.org; opp 11 quai François Mauriac, 13e; ☺bar noon-midnight Tue, club 11.30pm-6am; Ⓜ Quai de la Gare or Bibliothèque).

❾ Heading to the 'Hood

To dine on terra firma, head to small bistro **Chez Nathalie** (☑01 45 80 20 42; www.cheznathalie.fr; 41 rue Vandrezanne, 13e; mains €18-30; ☺noon-2.30pm & 7-11pm Mon-Sat; Ⓜ Corvisart) in the bar-filled Butte aux Cailles neighbourhood.

Explore

Musée d'Orsay & St-Germain des Prés

Literary buffs, antique collectors and fashionistas flock to this mythological part of Paris. Legendary writers such as Sartre, de Beauvoir, Camus, Hemingway and Fitzgerald hung out here and further south at Montparnasse, where despite late 20th-century eyesores like the '70s smoked-glass Tour Montparnasse skyscraper you'll find surviving brasseries and re-energised backstreets.

The Sights in a Day

☀ Get your bearings from the panoramic observation deck of **Tour Montparnasse** (p156; pictured left), before paying homage to writers Sartre and de Beauvoir and singer Serge Gainsbourg in the **Cimetière du Montparnasse** (p156) and getting a contemporary-art fix at the **Fondation Cartier pour l'Art Contemporain** (p158).

☀ After lunch at **Bouillon Racine** (p160) or a picnic in the **Jardin du Luxembourg** (p150), stroll through this beautiful park en route to viewing Delacroix' works in the **Église St-Sulpice** (p158) and **Musée National Eugène Delacroix** (p157). Stop by **Église St-Germain des Prés** (p157) before people-watching at famous literary cafes like **Les Deux Magots** (p162) and browsing designer boutiques.

🌙 Entry to the **Musée d'Orsay** (p148) is cheaper late afternoon, so it's an ideal time to check out its breathtaking collections. Dine nearby at **Les Climats** (p161), then return to one of Montparnasse's late-night cafes, such as **La Closerie des Lilas** (p162).

For a local's day in St-Germain des Prés, see p152.

👁 Top Sights

Musée d'Orsay (p148)

Jardin du Luxembourg (p150)

◯ Local Life

St-Germain des Prés' Historic Shops (p152)

💗 Best of Paris

Architecture
Fondation Cartier pour l'Art Contemporain (p158)

Churches
Église St-Sulpice (p158)

Église St-Germain des Prés (p157)

For Kids
Jardin du Luxembourg (p150)

Getting There

Ⓜ **Metro** St-Germain des Prés (line 4), Mabillon (line 10) and Odéon (lines 4 and 10) are in the heart of the action.

Ⓜ **Metro** Montparnasse Bienvenüe (lines 4, 6, 12 and 13) is Montparnasse's hub.

⚓ **Boat** The hop-on, hop-off Batobus stops outside the Musée d'Orsay and at quai Malaquais in St-Germain des Prés.

Top Sights
Musée d'Orsay

The home of France's national collection from the impressionist, postimpressionist and art nouveau movements spanning from 1848 to 1914 is the glorious former Gare d'Orsay railway station – itself an art nouveau showpiece – where a roll-call of masters and their world-famous works are on display.

◉ Map p154, B1

www.musee-orsay.fr

62 rue de Lille, 7e

adult/child €12/free

⊙9.30am-6pm Tue, Wed & Fri-Sun, to 9.45pm Thu

Ⓜ Assemblée Nationale or RER Musée d'Orsay

Main hall, Musée d'Orsay

Don't Miss

The Building

Built for the 1900 Exposition Universelle, by 1939 the Gare d'Orsay's platforms were too short for trains, and in a few years all rail services ceased. In 1962 Orson Welles filmed Kafka's *The Trial* in the then abandoned building before the government set about transforming it into the country's premier showcase for art from 1848 to 1914. Don't miss the panorama through the station's giant glass clockface and from the adjacent terrace.

Painting Collections

Masterpieces include Manet's *On the Beach;* Monet's gardens at Giverny and *Rue Montorgueil, Paris, Festival of June 30, 1878;* Cézanne's card players, *Green Apples* and *Blue Vase;* Renoir's *Ball at the Moulin de la Galette* and *Girls at the Piano;* Degas' ballerinas; Toulouse-Lautrec's cabaret dancers; Pissarro's *The Harvest;* Sisley's *View of the Canal St-Martin;* and Van Gogh's *Starry Night.*

Decorative Arts Collections

Household items from 1848 to 1914, such as hat stands, desks, chairs, bookcases, vases, water pitchers, decorated plates, goblets, bowls – and even kettles and cutlery – are true works of art and incorporate exquisite design elements.

Sculptures

Sculptures by Degas, Gauguin, Camille Claudel, Renoir and Rodin are housed in the museum.

Graphic Arts Collections

Drawings and sketches from major artists are another of the Musée d'Orsay's highlights. Look for Georges Seurat's crayon on paper work *The Black Bow* (c 1882) and Paul Gauguin's poignant self-portrait (c 1902–03).

☑ Top Tips

▶ Combined tickets with the Musée de l'Orangerie (p60) cost €14, while combined tickets wtih the Musée Rodin (p26) are €18; both combination tickets are valid for a single visit to the museums within three months.

▶ Musée d'Orsay admission drops to €9 after 4.30pm (after 6pm on Thursday).

▶ Photography (including from mobile phones) is forbidden.

✗ Take a Break

Designed like a fantasy underwater world, on-site **Café Campana** (dishes €9-18; ◷10.30am-5pm Tue, Wed & Fri-Sun, 11am-9pm Thu) serves a short, stylish menu.

Time has scarcely changed the museum's sumptuous **Restaurant Musée d'Orsay** (☎01 45 49 47 03; 2-/3-course lunch menus €22/32, mains €16-23; ◷11.45am-5.30pm Tue, Wed & Fri-Sun, 11.45am-2.45pm & 7-9.30pm Thu).

Top Sights
Jardin du Luxembourg

This inner-city oasis of formal terraces, chestnut groves and lush lawns has a special place in Parisians' hearts. Napoléon dedicated the 23 gracefully laid-out hectares of the Luxembourg Gardens to the children of Paris, and many residents spent their childhood prodding little wooden sailboats with long sticks on the octagonal pond, watching puppet shows and riding the carousel or ponies.

◎ Map p154, D5

www.senat.fr/visite/jardin

numerous entrances

⊙vary

Ⓜ Mabillon, St-Sulpice, Rennes, Notre Dame des Champs or RER Luxembourg

Grand Bassin, Jardin du Luxembourg

Don't Miss

Grand Bassin

All ages love the octagonal **Grand Bassin**, a serene ornamental pond where adults can lounge and kids can play with 1920s **toy sailboats** (30/60min €2/3.30; ⏱Apr-Oct). Nearby, littlies can take **pony rides** (€3.50; ⏱3-6pm Wed, Sat, Sun & school holidays) or romp around the **playgrounds** (adult/child €1.20/2.50; ⏱hours vary) – the green half is for kids aged seven to 12 years, the blue half for under-sevens.

Puppet Shows

You don't have to be a kid or be able to speak French to be delighted by marionette shows, which have entertained audiences in France since the Middle Ages. The lively puppets perform in the Jardin du Luxembourg's little Théâtre du Luxembourg. Show times can vary; check the program online and arrive half an hour ahead.

Musée du Luxembourg

Prestigious temporary art exhibitions, such as *Cézanne et Paris,* take place in the beautiful **Musée du Luxembourg** (www.museeduluxembourg.fr; 19 rue de Vaugirard, 6e; most exhibitions adult/child €13.50/9; ⏱10am-7pm Tue-Thu, Sat & Sun, to 9.30pm Fri & Mon; M St-Sulpice or RER Luxembourg).

Around the back of the museum, lemon and orange trees, palms, grenadiers and oleanders shelter from the cold in the palace's **orangery**.

Palais du Luxembourg

The **Palais du Luxembourg** (www.senat.fr; rue de Vaugirard, 6e; M Mabillon or RER Luxembourg) was built in the 1620s and has been home to the Sénat (French Senate) since 1958. It's occasionally visitable by guided tour.

☑ Top Tips

▶ Kiosks and cafes are dotted throughout the park.

▶ If you're planning on picnicking, forget bringing a blanket – the elegantly manicured lawns are off-limits apart from a small wedge on the southern boundary. Instead, do as Parisians do, and corral one of the iconic 1923-designed green metal chairs.

✕ Take a Break

Polidor (☎01 43 26 95 34; www.polidor.com; 41 rue Monsieur le Prince, 6e; menus €22-35, mains €12-20; ⏱noon-2.30pm & 7pm-12.30am Mon-Sat, noon-2.30pm & 7-11pm Sun; ⚄; M Odéon) and its decor date from 1845 and it still serves family-style French cuisine.

For decadent-and-then-some hot chocolate and delicious dining, head to the excellent **Angelina** (www.angelina-paris.fr; 19 rue de Vaugirard; ⏱10am-7.30pm Sun-Thu, to 11.30pm Fri & Sat; M St-Sulpice) adjacent to the Musée du Luxembourg.

Local Life
St-Germain des Prés' Historic Shops

While St-Germain des Prés spills over with chic fashion and interior-design boutiques, it's also filled with locally patronised antique and vintage dealers, small shops specialising in everything from handmade umbrellas to tiny tin soldiers, and the city's oldest department store, the Gustave Eiffel–designed Le Bon Marché, which all provide an insight into the neighbourhood's soul.

❶ Arcade Exploration

Browse the shops in the 1735-built, glass-roofed passageway **Cour du Commerce St-André**, and have lunch at the world's oldest cafe, the 1686-founded **Le Procope** (www.procope.com; 13 rue de l'Ancienne Comédie, 6e; 2-/3-course menus from €29/36; ⏰11.30am-midnight Sun-Wed, to 1am Thu-Sat; 🚻; Ⓜ Odéon).

❷ Classic Candles

Claude Trudon began selling candles here in 1643, and **Cire Trudon** (www.trudon.com; 78 rue de Seine, 6e; ⏰10am-7pm Tue-Sat; Ⓜ Odéon), which officially supplied Versailles and Napoléon with light, is now the world's oldest candle-maker (look for the plaque to the left of the awning).

❸ Soldiering On

Miniature tin and lead soldiers have been sold at the tiny **Au Plat d'Étain** (www.auplatdetain.sitew.com; 16 rue Guisarde, 6e; ⏰10.30am-6.30pm Tue-Sat; Ⓜ Odéon or Mabillon) since 1775.

❹ Doll's House

Opposite the residence of the French Senate's president, the teensy shop **La Maison de Poupée** (☎06 09 65 58 68; 40 rue de Vaugirard, 6e; ⏰2.30-7pm Mon-Sat, by appointment Sun; Ⓜ Odéon or RER Luxembourg) sells its namesake doll's houses as well as *poupées anciennes* (antique dolls).

❺ Bathroom Beauty

The antique and retro mirrors (hand-held and on stands), perfume spritzers, soap dishes and even basins and tapware at long-established shop **Le Bain Rose** (www.le-bain-rose.fr; 11 rue d'Assas, 6e; ⏰11.30am-7pm Mon-Sat, closed Aug; Ⓜ Rennes) can transform your bathroom into a belle époque sanctum.

❻ Department Store Decadence

The 1852-established department store **Le Bon Marché** (www.bonmarche.fr; 24 rue de Sèvres, 7e; ⏰10am-8pm Mon-Wed & Sat, to 9pm Thu & Fri; Ⓜ Sèvres Babylone) houses fashion, homewares and food hall **La Grande Épicerie de Paris** (www.lagrandeepicerie.com; 36 rue de Sèvres, 7e; ⏰8.30am-9pm Mon-Sat; Ⓜ Sèvres Babylone), with displays of chocolates, pastries, biscuits, cheeses and more.

❼ Bakery Treats

Pierre Poilâne opened his *boulangerie* (bakery) **Poilâne** (www.poilane.com; 8 rue du Cherche Midi, 6e; ⏰7.15am-8.15pm Mon-Sat; Ⓜ Sèvres-Babylone) upon arriving from Normandy in 1932. Today his grand-daughter runs the company, which still turns out wood-fired, rounded sourdough loaves made with stone-milled flour and Guérande sea salt. The cafe next door uses Poilâne bread for gourmet *tartines* (open sandwiches).

❽ Rainy-Day Style

Pick up a *parapluie* (umbrella), parasol or walking cane handcrafted by **Alexandra Sojfer** (www.alexandrasojfer.com; 218 bd St-Germain, 7e; ⏰10am-7pm Mon-Sat; Ⓜ Rue du Bac) at this boutique, which has been in the trade since 1834.

❾ A Menagerie of Sorts

Overrun with creatures such as lions, tigers, zebras and storks, taxidermist **Deyrolle** (www.deyrolle.com; 46 rue du Bac, 7e; ⏰10am-1pm & 2-7pm Mon, 10am-7pm Tue-Sat; Ⓜ Rue du Bac) opened in 1831. In addition to stuffed animals (for rent and sale), it stocks minerals, shells, corals and crustaceans, stand-mounted ostrich eggs and pedagogical storyboards.

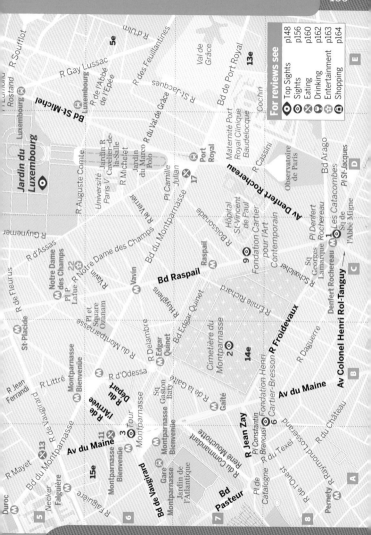

For reviews see

- ◉ Top Sights p148
- ◐ Sights p156
- ✕ Eating p160
- 🍷 Drinking p162
- ▶ Entertainment p163
- 🛍 Shopping p164

R Soufflot

R Gay Lussac

R d'Ulm

5e

R de l'Abbé de l'Epée

R des Feuillantines

Val de Grâce

13e

Bd St-Michel

Luxembourg Ⓜ

Luxembourg Ⓜ

Jardin du Luxembourg ◉

R Guynemer

R Auguste Comte

Université Paris V

Jardin R Cavelier-de-la-Salle

R Michelet

R du Marco Polo

R St-Jacques

Bd de Port Royal

R du Val de Grâce

Jardin du Luxembourg

Ⓜ Port Royal

Maternité Port Royal Clinique Baudelocque

Cochin

R de Fleurus

R de Vaugirard

Notre Dame des Champs Ⓜ

R de l'Abbé

Pl R Lafue 22

R Yavin R Notre Dame des Champs

R le Verrier

Pl Camille Julian ✕ 17

Bd du Montparnasse

Hôpital St-Vincent de Paul

R Boissonade

R Cassini

Observatoire de Paris

Bd Arago

R d'Assas

R Notre Dame des Champs

Ⓜ Vavin

R Huyghens

Ⓜ Raspail

Fondation Cartier pour l'Art Contemporain

9 ◐

R Schoelcher

Pl Denfert Rochereau

Pl Georges Lamarque

Sq de l'Abbé Migne

Les Catacombes

St-Placide Ⓜ

Bd Raspail

R d'Assas

R Delambre

Pl et Square Ozanam

Av Denfert Rochereau

Denfert Rochereau

1

R Froidevaux

Jean Ferrandi

R Littré

Ⓜ Montparnasse Bienvenüe

R d'Odessa

Edgar Quinet Ⓜ

Bd Edgar Quinet

R Emile Richard

Cimetière du Montparnasse

2 ◐

14e

R Daguerre

St Placide

R Jean Ferrandi

Sq Gaston Baty

R de la Gaîté

R Froidevaux

Av du Maine

R Mayet ✕13

Bd du Montparnasse

Av du Maine

11

Ⓜ Tour Montparnasse

3 ◐

Ⓜ Montparnasse Bienvenüe

Gare Montparnasse

R du Départ

R de l'Arrivée

R du Commandant René Mouchotte

R Jean Zay

Pl Constantin Brancusi

6 Fondation Henri Cartier-Bresson

Av Colonel Henri Rol-Tanguy

Necker

Falguière Ⓜ

15e

R Falguière

Bd de Vaugirard

Jardin de l'Atlantique

Pl de Catalogne

R de l'Ouest

R du Château

R du Texel

R Raymond Losserand

Pernety Ⓜ

Duroc Ⓜ

Bd Pasteur

7

8

Sights

Les Catacombes
CEMETERY

 Map p154, C8

Paris' most macabre sight is its underground tunnels lined with skulls and bones. In 1785 it was decided to rectify the hygiene problems of Paris' overflowing cemeteries by exhuming the bones and storing them in disused quarry tunnels and the Catacombes were created in 1810. After descending 20m (via 130 narrow, dizzying spiral steps) below street level, you follow the dark, subterranean passages to reach the ossuary (2km in all). Exit back up 83 steps onto rue Remy Dumoncel, 14e. (www.catacombes.paris.fr; 1 av Colonel Henri Roi-Tanguy, 14e; adult/child €12/free; ☺10am-8pm Tue-Sun; ⓂDenfert Rochereau)

Local Life

Les Berges de Seine

A breath of fresh air, the 2.3km-long expressway turned riverside promenade Les Berges de Seine is now a favourite spot to run, cycle, skate, play board games or take part in a packed program of events. Equally it's simply a great place to hang out – in a Zzz shipping-container hut (reserve at the information point just west of the Musée d'Orsay), on the archipelago of floating gardens, or at the burgeoning restaurants and bars (some floating aboard boats and barges).

Cimetière du Montparnasse
CEMETERY

 Map p154, B7

Opened in 1824, Montparnasse Cemetery, Paris' second-largest after Père Lachaise, sprawls over 19 hectares shaded by 1200 trees, including maples, ash, lime trees and conifers. Among its illustrious 'residents' are poet Charles Baudelaire, writer Guy de Maupassant, playwright Samuel Beckett, sculptor Constantin Brancusi, painter Chaim Soutine, photographer Man Ray, industrialist André Citroën, Captain Alfred Dreyfus of the infamous Dreyfus Affair, actress Jean Seberg, and philosopher-writer couple Jean-Paul Sartre and Simone de Beauvoir, as well as legendary singer Serge Gainsbourg. (www.paris.fr; 3 bd Edgar Quinet, 14e; ☺8am-6pm Mon-Fri, 8.30am-6pm Sat, 9am-6pm Sun; ⓂEdgar Quinet)

Tour Montparnasse
VIEWPOINT

3 ◉ Map p154, A6

Spectacular views unfold from this 209m-high smoked-glass and steel office block, built in 1973. (Bonus: it's about the only spot in the city you can't see this startlingly ugly skyscraper, which dwarfs low-rise Paris.) A speedy lift/elevator whisks visitors up in 38 seconds to the indoor observatory on the 56th floor, with multimedia displays. Finish with a hike up the stairs to the 59th-floor open-air terrace (with a sheltered walkway) and bubbly at the terrace's Champagne bar. (www.tourmontparnasse

Cimetière du Montparnasse

56.com; 33 av du Maine, 15e; adult/child €15/9.50; ⏱9.30am-11.30pm daily Apr-Sep, to 10.30pm Sun-Thu, to 11pm Fri & Sat Oct-Mar; Ⓜ Montparnasse Bienvenüe)

Église St-Germain des Prés
CHURCH

4 ◉ Map p154, D3

Paris' oldest standing church, the Romanesque St Germanus of the Fields, was built in the 11th century on the site of a 6th-century abbey and was the main place of worship in Paris until the arrival of Notre Dame. It's since been altered many times, but the **Chapelle de St-Symphorien** (to the right as you enter) was part of the original abbey and is believed to be the resting place of St Germanus (496–576), the first bishop of Paris. (www.eglise-stgermaindespres.fr; 3 place St-Germain des Prés, 6e; ⏱8am-7.45pm; Ⓜ St-Germain des Prés)

Musée National Eugène Delacroix
MUSEUM

5 ◉ Map p154, D3

In a courtyard off a magnolia-shaded square, this was the romantic artist's home and studio at the time of his death in 1863, and contains a collection of his oil paintings, watercolours, pastels and drawings, including many of his more intimate works, such as *An Unmade Bed* (1828) and his paintings of Morocco. A ticket from the Musée du Louvre (p50) allows entry to the museum on the same day (you can also buy tickets here and skip the Louvre's ticket queues). (www.musee-delacroix.fr; 6 rue de Furstenberg, 6e; adult/child €7/free; ⊙9.30am-5pm Wed-Mon; MMabillon)

Fondation Henri Cartier-Bresson
MUSEUM

6 ◎ Map p154, B8

Founded by renowned French humanist photographer Henri Cartier-Bresson (1908–2004), who pioneered artistic photojournalism, set up a photography department for the Resistance and co-founded the collective agency Magnum, and his portrait-photographer wife Martine Franck (1938–2012), this intimate gallery has a small permanent collection of their works and also mounts rotating exhibitions by French and international photographers, including the winner of the Henri Cartier-Bresson Award every two years. Take the laneway leading off rue Lebouis to find it tucked in a courtyard. (www.henricartierbresson.org; 2 impasse Lebouis, 14e; adult/child €7/4; ⊙1-6.30pm Tue, Thu, Fri & Sun, 1-8.30pm Wed, 11am-6.45pm Sat; MGaîté)

Musée des Lettres et Manuscrits
MUSEUM

7 ◎ Map p154, B2

Grouped into five themes – history, science, music, art and literature – the handwritten and annotated letters and works on display at this captivating museum provide a powerful emotional connection to their authors. They include Napoléon, Charles de Gaulle, Marie Curie, Albert Einstein, Mozart, Beethoven, Piaf, Monet, Toulouse-Lautrec, Van Gogh, Victor Hugo, Hemingway and F Scott Fitzgerald; there are many, many more. It's thoroughly absorbing – allow at least a couple of hours. Temporary exhibitions also take place regularly. (MLM; Letters & Manuscripts Museum; 222 bd St-Germain, 7e; adult/child €7/5; ⊙10am-7pm Tue, Wed & Fri-Sun, to 9.30pm Thu May-Sep, shorter hours Oct-Apr; MRue du Bac)

Église St-Sulpice
CHURCH

8 ◎ Map p154, D4

In 1646 work started on the twin-towered Church of St Sulpicius, lined inside with 21 side chapels, and it took six architects 150 years to finish. It's famed for its striking Italianate façade with two rows of superimposed columns, its Counter-Reformation-influenced neoclassical decor and its frescoes by Eugène Delacroix – and its setting for a murderous scene in Dan Brown's *The Da Vinci Code*. You can hear the monumental, 1781-built organ during 10.30am Mass on Sunday or the occasional Sunday-afternoon concert. (www.pss75.fr/saint-sulpice-paris; place St-Sulpice, 6e; ⊙7.30am-7.30pm; MSt-Sulpice)

Fondation Cartier pour l'Art Contemporain
ART MUSEUM

9 ◎ Map p154, C7

Designed by Jean Nouvel, this stunning glass-and-steel building is a work

Understand

Paris in Print & on Screen

Paris has been the inspiration for countless works of literature over the centuries, and is at least as much a star as the actors who compete with it on the big screen. Below is a selection of some of the best books and films set in the city.

Books

Les Misérables (Victor Hugo; 1862) Epic novel adapted to the stage and screen, tracing 20 years in the life of convict Jean Valjean through the battles and barricades of early 19th-century Paris.

Life: A User's Manual (Georges Perec; 1978) Intricately structured novel distilling Parisian life through a parade of characters inhabiting an apartment block between 1833 and 1975.

Down and Out in Paris and London (George Orwell; 1933) Eric Blair's (aka Orwell's) first published work is a no-holds-barred account of early 20th-century Paris, recounting his days as a dishwasher.

A Moveable Feast (Ernest Hemingway; 1964) Wry work recalling the author's early writing career in the 1920s with priceless vignettes depicting his contemporaries, including F Scott Fitzgerald and Gertrude Stein.

Films

Midnight in Paris (2011) Paris' timeless magic is palpable in Woody Allen's love letter to the city.

À Bout de Souffle (Breathless; 1960) Filmed with hand-held cameras, this new-wave story of a thief who kills a policeman revolutionised cinema.

La Haine (Hate; 1995) Raw, angst- and violence-ridden film shot in black and white. Three teenagers from Paris' *banlieues* (suburbs), trapped by crime, poverty and xenophobia, wait for a train overnight.

La Môme (La Vie en Rose; 2007) Acclaimed biopic of 'little sparrow' Édith Piaf, uncannily played by Marion Cotillard. Most songs on the soundtrack use Piaf's own voice.

Hugo (2011) A tribute to cinema and the legendary Georges Méliès.

○ Local Life
'Little Brittany'

Gare Montparnasse links Paris with Brittany, and the station's surrounding streets, especially rue du Montparnasse and rue d'Odessa, 14e, are lined with dozens of authentic crêperies. Breton savoury buckwheat-flour *galettes* and sweet crêpes, with traditional toppings such as *caramel au beurre salé* (salty caramel), are served on a plate and eaten using cutlery. Try lace-curtain-screened **Crêperie Josselin** (☏01 43 20 93 50; 67 rue du Montparnasse, 14e; crêpes €7-10; ⊙11.30am-3pm & 5-11pm Tue-Fri, 11.30am-11pm Sat & Sun; ⚐; Ⓜ Edgar Quinet).

of art in itself. It hosts temporary exhibits on contemporary art (from the 1980s to today) in a diverse variety of media – from painting and photography to video and fashion, as well as performance art. Artist Lothar Baumgarten created the wonderfully rambling garden. (http://fondation. cartier.com; 261 bd Raspail, 14e; adult/child €10.50/7; ⊙11am-10pm Tue, to 8pm Wed-Sun; Ⓜ Raspail)

Eating

L'Avant Comptoir de la Mer

SEAFOOD TAPAS **$**

10 ✕ Map p154, D3

The latest in Yves Camdeborde's stunning line-up of Carrefour de l'Odéon

eateries, alongside **Le Comptoir** and **L'Avant Comptoir**, serves succulent oysters (Bloody Mary–style or with chipolata sausages), herring tartine, cauliflower and trout roe, blood-orange razor clams, lobster with almond milk foam, roasted scallops and salmon croquettes, complemented by its bar's artisan bread, flavoured butters, sea salt and Kalamata olives. (www.hotel-paris-relais-saint-germain.com; 3 Carrefour de l'Odéon, 6e; tapas €4-30; ⊙noon-11pm; Ⓜ Odéon)

Le Clos Y

MODERN FRENCH **$$**

11 ✕ Map p154, A6

One of Paris' rapidly rising star chefs Yoshitaka Ikeda creates utterly original *menus* that change daily but might start with foie gras ice cream and move on to perch sashimi with beetroot, apple and powdered olive oil; green peas in pea jelly with mascarpone; smoked salmon and egg with raspberry foam; and Madeira-marinated beef with butternut squash and carrot purée. (☏01 45 49 07 35; www. leclosy.com; 27 av du Maine, 15e; 2-/3-course lunch menus €26/31, 4-/6-course dinner menus €45/65; ⊙noon-2pm & 7.30-10pm Tue-Sat; Ⓜ Montparnasse Bienvenüe)

Bouillon Racine

BRASSERIE **$$**

12 ✕ Map p154, E4

Inconspicuously situated in a quiet street, this heritage-listed 1906 art nouveau 'soup kitchen', with mirrored walls, floral motifs and ceramic tiling, was built in 1906 to feed market workers. Despite the magnificent interior, the food – inspired by age-old recipes – is no afterthought but superbly executed (stuffed, spit-roasted suckling pig, pork shank in Rodenbach red beer, scallops and shrimps with lobster coulis). (🖉01 73 20 21 12; www.bouillonracine.com; 3 rue Racine, 6e; weekday lunch menu €16, menus €31-42; ⏲noon-11pm; 👪; Ⓜ Cluny-La Sorbonne)

Chez Dumonet
BISTRO $$

13 Map p154, A5

Fondly known by its former name, Joséphine, this lace-curtained, mosiac-tiled place with white-clothed tables inside and out is the Parisian bistro of many people's dreams, serving time-less standards such as confit of duck, *millefeuille* of pigeon, and grilled chateaubriand steak with Bearnaise sauce. Be sure to order its enormous signature Grand Marnier soufflé at the start of your meal. (Joséphine; 🖉01 45 48 52 40; 117 rue du Cherche Midi, 6e; mains €25-42; ⏲noon-2.30pm & 7.30-9.30pm Mon-Fri; Ⓜ Duroc)

Au Pied de Fouet
BISTRO $

14 Map p154, D2

At this tiny, lively, cherry-red-coloured bistro, wholly classic dishes such as *entrecôte* (steak), *confit de canard* (duck cooked slowly in its own fat) with creamy potatoes and *foie de volailles sauté* (pan-fried chicken livers) are astonishingly good value. Round off your meal with a *tarte Tatin*

Bouillon Racine's art nouveau interior

(upside-down apple tart), wine-soaked prunes, or deliciously rich *fondant au chocolat*. (🖉01 43 54 87 83; www.aupieddefouet.com; 3 rue St-Benoît, 6e; mains €9-12.50; ⏲noon-2.30pm & 7-11pm Mon-Sat; Ⓜ St-Germain des Prés)

Les Climats
TRADITIONAL FRENCH $$$

15 Map p154, C1

Like the neighbouring Musée d'Orsay, this is a magnificent art nouveau treasure – a 1905-built former home for female telephone, telegram and postal workers – featuring soaring vaulted ceilings and original stained glass, along with a lunchtime summer garden and glassed-in winter garden.

Exquisite Michelin-starred dishes complement its 150-page list of wines, sparkling wines and whiskies purely from the Burgundy region. (☎ 01 58 62 10 08; www.lesclimats.fr; 41 rue de Lille, 7e; 2-/3-course lunch menus €36/42, 5-course dinner menu €98, mains €44-58, bar snacks €7-22; ⏱ restaurant noon-2.30pm & 7-10pm Tue-Sat, bar noon-2.30pm & 7-10.30pm Tue-Sat; M Solférino)

Goût de Brioche

PATISSERIE $

16 🍴 Map p154, D2

After relocating his **eponymous triple-Michelin-starred restaurant** (☎ 01 43 80 40 61; www.guysavoy.com; Monnaie de Paris, 11 quai de Conti, 6e; lunch menu via online booking €110, 12-/18-course tasting menus €420/490; ⏱ noon-2pm & 7-10.30pm Tue-Fri, 7-10.30pm Sat; M Pont Neuf) to the Monnaie de Paris complex, Guy Savoy and his pastry chef, Christian Boudard, opened this nearby boutique specialising in light, fluffy brioche loaves in savoury flavours ranging from Parmesan to mushroom, Lorraine (with ham) and duck, and sweet varieties such as chocolate, pink praline, pistachio and apricot, and ginger confit with cashew nuts. (www.goutde brioche.com; 54 rue Mazarine, 6e; brioche €4-7; ⏱ 8.30am-7.30pm Tue-Fri, 8am-7.30pm Sat & Sun; M Odéon)

La Closerie des Lilas

BRASSERIE $$

17 🍴 Map p154, D7

Brass plaques tell you exactly where Hemingway (who wrote much of *The Sun Also Rises* here) and luminaries like Picasso, Apollinaire, Man Ray, Jean-Paul Sartre and Samuel Beckett stood, sat or fell at the 1847-opened 'Lilac Enclosure'. It's split into a late-night piano bar, upmarket restaurant and more lovable (and cheaper) brasserie with a hedged-in pavement terrace. (☎ 01 40 51 34 50; www.closeriedeslilas.fr; 171 bd du Montparnasse, 6e; mains restaurant €28-55, brasserie €24-33; ⏱ restaurant noon-2.30pm & 7-11.30pm, brasserie noon-12.30am, piano bar 11am-1.30am; M Vavin or RER Port Royal)

Drinking

Les Deux Magots

CAFE

18 🍷 Map p154, C3

If ever there was a cafe that summed up St-Germain des Prés' early 20th-century literary scene, it's this former hang-out of anyone who was anyone. You will spend *beaucoup* to sip a coffee in a wicker chair on the terrace shaded by dark-green awnings and geraniums spilling from window boxes, but it's an undeniable piece of Parisian history. (www.lesdeuxmagots.fr; 170 bd St-Germain, 6e; ⏱ 7.30am-1am; M St-Germain des Prés)

Au Sauvignon

WINE BAR

19 🍷 Map p154, C3

Grab a table in the evening light at this wonderfully authentic *bar à vins* or head to the quintessential bistro interior, with an original zinc bar, tightly packed tables and hand-painted ceiling celebrating French viticultural tradition. A plate of *casse-croûtes au pain Poilâne* – toast with ham, pâté, terrine, smoked salmon and foie gras – is the perfect accompaniment. (www.ausauvignon.com; 80 rue des Sts-Pères, 7e; ⏱8am-11pm Mon-Sat, 9am-10pm Sun; Ⓜ Sèvres-Babylone)

Tiger Bar
COCKTAIL BAR

20 Map p154, D3

Suspended bare-bulb lights and fretted timber make this split-level space a stylish spot for specialist gins (45 different varieties). Its 24 cocktails include a Breakfast Martini (gin, triple sec, orange marmalade and lemon juice) and Oh My Dog (white-pepper-infused gin, lime juice, raspberry and rose cordial and ginger ale). You can also sip Japanese sake, wine and craft beer. (www.tiger-paris.com; 13 rue Princesse, 6e; ⏱6pm-2am Tue-Sat; Ⓜ Mabillon)

Café de Flore
CAFE

21 Map p154, C3

The red upholstered benches, mirrors and marble walls at this art deco landmark haven't changed much since the days when Jean-Paul Sartre and Simone de Beauvoir essentially set up office here, writing in its warmth during the Nazi occupation. It also hosts a monthly English-language *philocafé* (philosophy discussion) session. (172 bd St-Germain, 6e; ⏱7am-2am; Ⓜ St-Germain des Prés)

Entertainment

Le Lucernaire
CULTURAL CENTRE

22 Map p154, C5

Sunday-evening concerts are a fixture on the impressive repertoire of the dynamic Centre National d'Art et d'Essai (National Arts Centre). Whether it's classical guitar, baroque, French *chansons* or East Asian music, these weekly concerts starting from 4pm (hours vary) are a real treat. Art and photography exhibitions, cinema, theatre, lectures, debates and guided walks round off the packed cultural agenda. (☎reservations 01 45 44 57 34; www.lucernaire.fr; 53 rue Notre Dame des Champs, 6e; ⏱bar 11am-9pm Mon, 11am-12.30am Tue-Fri, 4pm-12.30am Sat, 4-10pm Sun; Ⓜ Notre Dame des Champs)

Shopping

Gab & Jo
CONCEPT STORE

23 Map p154, D2

Forget mass-produced, imported souvenirs: for quality local gifts, browse the shelves of the country's first-ever concept store stocking only made-in-France items. Designers include La Note Parisienne (scented candles for each Parisian *arrondissement*, such as the 6e, with notes of lipstick, cognac, orange blossom, tuberose, jasmine, rose and fig), Marius Fabre (Marseille soaps), Germaine-des-Prés (lingerie), MILF (sunglasses) and Monsieur Marcel (T-shirts). (www.gabjo.fr; 28 rue Jacob, 6e; ⏰11am-7pm Mon-Sat; MSt-Germain des Prés)

Local Life
Rue Daguerre

Paris' traditional village atmosphere thrives along rue Daguerre, 14e.

Tucked just southwest of the Denfert-Rochereau metro and RER stations, this narrow street is lined with florists, *fromageries* (cheese shops), *boulangeries* (bakeries), patisseries, greengrocers, delis (including Greek, Asian and Italian) and classic cafes where you can watch the local goings on.

Shops set up market stalls on the pavement; Sunday mornings are especially lively. It's a great option for packing a picnic to take to one of the area's parks and squares.

Magasin Sennelier
ARTS & CRAFTS

24 Map p154, C1

Cézanne and Picasso were among the artists who helped develop products for this venerable 1887-founded art supplier on the banks of the Seine, and it remains an exceptional place to pick up canvases, brushes, watercolours, oils, pastels, charcoals and more. The shop's forest-green façade with gold lettering, exquisite original timber cabinetry and glass display cases also fuel artistic inspiration. (www.magasinsennelier.com; 3 quai Voltaire, 7e; ⏰2-6.30pm Mon, 10am-12.45pm & 2-6.30pm Tue-Sat; MSt-Germain des Prés)

JB Guanti
FASHION & ACCESSORIES

25 Map p154, C4

For the ultimate finishing touch, the men's and women's gloves at this boutique, which specialises solely in gloves, are the epitome of both style and comfort, whether unlined, silk lined, cashmere lined, lambskin lined or trimmed with rabbit fur. (www.jbguanti.com; 59 rue de Rennes, 6e; ⏰10am-7pm Mon-Sat; MSt-Sulpice)

Marie Mercié
FASHION & ACCESSORIES

26 Map p154, D3

Stand out in the crowd in a unique hat handcrafted by Fontainebleau-born milliner Marie Mercié, who has collaborated with designers including Hermès, Kenzo, John Galliano and Agnès B and combines traditional methods with modern materials and

BERTRAND GUAY/AFP/GETTY IMAGES ©

Macarons by Pierre Hermé

humorous twists. She's also authored two books on her work and the history of millinery. (www.mariemercie.com; 23 rue St-Sulpice, 6e; ☺11am-7pm Mon-Sat; Ⓜ Mabillon)

Fermob HOMEWARES

27 🔒 Map p154, B3

Famed for manufacturing iconic French garden furniture, including the Jardin du Luxembourg's signature chairs, Fermob has now opened this large, white 120-sq-metre Left Bank boutique in addition to its **Bastille premises** (81-83 av Ledru-Rollin, 12e; ☺10am-7pm Mon-Sat; Ⓜ Ledru-Rollin). Choose from a spectacular array of colours (23 at last count) for your own

garden or terrace. Seasonal opening hours can vary. (www.paris.fermob.com; 17 bd Raspail, 7e; ☺10am-7pm Mon-Sat Apr-Oct, 10am-1pm & 2-7pm Tue-Sat Nov-Mar; Ⓜ Rue du Bac)

Pierre Hermé FOOD

28 🔒 Map p154, C3

It's the size of a chocolate box, but once you're in Pierre Hermé your taste buds will go wild. This boutique, one of Paris' top chocolatiers, is a veritable feast of perfectly presented petits fours, cakes, chocolates, nougats, macarons and jams. There are several other branches around Paris. (www.pierreherme.com; 72 rue Bonaparte, 6e; ☺10am-8pm; Ⓜ Odéon)

Top Sights
Versailles

Getting There

Versailles is about 22km southwest of Notre Dame.

🚆 **RER** C5 (€4.20, 40 minutes, frequent) goes from Paris' Left Bank RER stations to Versailles-Château–Rive Gauche station.

The opulent-and-then-some Château de Versailles sits amid 900 hectares of fountain-graced gardens, pond-filled parks and woods. Louis XIV transformed his father's hunting lodge into the colossal Château de Versailles in the mid-17th century and the baroque palace was the kingdom's political capital and the seat of the royal court from 1682 until the fateful events of 1789, when revolutionaries massacred the palace guard. Louis XVI and Marie Antoinette were ultimately dragged back to Paris and ingloriously guillotined.

Château de Versailles viewed from the Bassin d'Apollon

Don't Miss

Château de Versailles in Numbers
Louis XIV ordered 700 rooms, 2153 windows, 352 chimneys and 11 hectares of roof for the 580m-long main palace. It housed the entire court of 6000 (plus 5000 servants). The finest talent of the day installed some 6300 paintings, 2000 sculptures and statues, 15,000 engravings and 5000 furnishings and objets d'art.

Hall of Mirrors
The palace's opulence peaks in its shimmering, sparkling Galerie des Glaces (Hall of Mirrors). This 75m-long ballroom with 17 giant mirrors on one side and an equal number of windows on the other has to be seen to be believed.

King's & Queen's State Apartments
Luxurious, ostentatious appointments – frescoes, marble, gilt and woodcarvings, with themes and symbols drawn from Greek and Roman mythology – emanate from every last moulding, cornice, ceiling and door in the palace's Grands Appartements du Roi et de la Reine.

Guided Tours
To access areas that are otherwise off-limits and learn more about Versailles' history, take a 90-minute **guided tour** (☏ 01 30 83 77 88; www.chateauversailles.fr; Château de Versailles; tours €7, plus palace entry; ⊙ English-language tours 9.30pm Tue-Sun) of the Private Apartments of Louis XV and Louis XVI and the Opera House or Royal Chapel. Tours include access to the most famous parts of the palace; book online.

The Gardens
Celebrated landscape artist André Le Nôtre was commissioned by Louis XIV to design the

☏ 01 30 83 78 00

www.chateauversailles.fr

place d'Armes

passport ticket incl estate-wide access adult/child €18/free, with musical events €25/free, palace €15/free

⊙ 9am-6.30pm Tue-Sun Apr-Oct, to 5.30pm Tue-Sun Nov-Mar

☑ Top Tips

▶ By noon queues are out of control: arrive early morning and avoid Tuesday, Saturday and Sunday, its busiest days.

▶ Prepurchase tickets on the château's website or at **Fnac** (☏ 08 92 68 36 22; www.fnactickets.com) and head to **Entrance A**.

▶ Versailles is free on the first Sunday of every month (Nov-Mar).

✗ Take a Break

Eateries around the estate include tearoom **Angelina** (www.angelina-paris.fr; Domaine de Marie-Antoinette; mains €24-36; ⊙ 10am-6pm Tue-Sun Apr-Oct, to 5pm Tue-Sun Nov-Mar).

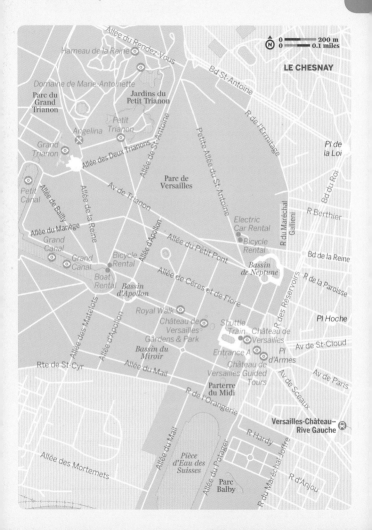

0   200 m
0   0.1 miles

LE CHESNAY

Allée du Rendez-Vous

Hameau de la Reine

Bd St-Antoine

Domaine de Marie-Antoinette

Parc du
Grand
Trianon

Jardins du
Petit Trianon

R de l'Ermitage

Pl de
la Loi

Angelina

Petit
Trianon

Allée des Deux Trianons

Petite Allée du St-Antoine

Allée du St-Antoine

Bd du Roi

Grand
Trianon

Petit
Canal

Parc de
Versailles

Av de Trianon

Allée de Bailly

Allée de la Reine

R du Maréchal
Gallieni

R Berthier

Allée du Manège

Grand
Canal

Bd de la Reine

Electric
Car Rental

Bicycle
Rental

Allée d'Apollon

Allée du Petit Pont

Bassin
de Neptune

R de la Paroisse

Grand
Canal

Bicycle
Rental

Boat
Rental

Bassin
d'Apollon

Allée de Cérès et de Flore

R des Reservoirs

Pl Hoche

Royal Walk

Château de
Versailles

Shuttle
Train

Château de
Versailles

Av de St-Cloud

Allée des Matelots

Allée d'Apollon

Château de
Versailles Guided
Tours

Entrance A

Pl
d'Armes

Av de Paris

Rte de St-Cyr

Bassin du
Miroir

Allée du Mail

Av de Sceaux

Parterre
du Midi

R de l'Orangerie

Versailles-Château–
Rive Gauche

Allée des Mortemets

Allée du Mail

Pièce
d'Eau des
Suisses

Allée du Potager

Parc
Balby

R Hardy

R du Maréchal Joffre

R d'Anjou

château's magnificent **gardens** (free except during musical events; ⊘gardens 8am-8.30pm Apr-Oct, to 6pm Nov-Mar, park 7am-8.30pm Apr-Oct, 8am-6pm Nov-Mar). The best view over the rectangular pools is from the Hall of Mirrors. Pathways include the Royal Walk's verdant 'green carpet', with smaller paths leading to leafy groves.

The Canals
Oriented to reflect the sunset, the **Grand Canal**, 1.6km long and 62m wide, is traversed by the 1km-long **Petit Canal**, creating a cross-shaped body of water with a perimeter of more than 5.5km.

Marie Antoinette's Estate
Northwest of the main palace is the **Domaine de Marie-Antoinette** (Marie Antoinette's Estate; adult/child €10/ free, with passport ticket free; ⊘noon-6.30pm Tue-Sun Apr-Oct, to 5.30pm Tue-Sat Nov-Mar). Tickets include the Grand and Petit Trianon palaces, and the **Hameau de la Reine** (Queen's Hamlet), a mock village of thatched cottages where Marie Antoinette played milkmaid.

Trianon Palaces
The pink-colonnaded **Grand Trianon** was built in 1687 for Louis XIV and his family as a place of escape from the rigid etiquette of the court, and renovated under Napoléon I in the Empire style. The ochre-coloured 1760s **Petit Trianon** was redecorated

PACK-SHOT/SHUTTERSTOCK ©

Building in the Hameau de la Reine

in 1867 by the consort of Napoléon III, Empress Eugénie, who added Louis XVI-style furnishings.

Musical Fountain Shows
Try to time your visit for the magical **Grandes Eaux Musicales** (adult/child €9/7.50; ⊘11am-noon & 2.30-4pm Tue, 11am-noon & 3.30-5pm Sat & Sun mid-May–late Jun, 11am-noon & 3.30-5pm Sat & Sun Apr–mid-May & Jul-Oct) or the after-dark **Grandes Eaux Nocturnes** (adult/child €24/20; ⊘from 8.30pm Sat mid-Jun–mid-Sep), 'dancing water' displays set to music composed by baroque- and classical-era composers.

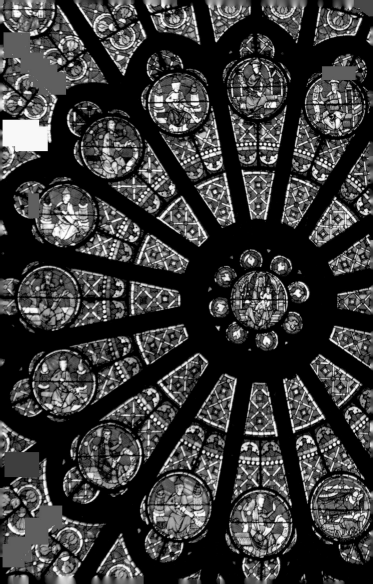

The Best of
Paris

Paris' Best Walks

Left Bank Literary Loop 172

Seine-Side Romantic Meander 174

Right Bank Covered Passages 176

Paris' Best...

Museums 178

Architecture.................... 180

History........................ 182

Parks & Gardens 184

Of the Seine 185

Churches....................... 186

Panoramas 187

Eating 188

Markets........................ 190

For Kids........................ 191

Drinking 192

Nights Out 194

Gay & Lesbian Paris 196

For Free 197

Fashion 198

Multicultural Paris 200

Tours 201

Cooking & Wine-Tasting Courses .. 202

Notre Dame's northern rose window (p111)
AYHAN ALTUN/GETTY IMAGES ©

Best Walks
Left Bank Literary Loop

🏃 The Walk

It wasn't only Paris' reputation for liberal thought and relaxed morals that lured writers in the early 20th century – Left Bank Paris was cheap and, unlike Prohibition-era America, you could drink to your heart's content. This walk through the area's long-gentrified streets takes in pivotal places from the era.

Start Rue du Cardinal Lemoine; **M** Cardinal Lemoine

Finish Rue Notre Dame des Champs; **M** Vavin

Length 6.5km; three hours

🍴 Take a Break

The route is littered with cafes and brasseries with literary associations, including favourites of Jean-Paul Sartre and Simone de Beauvoir **Les Deux Magots** (p162) and **Café de Flore** (p163), Hemingway's favoured **La Closerie des Lilas** (p162), and other literary-luminary magnets such as **Le Dôme** (108 bd du Montparnasse, 14e; mains €43-66.50, seafood platters €66; ⏱ noon-3pm & 7-11.30pm; **M** Vavin).

JOHN ELK III/GETTY IMAGES ©

Les Deux Magots (p162)

❶ Rue du Cardinal Lemoine

Walk southwest along rue du Cardinal Lemoine, peering down the passageway at **No 71**, where James Joyce finished *Ulysses* in apartment E. From 1922 to 1923, Ernest Hemingway lived at **No 74**.

❷ Paul Verlaine's Garret

Hemingway wrote in a top-floor garret of a hotel at **39 rue Descartes** – the same hotel where the poet Paul Verlaine died. Ignore the incorrect plaque.

❸ George Orwell's Boarding House

In 1928 George Orwell stayed in a boarding house above **6 rue du Pot de Fer**, which he called 'rue du Coq d'Or' in *Down and Out in Paris and London* (1933).

❹ Jack Kerouac's Hotel

The **Relais Hôtel du Vieux Paris** at 9 rue Gît le Cœur was a favourite of poet Allen Ginsberg and Beat writer Jack Kerouac in the 1950s.

❺ Shakespeare & Company

The original **Shakespeare & Company** (p142) bookshop stood at 12 rue de l'Odéon, where owner Sylvia Beach lent books to Hemingway and published *Ulysses* for Joyce in 1922. It was closed during WWII's Nazi occupation.

❻ Henry Miller's Room

Henry Miller stayed on the 5th floor of **36 rue Bonaparte** in 1930; he wrote about the experience in *Letters to Emil* (1989).

❼ Oscar Wilde's Hotel

The former Hôtel d'Alsace (now **L'Hôtel**), 13 rue des Beaux-Arts, is where Oscar Wilde died in 1900.

❽ Hemingway's First Night in Paris

Hemingway spent his first night in the city at the **Hôtel d'Angleterre**, 44 rue Jacob.

❾ Gertrude Stein's Home

Ezra Pound and Hemingway were among those entertained at **27 rue de Fleurus**, where Gertrude Stein lived with Alice B Toklas.

❿ Rue Notre Dame des Champs

Pound lived at **70bis rue Notre Dame des Champs**, while Hemingway's first apartment in this area was above a sawmill at **No 113**.

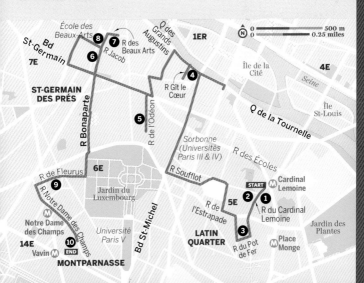

Best Walks
Seine-Side Romantic Meander

🏃 The Walk

The world's most romantic city has no shortage of beguiling spots, but the Seine and its surrounds are Paris at its most seductive. On this walk you'll pass graceful gardens, palaces, intimate parks, a flower market and an enchanting bookshop. Descend the steps along the quays wherever possible to stroll along the water's edge.

Start Place de la Concorde; Ⓜ Concorde

Finish Jardin des Plantes; Ⓜ Gare d'Austerlitz

Length 7km; three hours

✗ Take a Break

The Seine's islands – Île de la Cité and Île St-Louis – have plenty of enticing places to eat and/or drink, such as **Café Saint Régis** (p121), as well as some picturesque picnic spots. Or simply leave it to serendipity (which is, after all, the essence of every great romance).

Jardin des Tuileries (p60) and the Louvre (p50), left of the Seine

❶ Jardin des Tuileries

After taking in the panorama from **place de la Concorde** (p60), stroll through the **Jardin des Tuileries** (p60).

❷ Jardin du Palais Royal

Browse the arcades flanking the **Jardin du Palais Royal** (p62), adjoining the 17th-century palace where Louis XIV once lived.

❸ Cour Carrée

Walk through the **Jardin de l'Oratoire** to the Cour Carrée courtyard of the **Louvre** (p50) and exit at the **Jardin de l'Infante** (Garden of the Princess).

❹ Square du Vert Galant

From the **Pont Neuf** (p118), take the steps to the park at Île de la Cité's tip, **Square du Vert Galant**, before ascending to place du Pont Neuf to cross place Dauphine.

❺ Marché aux Fleurs Reine Elizabeth II

Parisians have been buying bouquets at the

Marché aux Fleurs Reine Elizabeth II (p124), newly renamed in honour of Britain's Queen Elizabeth II, for centuries. Choose carefully: tradition has it that chrysanthemums are only for cemeteries, carnations bring bad luck, and yellow roses imply adultery.

6 Shakespeare & Company

Amid handpainted quotations, make a wish in the wishing well, leave a message on the 'mirror of love' or curl up with a volume of poetry in the reading library of the magical bookshop **Shakespeare & Company** (p142).

7 Berthillon

Cross **Pont de l'Archevêché** to Île de la Cité, then take **Pont St-Louis** to Île St-Louis and share an ice cream from *glacier* (ice-cream maker) **Berthillon** (p119).

8 Musée de la Sculpture en Plein Air

Along quai St-Bernard, wander among more than 50 late-20th-century unfenced sculptures by artists such as César and Brancusi at the **Musée de la Sculpture en Plein Air** (p135; Open-Air Sculpture Museum).

9 Jardin des Plantes

End your romantic meander at the tranquil **Jardin des Plantes** (p134). For the ultimate denouement, cruise back along the Seine by Batobus.

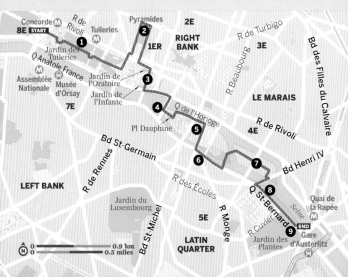

Best Walks
Right Bank Covered Passages

🏃 The Walk

Stepping into the *passages couverts* (covered shopping arcades) of the Right Bank is the best way to get a feel for what life was like in early-19th-century Paris. Around half a century later, Paris had around 150 of these decorated arcades. This walking tour is tailor-made for a rainy day, but it's best avoided on a Sunday, when some arcades are shut tight.

Start Galerie Véro Dodat; Ⓜ Palais Royal–Musée du Louvre

Finish Passage Verdeau; Ⓜ Le Peletier

Length 3km; two hours

🍴 Take a Break

Like visitors 150 years ago, on this walk you can dine and drink within the arcades as well as shop and even attend the theatre. For a two-Michelin-starred meal, book ahead to dine at **Passage 53** (p64) inside the Passage des Panoramas.

NEIL FARRIN/GETTY IMAGES ©

Galerie Vivienne

❶ Galerie Véro Dodat

At 19 rue Jean-Jacques Rousseau, **Galerie Véro Dodat** retains its 19th-century skylights, ceiling murals, Corinthian columns, tiled floor, gas globe fittings (now electric) and shopfronts including furniture restorers.

❷ Galerie Vivienne

Built in 1826, **Galerie Vivienne** is decorated with floor mosaics and bas-reliefs on the walls. Don't miss wine shop **Legrand Filles & Fils**, **Wolff et Descourtis**, selling silk scarves, and **Emilio Robba**, one of the most beautiful flower shops in Paris.

❸ Galerie Colbert

Enter this 1826-built passage, featuring a huge glass dome and rotunda, from rue Vivienne. Exit on rue des Petits Champs (and check out the fresco above).

❹ Passage Choiseul

This 1824-built, 45m-long passage has scores of shops including many specialising in discount and vintage clothing, beads and costume jewellery as well as cheap eateries. Comedies are performed at the **Théâtre des Bouffes Parisiens**, which backs onto the passage's northern end.

❺ Passage des Panoramas

From 10 rue St-Marc, enter Paris' oldest covered arcade (1800), the first to be lit by gas (1817). It was expanded in 1834 with four interconnecting passages – Feydeau, Montmartre, St-Marc and Variétés – and is full of eateries and unusual shops, such as autograph dealer **Arnaud Magistry**. Exit at 11 bd Montmartre.

❻ Passage Jouffroy

Enter at 10-12 bd Montmartre into passage Jouffroy, Paris' last major passage (1847). There's a wax museum, the **Musée Grévin**, and wonderful boutiques including bookshops, silversmiths and **M&G Segas**, where Toulouse-Lautrec bought his

walking sticks. Exit at 9 rue de la Grange Batelière.

❼ Passage Verdeau

Cross the road to 6 rue de la Grange Batelière to the last of

this stretch of covered arcades. There's lots to explore: vintage comic books, antiques, old postcards and more. The northern exit is at 31bis rue du Faubourg Montmartre.

Best
Museums

If there's one thing that rivals a Parisian's obsession with food, it's art. More than 200 museums pepper the city, and whether you prefer the classicism of the Musée du Louvre, the impressionists of the Musée d'Orsay or detailed exhibits of French military history, you can always be sure to find something new just around the corner.

ALARICO/SHUTTERSTOCK ©

Planning Your Visit

Most museums close one day a week, generally Monday or Tuesday; many open late one or more nights a week – usually the least crowded time to visit. You'll also save time by purchasing tickets online where possible. Remember that the cut-off for entry to museums is typically half an hour to an hour before the official closing times (including times listed in this guide). Audioguides are sometimes included with admission but often incur an extra charge.

National Museums Free Entry

If you can, time your trip to be here on the first Sunday of the month, when you can visit the *musées nationaux* (national museums; www.rmn.fr) as well as a handful of monuments for free (some during certain months only). Temporary exhibitions still incur a charge.

City Museums Free Entry

You can visit the permanent collections of most *musées municipaux* (city-run museums; www.paris.fr) for free any time. Temporary exhibitions incur a charge.

☑ **Top Tips**

▶ Save time and money by investing in a Paris Museum Pass or Paris Passlib' (which includes public transport) and bypass (or substantially reduce) ridiculously long ticket queues.

▶ Look out for museum combination tickets.

▶ EU citizens under 26 years get in for free at national monuments and museums.

Best Impressionist Collections

Musée d'Orsay France's national museum for impressionist and related artistic movements is a must. (p148)

Viewing platform, Musée National d'Art Moderne, Centre Pompidou (p88)

Musée de l'Orangerie
Monet conceived a stunning cycle of his Water Lilies series especially for this building. (p60)

Best Modern- & Contemporary-Art Museums

Musée National d'Art Moderne The country's national modern- and contemporary-art museum, located within the striking Centre Pompidou. (p88)

Musée d'Art Moderne de la Ville de Paris Paris' modern-art museum spans the 20th century to the present day. (p44)

Espace Dalí Showcases the work of the surrealist master. (p77)

Best Photography Museums

Jeu de Paume France's national photography centre. (p60)

Fondation Henri Cartier-Bresson Excellent photography displays and exhibitions. (p158)

Best Sculpture Museums

Musée Rodin Rodin's former mansion-set workshop and its rose gardens contain his masterworks. (p26)

Musée de la Sculpture en Plein Air Over 50 late 20th-century unfenced sculptures by artists including César and Brancusi. (p135)

Worth a Trip

Secluded in the Duke of Valmy's former hunting lodge, the intimate **Musée Marmottan** (☏ 01 44 96 50 33; www.marmottan.fr; 2 rue Louis Boilly, 16e; adult/child €11/6.50; ⏱10am-6pm Tue-Sun, to 9pm Thu; Ⓜ La Muette) houses the world's largest collection of Claude Monet's works, including *Impression: Sunrise* (1872), after which impressionism was named, plus paintings by Gauguin, Sisley, Renoir, Degas and Manet.

Best
Architecture

Several key eras define Paris' cityscape. From the 11th-century, magnificent cathedrals and palaces were built. Baron Haussmann's demolition of the city's disease-ridden streets made way for boulevards lined by neoclassical buildings. And, after the art nouveau movement, additions centred on French presidents' bold *grands projets* (great projects). For an architectural overview, visit the Cité de l'Architecture et du Patrimoine.

Haussmann's Renovation

Paris' appearance today is largely the work of Baron Georges-Eugène Haussmann (1809–91). Under Napoléon III, Haussmann completely rebuilt swathes of Paris between 1853 and 1870, replacing chaotic narrow streets (easy to barricade in an uprising) with arrow-straight, wide thoroughfares, including the 12 avenues radiating out from the Arc de Triomphe.

Art Nouveau Influence

Art nouveau swept through the Parisian cityscape from the mid-19th century until WWI, leaving its mark on architecture, interior design, furniture and graphics. Sinuous swirls, curls and floral tendrils characterise this 'new art' movement; materials that supported its signature motifs included wrought iron, glass, richly grained timbers and marble.

Rising Skyline

The outrage over the construction of the 1970s eyesore Tour Montparnasse prompted a clampdown on skyscrapers. However, due to Paris' chronic lack of housing space, the city council approved raising height limits to 180m in some areas. Advocates include Pritzker Prize–winning French architect Jean Nouvel (b 1945).

PHAS/GETTY IMAGES ©

Best Medieval Marvels

Notre Dame This incomparable medieval cathedral is the city's heart in every sense. (p110)

Musée National du Moyen Âge The 15th-century Hôtel de Cluny is a medieval treasure. (p128)

Best Art Nouveau Splendours

Eiffel Tower Paris' 'iron lady' is art nouveau at its best. (p24)

Abbesses metro entrance Hector Guimard's finest remaining metro entrance. (p75)

Bofinger Dine amid art nouveau brass, glass and mirrors in Paris' oldest brasserie. (p100)

Metro station in art nouveau style

Best Grands Projets

Centre Pompidou Former president Georges Pompidou's now-beloved cultural centre sparked a furore when it was unveiled in 1977. (p88)

Louvre glass pyramid IM Pei's pyramid, instigated by former president François Mitterrand, likewise created an uproar in 1989. (p53)

Opéra Bastille Mitterrand oversaw a slew of other costly *projets*, including the city's second, state-of-the-art opera house. (p102)

Best Jean Nouvel Buildings

Musée du Quai Branly President Jacques Chirac's pet *projet*, designed by Nouvel. (p30)

Institut du Monde Arabe The building that established Nouvel's reputation blends modern and traditional Arab elements with Western influences. (p134)

Fondation Cartier pour l'Art Contemporain Stunning contemporary-art space. (p158)

Best Contemporary Structures

Cinémathèque Française Frank Gehry–designed postmodern stunner housing two cinema museums and presenting screenings. (p145)

Forum des Halles Epicentral shopping mall now topped by a giant rainforest-inspired canopy. (p62)

Worth a Trip

The futuristic glass-and-chrome urban jungle of the La Défense business district rises just northwest of the *périphérique* (ring road), reached by a regular metro ticket. Its dramatic gateway is the 110m-high Carrara-marble-and-granite **Grande Arche** (www.grandearche. com; 1 Parvis de la Défense; M La Défense). Pick up a map and guided walking tour of sculpture installations at **Info Défense** (☏ 01 46 93 19 00; www.ladefense. fr; place de la Défense; ⏱ 9am-6pm Mon-Fri, 10am-5pm Sat & Sun; M La Défense).

Best
History

Paris' history is a saga of battles, bloodshed, grand-scale excesses, revolution, reformation, resistance, renaissance and constant reinvention. But this epic is not just consigned to museums and archives: reminders of the capital's and the country's history are evident all over the city.

CRAIG PERSHOUSE/GETTY IMAGES ©

Early Beginnings

Paris was born in the 3rd century BC, when the Parisii tribe of Celtic Gauls established a fishing village in the area. Julius Caesar ended centuries of conflict between the Gauls and Romans in 52 BC. Christianity was introduced in the 2nd century AD; in 508 Frankish king Clovis I united Gaul and made Paris his seat.

Conflicts

In the 12th century Scandinavian Vikings pushed towards Paris, heralding the Hundred Years' War with Norman England, which resulted in England gaining control of France in 1420. In 1429 Joan of Arc rallied French troops to defeat the English.

Revolution

The excesses of Louis XIV and his heirs triggered an uprising of Parisians on 14 July 1789, which kick-started the French Revolution. The government was consolidated in 1799 under Napoléon Bonaparte, who then conquered most of Europe before his defeat at Waterloo.

Reformation & Beyond

At the behest of Napoléon III, Baron Haussmann reshaped the cityscape. However, when Parisians heard of Napoléon III's capture in the war with Prussia in 1870, they demanded a republic. It gave rise to the glittering belle époque ('beautiful era').

Best Roman Legacies

Musée National du Moyen Âge Incorporates the remains of Gallo-Roman baths c AD 200. (p128)

Arènes de Lutèce Gladiatorial 2nd-century amphitheatre. (p135)

Best Medieval Milestones

Notre Dame Completed in the early 14th century. (p110)

Louvre Vast 12th-century fort turned palace turned museum. (p50)

Sainte-Chapelle Consecrated in 1248. (p118)

Sorbonne University founded in 1253. (p136)

Musée National du Moyen Âge Partly housed in the 15th-

Les Catacombes (p156)

century Hôtel de Cluny. (p128)

Best Revolutionary Sights

Place de la Bastille
Site of the former prison stormed on 14 July 1789, mobilising the Revolution. (p94)

Versailles The October 1789 March on Versailles forced the royal family to leave the château. (p167)

Place de la Concorde
Louis XVI and his queen, Marie Antoinette, were among thousands guillotined where the obelisk now stands. (p60; above left)

Conciergerie Marie Antoinette was one of the aristocrats tried and imprisoned here. (p118)

Parc du Champ de Mars This former military training ground was the site of revolutionary festivals. (p31)

Best Burial Places

Père Lachaise The world's most visited cemetery, with famous graves and time-honoured tomb traditions. (p105)

Cimetière du Montparnasse More famous graves, south of St-Germain des Prés. (p156)

Cimetière de Montmartre Yet more famous graves, west of Sacré-Cœur. (p77)

Les Catacombes Prowl the skull- and bone-packed tunnels of Paris' creepy ossuary. (p156)

Panthéon France's greatest thinkers are laid to rest in this immense mausoleum. (p134)

Best
Parks & Gardens

PATRICK ESCUDERO/HEMIS.FR/GETTY IMAGES ©

If Paris' cafes are the city's communal lounge rooms, its parks, gardens and squares are its backyards. The larger parks are idyllic for strolling or simply soaking up the sunshine, with plenty of seating as well as kiosks and cafes, while small, secret gardens are tucked between historic stone buildings or even perched in the middle of the Seine.

Best Traditional Gardens

Jardin du Luxembourg Paris' most popular park. (p150)

Jardin des Tuileries Part of Paris' historic axis and as classical as it gets. (p60)

Versailles Designed by André Le Nôtre, the château's gardens are fit for a king. (p169)

Best Parks

Promenade Plantée The world's first elevated park, atop a disused railway viaduct. (p95)

Jardin des Plantes Paris' botanic gardens include peony and rose gardens, an alpine garden, greenhouses and more. (p134; above)

Parc des Buttes Chaumont Hilly, forested haven with grottoes, waterfalls, a lake and an island. (p85)

Place des Vosges Paris' prettiest square, ringed by cloisters, with a park at its centre. (p96)

Best Hidden Gems

Square du Vert-Galant Romantically situated on the tip of the Île de la Cité. (p119)

Jardin de la Nouvelle France Enchanting little oasis between some of Paris' busiest boulevards. (p44)

Île aux Cygnes A tree-shaded walkway runs the length of the city's little-known third island. (p30)

 Top Tips

▶ Opening hours vary seasonally – check closing times posted at park gates to avoid being locked in.

▶ Look out for *murs végétaux* (vertical gardens) popping up around the city, such as outside the Musée du Quai Branly (p30).

▶ Ecominded city initiatives will see Paris become even greener, with many open areas being created.

Best
Of the Seine

La ligne de vie de Paris ('the lifeline of Paris'), the Seine, sluices through the city, spanned by 37 bridges. Its Unesco World Heritage–listed riverbanks offer picturesque promenades, parks, activities and events, including sandy summer-time beaches. After dark, watch the river dance with the watery reflections of city lights and tourist-boat floodlamps. You are in Paris.

JACQUES LOIC/GETTY IMAGES ©

Riverbank Rejuvenation

Paris' riverbanks have been reborn in recent years. On the Right Bank, east of the Hôtel de Ville, the former expressway is now home to walkways and cycleways. On the Left Bank from the Pont de l'Alma to the Musée d'Orsay (linked to the water's edge by a grand staircase that doubles as amphitheatre seating), the car-free stretch Les Berges de Seine (p156) is now a Parisian hot spot for outdoor activities.

Paris Plages

Palm trees, bars, cafes, sun lounges, parasols, water sprays and sand line the river from mid-July to early September during the 'Paris Beaches'.

Best River Cruises

Bateaux-Mouches (www.bateauxmouches.com; Port de la Conférence, 8e; adult/child €13.50/6; M Alma Marceau) The largest river cruise company in Paris and a favourite with tour groups. Cruises (70 minutes) run regularly from 10.15am to 10.30pm

April to September and 13 times a day between 11am and 9.20pm the rest of the year. Commentary is in French and English. It's located on the Right Bank, just east of the Pont de l'Alma.

Vedettes de Paris (www.vedettesdeparis.fr; Port de Suffren, 7e; adult/child €13.50/6) It might be a small company, but its one-hour sightseeing cruises on smaller boats are second to none. It runs themed cruises too, including imaginative 'Mysteries of Paris' tours for kids (adult/child €14/8).

Best
Churches

Some of the city's most magnificent buildings are its churches and other places of worship. Not only exceptional architecturally and historically, they also contain exquisite art, artefacts and other priceless treasures. And best of all, entry to general areas within them is, in most cases, free.

EURASIA PRESS-GETTY IMAGES ©

Classical Concerts

Paris' beautiful, centuries-old stone churches have magnificent acoustics and provide a meditative backdrop for classical-music concerts. Posters outside churches advertise upcoming events with ticket information, or visit www.ampconcerts.com, where you can make online reservations. Tickets cost around €23 to €30.

Etiquette

Bear in mind that, although many of Paris' places of worship are also major tourist attractions, Parisians come here to pray and celebrate significant events on religious calendars as part of their daily lives. Be respectful: keep noise to a minimum, obey photography rules (check signs), dress appropriately and try to avoid key times (eg Mass) if you're sightseeing only.

Best Landmark Churches

Notre Dame The city's mighty Gothic cathedral is without equal. (p110)

Sacré-Cœur Paris' domed basilica lords over the city. (p72)

Église St-Sulpice Featured in *The Da Vinci Code*, with frescoes by Eugène Delacroix. (p158)

Église St-Germain des Prés Built in the 11th century, this is Paris' oldest church. (p157)

Best Churches for Classical Concerts

Sainte-Chapelle Concerts provide the perfect opportunity to appreciate Sainte-Chapelle's beauty. (p118)

Église de la Madeleine Renowned for its monumental organ. (p60; above)

Église St-Eustache Concerts have long been a tradition at this beautiful central church. (p61)

Best Non-Christian Places of Worship

Mosquée de Paris Paris' 1920s art deco tiled mosque has a wonderful tearoom and *hammam* (steambath). (p134)

Art nouveau synagogue Designed in 1913 by Hector Guimard. (p97)

Best
Panoramas

OLENA MYKHAYLOVA/SHUTTERSTOCK ©

Paris is a photographer's dream. In addition to close-up shots of local street life, there are spectacular vantage points where you can snap vistas of the city – from the top of monuments, on hilltops, in vast squares and on bridges. Even without a camera, the views are unforgettable. Stroll around and you'll find your own favourite panoramas of Paris.

Best Buildings with a View

Eiffel Tower Not only the city's most iconic building but also its highest. (p24)

Tour Montparnasse The saving grace of this otherwise-hideous highrise is its panoramic observation deck. (p156)

Arc de Triomphe Climb to the top for the best views along Paris' historic axis. (p38; above)

Centre Pompidou Captivating views of Paris, including the Eiffel Tower. (p88)

Galeries Lafayette Incredible views of Paris unfold from this department store's rooftop – and they're free! (p68)

Le Printemps This magnificent department store also has mesmerising rooftop views for free. (p69)

Cité de l'Architecture et du Patrimoine Amazing Eiffel Tower views unfurl from the windows and terrace out front. (p42)

Best Open Spaces with a View

Île aux Cygnes Walk west to east along this artificial island for breathtaking Eiffel Tower views. (p30)

Promenade Plantée Get a bird's-eye view of local Parisian life three storeys up along this elevated park. (p95)

☑ Top Tips

▶ For transport with a view, hop on a Batobus (p208) or regular bus. Scenic bus routes include lines 21 and 27 (Opéra–Panthéon), line 29 (Opéra–Gare de Lyon), line 47 (Centre Pompidou–Gobelins), line 63 (Musée d'Orsay–Trocadéro), line 73 (Concorde–Arc de Triomphe) and line 82 (Montparnasse–Eiffel Tower).

Best
Eating

France pioneered what is still the most influential style of cooking in the Western world and Paris is its showcase par excellence. Colours, textures and garnishes are impeccably arranged everywhere from simple restaurants to *haute cuisine* establishments helmed by legendary chefs. The city doesn't have its own 'local' cuisine but is the crossroads for France's regional produce and flavours.

VISIONSI/SHUTTERSTOCK ©

Evolving Trends

In addition to classical French fare, look out for cuisines from around the globe. Neobistros offer some of Paris' most exciting dining options. Generally small and relatively informal, they're run by young, talented chefs who aren't afraid to experiment. Exclusively vegetarian establishments are emerging but still rare.

Dining Times

Breakfast (usually a baguette with butter and jam, and strong coffee) is seen as a mere precursor to lunch, the traditional main meal, starting around 12.30pm. Most restaurants open for dinner around 7pm or 7.30pm. Some high-end restaurants close at weekends, and many places close in August.

Menus

Eateries usually serve a *plat du jour* (dish of the day) at lunch (and occasionally at dinner), as well as *menus* (fixed-price meals) of an *entrée* (starter), *plat* (main course) and *fromage* (cheese) or dessert or both. These offer infinitely better value than ordering à la carte. Meals are often considerably cheaper at lunch than dinner.

☑ Top Tips

▶ Midrange restaurants will usually have a free table for lunch (arrive by 12.30pm); book a day or two in advance for dinner.

▶ Reservations are absolutely mandatory for lunch and dinner at popular/high-end restaurants – up to one or two months in advance, and you may need to reconfirm on the day.

Best Bistros

Le Bistrot Paul Bert Timeless vintage decor and perfectly executed classics. (p97)

Le Pantruche Superb, great-value modern French cuisine. (p78)

Macarons on display

Chez Dumonet (Joséphine) The Parisian bistro of your dreams. (p161)

Frenchie Hidden alleyway bistro serving sensational menus. (p62)

Le Miroir Stylish, creative bistro fare. (p80)

Best Gastronomic Extravaganzas

Restaurant David Toutain Mind-blowing mystery degustation menus. (p32)

Yam'Tcha Exquisitely fused French and Asian flavours, paired with teas. (p63)

La Tour d'Argent Centuries-old establishment overlooking Notre Dame serving signature pressed duck. (p138)

Best Picnic Fare

La Grande Épicerie de Paris Dazzling gourmet emporium. (p153)

Chambelland Exquisite gluten-free baked goods and sandwiches to take away. (p99)

Best Boulangeries

Poilâne Turning out distinctive wood-fired, rounded sourdough loaves since 1932. (p153)

Besnier Watch baguettes being made through the viewing window. (p27)

Huré Contemporary bakery near Notre Dame. (p123)

Worth a Trip

Hugo Desnoyer (01 46 47 83 00; www.hugodesnoyer. fr; 28 rue du Docteur Blanche, 16e; mains from €28; restaurant 11.30am-3.30pm Tue-Sat, 8-11pm Wed; Jasmin) is Paris' most famous butcher and the trip to his shop in the 16e is well worth it. Arrive by noon or reserve to snag a table and settle down to a *table d'hôte* feast of homemade terrines, quiches, foie gras and cold cuts followed by the finest meat in Paris.

Best
Markets

Nowhere encapsulates Paris' village atmosphere more than its markets. Not simply places to shop, the city's street markets are also social gatherings for the entire neighbourhood. Residents toting quintessentially Parisian canvas shopping bags on wheels chat with neighbours, fellow shoppers and stallholders and pick up culinary tips. Flea markets are full of antique, vintage and new treasures.

Street Markets

Nearly every little quarter has its own street market, held at least once a week, where tarpaulin-topped trestle tables bow beneath spit-roasted poultry, seafood on beds of crushed ice, meat, cheeses, sun-ripened fruit and vegetables, and pâtés, preserves and other delicacies. Many markets also sell clothes, accessories, homewares and more. *Marchés biologiques* (organic markets) abound.

Flea Markets

Exquisite antiques, vintage and retro clothing, jewellery, bric-a-brac, cheap brand-name clothing, footwear, African carvings, DVDs and electronic items are laid out at the city's colourful flea markets. Watch out for pickpockets! Just north of Montmartre, **Marché aux Puces de St-Ouen** (www.marcheauxpuces-saintouen.com; rue des Rosiers; ⊙varies; Ⓜ Porte de Clignancourt) has more than 2500 stalls.

Best Markets

Marché Bastille One of the city's largest, liveliest street markets laden with quality produce. (p99; above)

☑ **Top Tips**

▸ No street markets take place on Monday.

▸ The website www.paris.fr lists every market by *arrondissement*, including speciality markets.

Marché des Enfants Rouges Paris' oldest covered market, with communal tables for lunch. (p91)

Marché aux Puces d'Aligre Central flea market adjoining the wonderfully chaotic Marché d'Aligre. (p102)

Best
For Kids

JOEL ROBINE/AFP/GETTY IMAGES ©

Parisians adore *les enfants* (children) and welcome them with open arms just about everywhere. You'll notice French kids are generally quiet and polite, and you'll be expected to make sure yours are, too. But kids can still burn off plenty of energy: central Paris' residential design means you'll find playground equipment in parks and squares throughout the city.

Dining with Kids

Many restaurants accept little diners (confirm ahead). Children's menus aren't widespread, however, and most restaurants don't have highchairs. In fine weather, pick up sandwiches and crêpes from a street stall or pack a market-fresh picnic and head to the city's parks and gardens.

Accommodating Kids

Parisian buildings' limited space often means premium-priced family-size accommodation – apartments may be more economical. Check availability and costs for a *lit bébé* (cot).

Amusement Parks

Just outside central Paris are several amusement parks. The most high-profile is Disneyland Resort Paris (www. disneylandparis.com); French alternatives include Parc Astérix (www. parcasterix.fr; above) and, for tots, the adorable Jardin d'Acclimatation (www. jardindacclimatation.fr).

Best Attractions for Kids

Le Grand Rex Kids can become movie stars on entertaining behind-the-scenes tours. (p67)

Aquarium de Paris Cinéaqua Shark tank! (p45)

☑ Top Tips

▶ Children under four travel free on public transport and generally receive free admission to sights. Discounts vary for older kids (aged up to 18) – anything from a euro off to free.

▶ Be extra vigilant crossing roads as Parisian drivers frequently ignore green pedestrian lights.

Jardin du Luxembourg Pony rides, puppet shows and more. (p150)

Vedettes de Paris Special 'Paris Mystery' Seine cruises for kids. (p185)

Best
Drinking

For Parisians, drinking and eating go together like wine and cheese, and the line between a cafe, *salon de thé* (tearoom), bistro, brasserie, bar and even a *bar à vins* (wine bar) is blurred, while the line between drinking and clubbing is often nonexistent – a cafe that's quiet mid-afternoon might have DJ sets in the evening and dancing later on.

BERTRAND GARDEL/GETTY IMAGES ©

Cafe Culture

Paris' cafes have long been the city's communal lounge rooms: places to meet friends, read, write, philosophise, flirt and fall in – and out of – love.

Coffee

If you order *un café* (a coffee), you'll be served a single shot of espresso. A *café allongé* is lengthened with hot water, a *café au lait* comes with milk and a *café crème*, lengthened with steamed milk, is the closest to a latte. The city is in the throes of a coffee revolution, with local roasteries like Belleville Brûlerie and Coutume priming cafes citywide for outstanding brews made by professional baristas, often using cutting-edge extraction techniques.

Wine

Wine is easily the most popular beverage in Paris and house wine invariably costs less than bottled water. *Les vins naturels* (natural wines) contain little or no sulphites.

Cocktails

Cocktail bars are undergoing a resurgence; many hip restaurants pair cocktails with food. Paris Cocktail Week (www.pariscocktailweek.fr) takes place in late January.

☑ Top Tips

▶ Many establishments have a tiered pricing structure, with coveted terrace seats more expensive than perching at the counter.

▶ Most places serve at least small plates; it's normally fine to order coffee or alcohol if you're not dining.

▶ The French rarely go drunk-wild and tend to frown upon it.

Best Neighbourhood Cafes

Le Pure Café Still as quintessentially Parisian as Ethan Hawke's character found it in *Before Sunset*. (p102)

ALLEN ENRIQUEZ / GETTY IMAGES ©

La Fée Verte Absinthe specialist. (p101)

Le Progrès Montmartre local. (p80)

Best Coffee

Coutume Artisan roasters of premium beans, with a fab flagship cafe. (p35)

La Caféothèque Maze of a coffee house with serious tasting notes and seating made for lounging all day. (p101)

Lockwood Belleville-roasted beans. (p65)

Best Wine Bars

Le Baron Rouge Wonderfully convivial barrel-filled spot. (p102)

Taverne Henri IV Island-set stalwart serving cheese and charcuterie. (p123)

Au Sauvignon With an original zinc bar. (p162)

Le Garde Robe Excellent, affordable natural wines. (p65)

Best Cocktail Bars

Tiger Bar Split-level space serving specialist gins. (p163)

Harry's New York Bar Knockout cocktails from the inventor of the Bloody Mary. (p66)

Le Mary Céleste Ultrafashionable Marais cocktail bar. (p91)

Experimental Cocktail Club Fabulous cocktails in a setting that exudes spirit and soul. (p65)

Best
Nights Out

ANTON_IVANOV/SHUTTERSTOCK ©

From sipping cocktails in swanky bars to carving up cutting-edge clubs, rocking to live bands, being awed by operas, ballets and classical concerts, entertained by films, dazzled by cabarets, intrigued by avant-garde theatre productions or listening to smooth jazz or stirring *chansons,* a night out in Paris promises to be a night to remember.

Nightclubs

Paris' residential make-up means clubs aren't ubiquitous. Still, electronica, laced with funk and groove, remains its strong suit. DJs tend to have short stints in venues – check www.tribudenuit. com. Salsa and Latino also maintain a huge following. Admission to clubs is free to around €20.

Jazz, Chansons & Cabarets

Paris has some fantastic venues for jazz and *chansons* (heartfelt, lyric-driven music typified by Édith Piaf). Tickets to major cabaret spectacles start from around €90 (from €200 with dinner) and may include a half-bottle of Champagne for an extra €10.

Opera, Ballet, Theatre & Classical Music

France's Opéra National de Paris and Ballet de l'Opéra National de Paris perform at the Palais Garnier (above left) and Opéra Bastille opera houses. Virtually all theatre productions are in French but sometimes have English-language subtitles.

Cinema

Pariscope and *L'Officiel des Spectacles* list screening times; also check out http://cinema.leparisien.fr. Tickets cost around €11.50 for adults. Foreign films screened in their original language with French subtitles are labelled 'VO' (*version originale*); films labelled 'VF' (*version française*) are dubbed.

☑ Top Tips

▶ Paris Nightlife (www.parisnightlife. fr) is an all-encompassing listings site.

▶ On the day of a performance, tickets are often available at half price at **Kiosque Théâtre Madeleine** (opposite 15 place de la Madeleine, 8e; ⏱12.30-8pm Tue-Sat, to 4pm Sun; Ⓜ Madeleine).

▶ Fnac (www.fnac. fr) sells a wide range of entertainment and sport tickets.

Best Nightclubs

Point Éphémère Edgy club and performance venue booking exceptional emerging and established DJs, artists

The iconic exterior of the Moulin Rouge (p82)

and bands. Ubercool.
(p84)

Le Rex Club Paris' first
dedicated techno club
is still cutting edge and
has a phenomenal sound
system. (p66)

Social Club Subterranean
nightclub with superb DJs
and live bands. (p66)

Le Nouveau Casino
Intimate concerts and

top DJs play electro, pop,
deep house and rock.
(p85)

Best Jazz Clubs

Café Universel Brilliant
array of live jazz and
blues concerts. (p141)

Caveau de la Huchette
Always entertaining
medieval-cellar venue.
(p141)

Best Cabarets

Moulin Rouge The home
of the cancan is touristy
but spectacular all the
same. (p82)

Au Lapin Agile Historic
and authentic, in the
heart of Montmartre.
(p75)

Best
Gay & Lesbian Paris

There's less of a defined gay and lesbian 'scene' here than in other cities where it's more underground. While Le Marais – particularly around the intersection of rues Ste-Croix de la Bretonnerie and des Archives – is the mainstay of gay and lesbian nightlife, venues throughout the city attract a mixed crowd.

Background

Paris was the first-ever European capital to vote in an openly gay mayor when Bertrand Delanoë was elected in 2001, and the city itself is very open – same-sex couples commonly display affection in public and checking into a hotel room is unlikely to raise eyebrows. In 2013, France became the 13th country in the world to allow same-sex marriage (and adoption by same-sex couples). Typically, at least one partner needs to be a resident to get married here.

Festivities

Gay pride peaks during late June's Gay Pride March (www.gaypride.fr), with over-the-top floats and festivities.

Gay Guided Tours

For an insider's perspective of gay life in Paris and recommendations on where to eat, drink, sightsee and party, take a tour with the **Gay Locals** (www.thegaylocals. com; 3hr tour from €180) – two long-time resident expats who lead tours of Le Marais in English, as well as private tours of other popular neighbourhoods and customised tours based on your interests.

Best Gay & Lesbian Bars

Le Tango Mingle with a cosmopolitan gay and lesbian set in a historic 1930s dance hall. (p101)

☑ **Top Tips**

Useful resources:
▶ Centre Gai et Lesbien de Paris Île de France (www.cglparis.org)

▶ Paris-Gay.com (www.paris-gay.com)

Open Café The wide terrace is prime for talent-watching. (p101)

3w Kafé Flagship cocktail bar-pub on a street with several lesbian bars. (p101)

Quetzal Perennial favourite; cruisy at all hours. (p101)

Best
For Free

Paris' national museums offer free entry on the first Sunday of the month (some during certain months only), and permanent exhibits at city museums are free (temporary exhibitions incur a charge). A handful of Paris' national monuments also have free entry on the first Sunday of the month (also some in certain months only), including those listed below.

FREDERIC LEGRAND - COMEO/SHUTTERSTOCK ©

Free Music

Concerts, DJ sets and recitals regularly take place for free (or for the cost of a drink) at venues throughout the city.

Busking musicians and performers entertain crowds on Paris' streets, squares and even aboard the metro.

Free Literary Events

This literary-minded city is an inspired place to catch a reading, author signing or writing workshop. English-language bookshops such as Shakespeare & Company (p142) and Abbey Bookshop (p142) host literary events throughout the year and can point you towards others.

Free Festivals

Loads of Paris' festivals and events are free, such as the summertime Paris Plages riverside beaches. Catch free live-music gigs all over the city during the Fête de la Musique in mid-June. There's also many events during Nuit Blanche ('White Night', ie 'All Nighter') on the first Saturday and Sunday of October. For more, visit www.paris.fr.

Best Free Sights

Louvre Free entry on the first Sunday of the month October to March. (p50)

Arc de Triomphe Free entry to the top on the first Sunday of the month November to March. (p38)

Notre Dame Free tower entry on the first Sunday of the month November to March. (p110)

Versailles Free château entry on the first Sunday of the month November to March. (p167; above)

Père Lachaise This vast celebrity-filled cemetery is free to wander around. (p105)

Best
Fashion

MARZO PHOTOGRAPHY/GETTY IMAGES ©

Home to iconic labels like Chanel and Dior, Paris is a world trendsetter. Yet, although its well-groomed residents mean the city can look and feel like a giant catwalk, fashion here is about style and quality rather than status or brand names. Note most shops close at least one or two days a week, usually Sunday and Monday.

Fashion Districts

Shopping opportunities exist throughout the city, but certain neighbourhoods have especially concentrated options.

Look for luxury flagships in the Triangle d'Or (Golden Triangle; bordered by avs Georges V, Champs-Élysées and Montaigne) and St-Germain des Prés, particularly the northern wedge between Église St-Germain des Prés and the Seine, as well as the western half of bd St-Germain and rue du Bac.

Paris' traditional garment-making district is the 2e around the metro station Sentier, and there are plenty of boutiques here and on nearby rue Montmartre and rue Tiquetonne, which are the places to find streetwear and avant-garde designs.

The hip Haut Marais and Canal St-Martin are fertile grounds for experimental designers.

Arcades & Department Stores

Paris' covered passages are treasure chests of boutiques, while the city's *grands magasins* (department stores) such as Galeries Lafayette (above left), Le Printemps and Le Bon Marché sell quality wares.

Speciality Shops

What sets Paris apart is its incredible array of speciality shops dedicated to individual items such as hats, gloves, handbags, umbrellas, stockings and tights, and chic children's wear.

☑ **Top Tips**

▸ Paris' twice-yearly *soldes* (sales) generally last five to six weeks, starting around mid-January and again around mid-June.

▸ Ring the bell to access ultra-exclusive designer boutiques.

◂ Head to a *cabine d'essayage* (fitting room), or check sizes at www.onlineconversion.com/clothing.

Best Boutiques

Maison Kitsuné The secret to looking effortlessly French. (p83)

La Boutique Extraordinaire Exquisite hand-knitted garments. (p91)

Boutiques on the Avenue des Champs-Élysées

Pigalle Leading Parisian menswear brand. (p83)

Best Accessories

JB Guanti Gorgeous gloves. (p164)

Marie Mercié Handmade hats. (p164)

Alexandra Sojfer Handcrafted umbrellas. (p153)

Best Secondhand, Vintage & Discount Boutiques

Didier Ludot Couture creations of yesteryear. (p68)

L'Habilleur Discount designer wear. (p91)

Frivoli Brand-name cast-offs by the Canal St-Martin. (p85)

Kiliwatch New and used streetwear; vintage hats and boots. (p69)

Best Concept Stores

Merci Fabulously fashionable and unique: all profits go to a children's charity in Madagascar. (p90)

Gab & Jo The country's first concept store stocking only French-made items. (p164)

Colette Uber-hip designer fashion and basement 'water bar'. (p69)

Worth a Trip

For previous seasons' collections, surpluses and seconds by name-brand designers such as Sonia Rykiel, save money at discounted outlet stores along **rue d'Alésia**, 14e, particularly west of the Alésia metro station between av de Maine and rue Raymond-Losserand. Shops here pop up regularly and close just as often, so you can never be sure what you'll find.

Best
Multicultural Paris

Paris might be the bastion of French culture, but these days that definition incorporates myriad nationalities who call this cosmopolitan city home. Throughout the capital you'll find vibrant hubs of cultural life that make up *mondial* (multicultural) Paris. Visiting grocery stores, delis, markets, shops and places of worship as you explore the city offers a mini world tour.

Multicultural Background

Waves of immigration over the centuries, including a large number of immigrants from France's former colonies since the middle of last century, have given rise to an exhilarating mix of ethnicities, cuisines and the arts – and to debates like the 2004 ban at state-run schools on Muslim headscarves (and all other religious symbols, such as crucifixes) in favour of secularism, and the controversial 2011 ban on women wearing burqas in public (France was the first European country to impose one). Under French law, censuses can't ask questions about ethnicity or religion, but they do collect country-of-birth statistics, which confirm Paris as one of the most multicultural cities in Europe.

Best Mondial Museums

Musée du Quai Branly Indigenous art, artefacts, music and more from every continent bar Europe. (p30)

Institut du Monde Arabe Arabian arts are displayed in stunning surrounds; also hosts concerts and film screenings. (p134; above)

Musée Guimet des Arts Asiatiques Exceptional collection of Asian art and artefacts. (p42)

Louvre Antiquities from Greece and Egypt and other extraordinary global treasures. (p50)

La Pinacothèque Look out for mondial exhibitions at Paris' top private museum. (p61)

Best
Tours

Parisien d'un jour – Paris Greeters (www. greeters.paris; by donation) See Paris through local eyes with these two- to three-hour city tours. Volunteers – knowledge-able Parisians passion-ate about their city in the main – lead groups (maximum six people) to their favourite spots. Minimum two weeks' notice needed.

Paris Walks (☑01 48 09 21 40; www.paris-walks. com; 2hr tours adult/child €15/8) Long established and well respected, Paris Walks offers two-hour thematic walking tours (art, fashion, chocolate, the French Revolution etc).

Fat Tire Bike Tours (☑01 85 08 19 76; www. fattirebiketours.com; tours from €32) Day and night bike tours of the city, both in central Paris and further afield to Versailles and Monet's Garden in Giverny.

Set in Paris (☑09 84 42 35 79; www.setinparis. com; 3 rue Maître Albert, 5e; 2hr tours €25; ⊙2hr tours 10am & 3pm; Ⓜ Maubert-Mutualité) From its cinema-style 'box office' HQ in the Latin Quarter, Set in Paris' two-hour walking tours take you to locations throughout Paris where movies including *The Devil Wears Prada, The Bourne Identity, The Three Musket-eers, The Hunchback of Notre Dame, Ratatouille, Before Sunset,* several James Bond instalments and many others were filmed. Advance reserva-tions are recommended.

Canauxrama (www. canauxrama.com; opposite 50 bd de la Bastille, 12e, Port de l'Arsenal; adult/child €18/9; Ⓜ Bastille) Runs 2½-hour trips along the Canal St-Martin, chug-ging back and forth between central Paris and Parc de la Villette. Boats go at a leisurely pace,

FABRICE LEROUGE/GETTY IMAGES ©

passing through four double locks, two swing bridges and an under-ground section (with an art installation).

L'Open Tour (☑01 42 66 56 56; www.paris.opentour. com; 1-day pass adult/child €32/16) Hop-on, hop-off bus tours aboard open-deck buses with four different circuits and 50 stops – good for a whirlwind city tour.

Localers (☑01 83 64 92 01; www.localers.com) Classic walking tours and behind-the-scenes urban discoveries with local Paris experts: *pétanque,* photo shoots, market tours, cooking classes, foie gras–tasting et al.

Best
Cooking & Wine-Tasting Courses

If dining in the city's restaurants whets your appetite, Paris has stacks of cookery schools with courses for all budgets and levels of ability. Where there's food in Paris, wine is never more than an arm's length away; plenty of places offer wine tastings and instruction for beginners through to connoisseurs.

GREENART PHOTOGRAPHY/GETTY IMAGES ©

Best Culinary Classes

Cook'n With Class (www.cooknwithclass.com) International chefs, small classes.

Le Cordon Bleu (www.cordonbleu.edu/paris) One of the world's foremost culinary-arts schools.

La Cuisine Paris (www.lacuisineparis.com) Courses from bread, croissants and macarons to market classes and 'foodie walks'.

Le Foodist (www.lefoodist.com) Cooking classes and wine pairings.

Best Wine Appreciation Sessions

Ô Château (www.o-chateau.com; 68 rue Jean-Jacques Rousseau, 1er; ⏰4pm-midnight Mon-Sat; 📶; Ⓜ Les Halles, Étienne Marcel) Wine aficionados can thank this young, fun, cosmopolitan *bar à vins* for bringing affordable tasting to Paris.

Musée du Vin (📞01 45 25 63 26; www.museeduvinparis.com; 5 sq Charles Dickens, 16e; adult/child €10/free; ⏰10am-6pm Tue-Sun; Ⓜ Passy) In addition to its displays, Paris' wine museum offers instructive tastings.

Wine Tasting in Paris (📞06 76 93 32 88; www.wine-tasting-in-paris.com; 14 rue des Boulangers, 5e; 2hr tastings from €60; ⏰tastings 5-7pm Tue, Thu & Sat; Ⓜ Jussieu) Tastings include the popular French Wine Tour (two hours, six wines), covering tasting methodology,

wine vocabulary, and interpreting wine labels as well as French wine-growing regions.

Survival Guide

Before You Go   204

When to Go 204

Book Your Stay .204

Arriving in Paris   205

Getting Around   208

Bicycle 208

Boat 208

Bus 209

Metro & RER 209

Taxi 209

Essential Information   210

Business Hours 210

Discount Cards 211

Electricity 211

Emergency 211

Internet Access 211

Money 212

Public Holidays 212

Safe Travel 212

Telephone 212

Toilets 213

Tourist Information 213

Travellers with Disabilities 214

Visas 214

Language   215

Survival Guide

Before You Go

When to Go

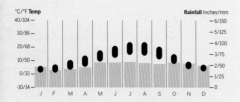

Winter (Nov–Feb)
Cold and dark, occasional snow. Museums are quieter and accommodation prices are lower.

Spring (Mar–May)
Mild, sometimes wet. Major sights start getting busier; parks and gardens begin to come into their own.

Summer (Jun–Aug)
Warm to hot, generally sunny. Main tourist season. Some businesses close for August.

Autumn (Sep–Nov)
Mild, generally sunny. Cultural life moving into top gear after the summer lull.

Book Your Stay

➡ Paris has a wealth of accommodation for all budgets, but it's often *complet* (full) well in advance. Reservations are recommended year-round and essential during the warmer months (April to October) and all public and school holidays.

➡ Although marginally cheaper, accommodation outside central Paris is invariably a false economy given travel time and costs. Choose somewhere within Paris' 20 *arrondissements* to experience Parisian life the moment you step out the door.

➡ The city of Paris levies a *taxe de séjour* (tourist tax) per person per night on all accommodation, from €0.83 to €4.40 per person per night (normally added to your bill).

➡ Breakfast is rarely included; cafes often offer better value.

➔ To live like a Parisian, consider renting a short-stay apartment.

Useful Websites

Lonely Planet (www.lonelyplanet.com/france/paris/hotels) Reviews of Lonely Planet's top choices.

Paris Hotel Service (www.parishotelservice.com) Boutique hotel gems.

Paris Hotel (www.hotels-paris.fr) Well-organised hotel booking site with lots of user reviews.

Room Sélection (www.room-selection.com) Select apartment rentals centred on Le Marais.

Paris Attitude (www.parisattitude.com) Thousands of apartment rentals, professional service, reasonable fees.

Best Budget

Cosmos Hôtel (www.cosmos-hotel-paris.com) Cheap, brilliant value and footsteps from the nightlife of Le Marais' rue JPT.

Hôtel du Nord – Le Pari Vélo (www.hoteldunord-leparivelo.com) Bric-a-brac charm and bikes on loan.

Mama Shelter (www.mamashelter.com) Philippe Starck–designed hipster haven with a cool in-house pizzeria.

Hôtel St-André des Arts (www.hotel-saintandredesarts.fr) Old-school charm in St-Germain's beating heart.

Generator Hostel (www.generatorhostels.com) Shout out to design, street art and French *art de vivre*.

Les Piaules (www.lespiaules.com) Designer hostel and bar with rooftop terrace in Belleville.

Best Midrange

Hôtel Exquis (www.hotelexquisparis.com) Surrealist design hotel east of Bastille.

Hôtel Amour (www.hotelamourparis.fr) Stylish choice for a romantic getaway.

Familia Hôtel (www.familiahotel.com) Sepia murals and flower-bedecked balconies in the Latin Quarter.

Hôtel Jeanne d'Arc (www.hoteljeannedarc.com) Gorgeous, like a family home in a quiet Marais backstreet.

Best Top End

Les Bains (www.lesbains-paris.com) Nineteenth-century thermal baths turned nightclub, turned rockstar-hot lifestyle hotel.

Hôtel Molitor (www.mltr.fr) Stunningly restored art deco swimming pool with gallery-style poolside rooms.

Hôtel Crayon (www.hotelcrayon.com) Line drawings, retro furnishings and coloured-glass shower doors.

Hôtel du Jeu de Paume (www.jeudepaumehotel.com) Romantic haven on the serene Île St-Louis.

Arriving in Paris

☑ For the best way to get to your accommodation, see p17.

Charles de Gaulle Airport

Most international airlines fly to **Aéroport de Charles de Gaulle** (CDG; ☎ 01 70 36 39 50; www.aeroportsdeparis.fr), 28km

Bus

There are six main bus lines linking CDG with Paris:

LINE	FARE	DURATION	FREQUENCY	ROUTE
Le Bus Direct line 2	€17	1hr	every 30min, 5.45am-11pm	Links the airport with the Arc de Triomphe via the Eiffel Tower and Trocadéro. Children under four travel free.
Le Bus Direct line 4	€17	50-80min	every 30 min from the airport (6am-10.30pm) and from Montparnasse (5.30am-10.30pm)	Links the airport with Gare Montparnasse (80 minutes) in southern Paris via Gare de Lyon (50 minutes) in eastern Paris. Under fours travel free.
Noctilien bus 140 & 143	€8 or 4 metro tickets	line 140 1¼hr; line 143 2hr	hourly, 12.30am-5.30am	Part of the RATP night service, Noctilien has two buses that go to CDG: bus 140 from Gare de l'Est, and 143 from Gare de l'Est and Gare du Nord.
RATP bus 350	€6	70min	every 30min, 5.30am-11pm	Links the airport with Gare de l'Est in northern Paris.
RATP bus 351	€6	70min	every 30min, 5.30am-11pm	Links the airport with place de la Nation in eastern Paris.
Roissybus	€11.50	1hr	from CDG every 15min 5.30am-10pm and every 30min, 10pm and 11pm; from Paris every 15min 5.15am-10pm and every 30min 10pm-12.30am	Links the airport with the Opéra.

northeast of central Paris. In French the airport is commonly called 'Roissy' after the suburb in which it is located. A €1.7 billion project to create a high-speed train link between Charles de Gaulle and Gare de l'Est in central Paris is on the table, but no track will be laid until 2017. When complete in 2023, the CDG Express will cut the current 50-odd minute journey to 20 minutes. A fourth terminal is due to open in 2020.

Train

Charles de Gaulle is served by the RER B line (€9.75, approximately 50 minutes, every 10 to 20 minutes), which connects with the Gare du Nord, Châtelet–Les Halles and St-Michel–Notre Dame stations in the city centre. Trains run from 5am to 11pm; there are fewer trains on weekends.

Taxi

➡ A taxi to the city centre takes 40 minutes. From

2016, fares have been standardised to a flat rate: €50 to the Right Bank and €55 to the Left Bank. The fare increases by 15% between 5pm and 10am and on Sundays.

➡ Only take taxis at a clearly marked rank. Never follow anyone who approaches you at the airport and claims to be a driver.

Orly Airport

Aéroport d'Orly (ORY; 📞 01 70 36 39 50; www. aeroportsdeparis.fr) is 19km south of central Paris but, despite being closer than CDG, it is not as frequently used by international airlines, and public transport options aren't quite as straightforward. That will change by 2024, when metro line 14 will be extended to the airport. A TGV station is due to arrive here in 2025.

Orly's south and west terminals are currently being unified into one large terminal suitable for bigger planes such as A380s; completion is due in 2018.

Train

There is currently no direct train to/from Orly;

you'll need to change halfway. Note that while it is possible to take a shuttle to the RER C line, this service is quite long and not recommended.

RER B (€12.05, 35 minutes, every four to 12 minutes) This line connects Orly with the St-Michel–Notre Dame, Châtelet–Les Halles and Gare du Nord stations in the city centre. In order to get from Orly to the RER station (Antony), you must first take the Orlyval automatic train. The service runs from 6am to 11pm (less frequently on weekends). You only need one ticket to take the two trains.

Tram

Tramway T7 (€1.80, every six minutes, 40 minutes, 5.30am to 12.30am) This tramway links Orly with Villejuif–Louis Aragon metro station in southern Paris; buy tickets from the machine at the tram stop as no tickets are sold on board.

Taxi

A taxi to the city centre takes roughly 30 minutes. Standardised flat-rate fares since 2016

mean a taxi costs €30 to the Left Bank and €35 to the Right Bank. The fare increases by 15% between 5pm and 10am and on Sundays.

Bus

Two bus lines serve Orly:

Les Cars Air France line 1 (€12.50, one hour, every 20 minutes, 6am to 11.40pm from Orly, 5am to 10.40pm from Invalides) Runs to/from the Gare Montparnasse (35 minutes) in southern Paris, Invalides in the 7e, and the Arc de Triomphe. Children aged two to 11 pay half price.

Orlybus (€7.50, 30 minutes, every 15 minutes, 6am to 12.30pm from Orly, 5.35am to midnight from Paris) Runs to/from the metro station Denfert Rochereau in southern Paris, making several stops en route.

Beauvais Airport

Aéroport de Beauvais (BVA; 📞 08 92 68 20 66; www.aeroportbeauvais.com) is 75km north of Paris and is served by a few low-cost flights. Before you snap up that bargain, consider if the postarrival journey is worth it.

Shuttle (€17, 1¼ hours) The Beauvais shuttle bus links the airport with metro station Porte de Maillot. See the airport website for details and tickets.

Gare du Nord

Located in northern Paris, **Gare du Nord** (rue de Dunkerque, 10e; M Gare du Nord) is the terminus for northbound domestic trains as well as several international services.

Eurostar (www.eurostar. com) The London–Paris line runs from St-Pancras International to Gare du Nord. Voyages take 2¼ hours.

Thalys (www.thalys.com) Trains pull into Paris' Gare du Nord from Brussels, Amsterdam and Cologne.

Other Mainline Stations

➡ Paris has five other stations for long-distance trains, each with its own metro station: Gare d'Austerlitz, Gare de l'Est, Gare de Lyon, Gare Montparnasse and Gare St-Lazare. The station

used depends on the direction from Paris.

➡ Contact Voyages SNCF (www.voyages-sncf. com) for connections throughout France and continental Europe.

Getting Around

Bicycle

The **Vélib'** (📞 01 30 79 79 30; http://en.velib.paris. fr; day/week subscription €1.70/8, bike hire up to 30/60/90/120min free/€1/2/4) bike-share scheme puts 23,600 bikes at the disposal of Parisians and visitors for getting around the city. There are some 1800 stations throughout the city, each with anywhere from 20 to 70 bike stands. The bikes are accessible around the clock.

➡ To get a bike, you first need to purchase a one- or seven-day subscription. There are two ways to do this: either at the terminals found at docking stations or online.

➡ The terminals require a credit card with an embedded smart chip (which precludes many North American cards), and, even then, not all foreign chip-embedded cards will work. Alternatively, you can purchase a subscription online before you leave your hotel.

➡ After you authorise a deposit (€150) to pay for the bike should it go missing, you'll receive an ID number and PIN code and you're ready to go.

➡ Bikes are rented in 30-minute intervals. If you return a bike before a half-hour is up and then take a new one, you will not be charged.

➡ If the station you want to return your bike to is full, log in to the terminal to get 15 minutes for free while you find another station.

➡ Bikes are geared to cyclists aged 14 and over, and are fitted with gears, an antitheft lock with key, reflective strips and front/rear lights. Bring your own helmet (they are not required by law).

Boat

Batobus (www.batobus. com; adult/child 1-day pass €17/10, 2-day pass €19/10;

⏱10am-9.30pm Apr-Aug, to 7pm Sep-Mar) runs glassed-in trimarans that dock every 20 to 25 minutes at nine small piers along the Seine: Beaugrenelle, Eiffel Tower, Musée d'Orsay, St-Germain des Prés, Notre Dame, Jardin des Plantes/Cité de la Mode et du Design, Hôtel de Ville, Musée du Louvre and Champs-Élysées.

Buy tickets online, at ferry stops or at tourist offices. You can also buy a two-/three-day Paris À La Carte Pass that includes **L'Open Tour** (✆01 42 66 56 56; www.paris.opentour. com; 1-day pass adult/child €32/16) buses for €45/49.

Bus

➡ Paris' bus system, operated by RATP, runs from 5.30am to 8.30pm Monday to Saturday; after that, certain evening-service lines continue until between midnight and 12.30am. Services are drastically reduced on Sunday and public holidays, when buses run from 7am to 8.30pm.

➡ The RATP runs 47 night bus lines known as Noctilien (www.vianavigo. com), which depart hourly

from 12.30am to 5.30am. You pay a certain number of standard €1.80 metro/ bus tickets, depending on the length of your journey.

Metro & RER

Paris' underground network is run by RATP and consists of two separate but linked systems: the metro and the Réseau Express Régional (RER) suburban train line.

➡ The metro has 14 numbered lines; the RER has five main lines (but you'll probably only need to use A, B and C).

➡ When buying tickets consider how many zones your journey will cover; there are five concentric transport zones rippling out from Paris (5 being the furthest); if you travel from Charles de Gaulle airport to Paris, for instance, you will have to buy a zone 1–5 ticket.

➡ For information and route maps for the metro, RER and bus systems, visit www.ratp.fr.

➡ Each metro line has a different colour, number and final destination. Signs in stations indicate the way to the platform for your line. The direction signs on each

platform indicate the terminus. On lines that split into several branches, the terminus served by each train is indicated on the cars, and signs on each platform give the number of minutes until the next train.

➡ Signs marked *correspondance* (transfer) show how to reach connecting trains. At stations with many intersecting lines, such as Châtelet and Montparnasse Bienvenüe, the connection can take a long time.

➡ Each line has its own schedule but trains usually start at around 5.30am, with the last train beginning its run between 12.35am and 1.15am (2.15am on Friday and Saturday).

Taxi

➡ The *prise en charge* (flagfall) is €2.60. Within the city limits, it costs €1.04 per kilometre for travel between 10am and 5pm Monday to Saturday (*Tarif A*; white light on taxi roof and meter).

➡ At night (5pm to 10am), on Sunday from 7am to midnight, and in the inner suburbs the rate is €1.27

Tickets & Passes

➡ The same RATP tickets are valid on the metro, the RER (for travel within the city limits), buses, trams and the Montmartre funicular.

➡ A ticket – white in colour and called *Le Ticket t+* – costs €1.80 (half price for children aged four to nine years) if bought individually and €14.10 for adults for a *carnet* (book) of 10.

➡ Tickets are sold at all metro stations. Ticket windows accept most credit cards; however, automated machines do not accept credit cards without embedded chips (and even then, not all foreign chip-embedded cards).

➡ One ticket lets you travel between any two metro stations (no return journeys) for a period of 1½ hours, no matter how many transfers are required. You can also use it on the RER for travel within zone 1, which encompasses all of central Paris.

➡ Transfers from the metro to bus or vice versa are not possible.

➡ Always keep your ticket until you exit from your station or risk a fine.

➡ If you're staying in Paris for a week or more, ask at metro station offices about rechargeable Navigo (www.navigo.fr) passes.

➡ Tourist passes Mobilis and Paris Visite cover transport.

per kilometre (*Tarif B*; orange light).

➡ Travel in the city limits and inner suburbs on Sunday night (midnight to 7am Monday) and in the outer suburbs is at *Tarif C*, €1.54 per kilometre (blue light).

➡ The minimum taxi fare for a short trip is €6.86.

➡ Flat fees have been introduced for taxis to/from the major airports, Charles de Gualle (p206) and Orly (p207).

➡ There's a €3 surcharge for taking a fourth passenger, but drivers sometimes refuse for insurance reasons. The first piece of baggage is free; additional pieces over 5kg cost €1 extra.

➡ Flagging down a taxi in Paris can be difficult; it's best to find an official taxi stand.

➡ To order a taxi, call or reserve online with **Taxis G7** (☎01 41 27 66 99, 3607; www.taxisg7.com), **Taxis Bleus** (☎08 91 70 10 10, 3609; www.taxis-bleus.com) or **Alpha Taxis** (☎01 45 85 85 85; www.alphataxis.fr).

Essential Information

Business Hours

The following list shows *approximate* standard opening hours for businesses. Hours can vary by season. Many businesses close for the entire month of August for summer holidays.

Banks 9am–1pm and 2–5pm Monday to Friday, some Saturday morning

Bars and cafes 7am–2am

Museums 10am–6pm, closed Monday or Tuesday

Post offices 8am–7pm Monday to Friday, and until noon Saturday

Restaurants noon–2pm and 7.30–10.30pm

Shops (clothing) 10am–7pm Monday to Saturday, occasionally close in the early afternoon for lunch and sometimes all day Monday

Shops (food) 8am–1pm and 4–7.30pm, closed Sunday afternoon and sometimes Monday

Discount Cards

➡ If you plan on visiting a lot of museums, pick up a **Paris Museum Pass** (www.en.parismuseumpass.com; 2/4/6 days €48/62/74) or a **Paris Passlib'** (www.parisinfo.com; 2/3/5 days €109/129/155); the latter also includes public transport and various extras. The passes get you into 60-odd venues in and around Paris, bypassing (or reducing) long ticket queues. Both passes are available from the **Paris**

Convention & Visitors Bureau (Office du Tourisme et des Congrès de Paris; Map p58, D3; www.parisinfo.com; 27 rue des Pyramides, 1er; ⏱7am-7pm May-Oct, 10am-7pm Nov-Apr; Ⓜ Pyramides).

➡ **Mobilis** and **Paris Visite** passes are valid on the metro, RER, SNCF's suburban lines, buses, night buses, trams and Montmartre funicular railway. Passes are sold at larger metro and RER stations, SNCF offices in Paris, and the airports.

➡ **Mobilis** Allows unlimited travel for one day and costs €7 (two zones) to €16.60 (five zones). Buy it at any metro, RER or SNCF station in the Paris region. Depending on how many times you plan to hop on/off the metro in a day, a *carnet* (book of tickets) might work out cheaper.

➡ **Paris Visite** Allows unlimited travel as well as discounted entry to certain museums and other discounts and bonuses. The 'Paris+Suburbs+Airports' pass includes transport to/from the airports and costs €23.50/ 35.70/ 50.05/ 61.25 for one/ two/three/five days. The cheaper 'Paris Centre' pass, valid for zones 1 to

3, costs €11.15/ 18.15/ 24.80/ 35.70 for one/ two/three/five days. Children aged four to 11 years pay half price.

Electricity

230V/50Hz

Emergency

Ambulance (SAMU) (☏15)

Fire (☏18)

Police (☏17)

EU-wide emergency (☏112)

Internet Access

➡ Wi-fi (pronounced 'wee-fee' in France) is available in most Paris hotels, usually at no extra cost, and in some museums.

➡ Free wi-fi is available in some 300 public places, including parks, libraries and municipal buildings, between 7am and 11pm daily. In parks look for a purple 'Zone Wi-Fi' sign near the entrance. To connect, select the 'PARIS_WI-FI_' network and connect; sessions are limited to two hours. For complete details and a map of hot spots see www.paris.fr/wifi.

Money

➡ France uses the euro (€). For updated exchange rates, check www.xe.com.

➡ Visa is the most widely accepted credit card, followed by MasterCard. American Express and Diners Club cards are accepted only at more exclusive establishments. Some restaurants don't accept credit cards.

➡ Many automated services, such as ticket machines, require a chip-and-PIN credit card (even some foreign chip-enabled cards won't work). Ask your bank for advice before you leave.

Public Holidays

New Year's Day (Jour de l'An) 1 January

Easter Sunday & Monday (Pâques & Lundi de Pâques) Late March/ April

May Day (Fête du Travail) 1 May

Victory in Europe Day (Victoire 1945) 8 May

Ascension Thursday (L'Ascension) May; celebrated on the 40th day after Easter

Whit Monday (Lundi de Pentecôte) Mid-May to mid-June; seventh Monday after Easter

Bastille Day/National Day (Fête Nationale) 14 July

Assumption Day (L'Assomption) 15 August

All Saints' Day (La Toussaint) 1 November

Armistice Day/Remembrance Day (Le Onze Novembre) 11 November

Christmas (Noël) 25 December

Safe Travel

➡ In general, Paris is a safe city but pickpockets prey on busy places; *always* stay alert to the possibility of someone surreptitiously reaching for your pockets or bags, especially where there

are tourist crowds, such as the base of Sacré-Cœur.

➡ Common 'distraction' scams include would-be pickpockets pretending to 'find' a gold ring, brandishing fake petitions, dropping items, and tying 'friendship bracelets' to your wrist.

➡ The metro is safe to use until it closes, including for women travelling alone, but stations best avoided late at night include the long passageways of Châtelet–Les Halles and Montparnasse–Bienvenüe, as well as Château Rouge, Gare du Nord, Strasbourg St-Denis, Réaumur Sébastopol and Stalingrad. *Bornes d'alarme* (alarm boxes) are located in the centre of each metro/ RER platform and in some station corridors.

Telephone

➡ Check with your provider before you leave about roaming costs and/ or ensure your phone's unlocked to use a French SIM card (available in Paris).

➡ France doesn't use separate area codes – you always dial the full

10-digit number. Drop the initial '📞0' if calling France from abroad.

➡ France's country code is 📞33.

➡ To call abroad from Paris, dial France's international access code (📞00).

Toilets

➡ Public toilets in Paris are signposted *toilettes* or *WC*. The self-cleaning cylindrical toilets you see on Parisian pavements are open 24 hours, reasonably clean and free of charge, though, of course, they never seem to be around when you need them. Look for the words *libre* ('available'; green-coloured) or *occupé* ('occupied'; red-coloured).

➡ Cafe owners do not appreciate you using their facilities if you are not a paying customer (a coffee can be a good investment); however, if you have young children they may make an exception (ask first!). Other good bets are major department stores and big hotels.

➡ There are free public toilets in front of Notre Dame cathedral, near the Arc de Triomphe,

Dos & Don'ts

➡ Always greet/farewell anyone you interact with, such as shopkeepers, with '*Bonjour* (*bonsoir* at night)/*Au revoir*'.

➡ Particularly in smaller shops, staff may not appreciate you touching the merchandise until invited to do so, nor taking photographs.

➡ Parisians don't speak loudly – modulate your voice to a similarly low pitch.

➡ *Tu* and *vous* both mean 'you' but *tu* is only used with people you know very well, children or animals. Use *vous* until you're invited to use *tu*.

➡ Talking about money (eg salaries or spending outlays) is generally taboo in public.

➡ Never use '*garçon*' ('boy') to summon a waiter, rather 'Monsieur' or 'Madame'.

east down the steps at Sacré-Cœur and at the northwestern entrance to the Jardins des Tuileries.

Tourist Information

Paris Convention & Visitors Bureau (Office du Tourisme et des Congrès de Paris; Map p58, D3; www.parisinfo.com; 27 rue des Pyramides, 1er; ⏰7am-7pm May-Oct, 10am-7pm Nov-Apr; Ⓜ Pyramides) The main branch is 500m northwest of the Louvre. It sells tickets for tours and several attractions, plus museum and transport passes. Also books accommodation.

Anvers-Montmartre Welcome Desk (http://en.parisinfo.com; opp 72 bd Rochechouart, 18e; ⏰10am-6pm; Ⓜ Anvers) At the foot of Montmartre, next to Anvers metro station.

Gare de l'Est Welcome Desk (place du 11 Novembre 1918, 10e; ⏰8am-7pm Mon-Sat; Ⓜ Gare de l'Est) Inside Gare de l'Est train station, facing platforms 1–2.

Gare de Lyon Welcome Desk (20 bd Diderot, 12e; ⏰8am-6pm Mon-Sat; Ⓜ Gare de Lyon) Inside Gare de Lyon train station, facing platforms L–M.

Gare du Nord Welcome Desk (18 rue de Dunkerque, 10e; ⏰8am-6pm; Ⓜ Gare du Nord) Inside Gare du Nord station, under the glass roof of the Île de France departure and arrival area (eastern end of station).

Syndicate d'Initiative de Montmartre (☎01 42 62 21 21; www.montmartre-guide.com; 21 place du Tertre, 18e; ⏰10am-6pm summer, 10am-4pm Mon-Thu, 10am-5pm Fri, 10am-1pm & 2-5pm Sat rest of year; Ⓜ Abbesses) Locally run tourist office and shop on Montmartre's most picturesque square. It sells maps of Montmartre and organises guided tours.

Travellers with Disabilities

➡ For information about which cultural venues in Paris are accessible to people with disabilities, surf Accès Culture (www.accesculture.org).

➡ *Access in Paris,* a 245-page guide to the French capital for people with disabilities, can be downloaded in PDF form at Access Project (www.accessinparis.org).

➡ **Mobile en Ville** (☎09 52 29 60 51; www.mobile-en-ville.asso.fr; 8 rue des Mariniers, 14e) works hard to make independent travel within the city easier for people in wheelchairs. Among other things it organises wheelchair *randonnées* (walks) in and around Paris; those in wheelchairs are pushed by 'walkers' on rollerskates.

➡ Download Lonely Planet's free *Accessible Travel* guide from http://lptravel.to/AccessibleTravel.

Transport

➡ For information on the accessibility of all forms of public transport in the Paris region, get a copy of the *Guide Practique à l'Usage des Personnes à Mobilité Réduite* (Practical Usage Guide for People with Reduced Mobility) from the Syndicate des Transports d'Île de France (www.stif.info). Its info service for travellers with disabilities, **Info Mobi** (☎09 70 81 83 85; www.infomobi.com), is especially useful.

➡ **Taxis G7** (☎01 41 27 66 99, 3607; www.taxisg7.com) has 120 cars especially adapted to carry wheelchairs, and drivers trained in helping passengers with disabilities.

Visas

➡ There are no entry requirements for nationals of EU countries and a handful of other European countries (including Switzerland). Citizens of Australia, the USA, Canada and New Zealand do not need visas to visit France for up to 90 days.

➡ Everyone else, including citizens of South Africa, needs a Schengen Visa, named after the Schengen Agreement that has abolished passport controls among 26 EU countries and which has also been ratified by the non-EU governments of Iceland, Norway and Switzerland. Note that the UK and Ireland are not Schengen countries.

➡ Check www.france.diplomatie.fr for the latest visa regulations and the closest French embassy to your current residence.

Language

The sounds used in spoken French can almost all be found in English. There are a couple of exceptions: nasal vowels (represented in our pronunciation guides by 'o' or 'u' followed by an almost inaudible nasal consonant sound 'm', 'n' or 'ng'), the 'funny' *u* sound ('ew' in our guides) and the deep-in-the-throat *r*. Bearing these few points in mind and reading our pronunciation guides below as if they were English, you'll be understood just fine. The markers (m) and (f) indicate the forms for male and female speakers respectively.

To enhance your trip with a phrasebook, visit **lonelyplanet.com**. Lonely Planet iPhone phrasebooks are available through the Apple App store.

Basics

Hello.
Bonjour.   bon·zhoor

Goodbye.
Au revoir.   o·rer·vwa

How are you?
*Comment
allez-vous?*   ko·mon
ta·lay·voo

I'm fine, thanks.
Bien, merci.   byun mair·see

Please.
S'il vous plaît.   seel voo play

Thank you.
Merci.   mair·see

Excuse me.
Excusez-moi.   ek·skew·zay·mwa

Sorry.
Pardon.   par·don

Yes./No.
Oui./Non.   wee/non

I don't understand.
*Je ne comprends
pas.*   zher ner kom·pron
pa

Do you speak English?
*Parlez-vous
anglais?*   par·lay·voo
ong·glay

Eating & Drinking

..., please.
..., s'il vous plaît.   ... seel voo play

A coffee	*un café*	un ka·fay
A table for two	*une table pour deux*	ewn ta·bler poor der
Two beers	*deux bières*	der bee·yair

I'm a vegetarian.
*Je suis
végétarien/
végétarienne.* (m/f)   zher swee
vay·zhay·ta·ryun/
vay·zhay·ta·ryen

Cheers!
Santé!   son·tay

That was delicious!
C'était délicieux!   say·tay day·lee·syer

The bill, please.
*L'addition,
s'il vous plaît.*   la·dee·syon
seel voo play

Shopping

I'd like to buy ...
*Je voudrais
acheter ...*   zher voo·dray
ash·tay ...

I'm just looking.
Je regarde.   zher rer·gard

How much is it?
C'est combien?   say kom·byun

It's too expensive.
C'est trop cher.   say tro shair

Can you lower the price?
Vous pouvez baisser le prix? — voo poo·vay bay·say ler pree

Emergencies

Help!
Au secours! — o skoor

Call the police!
Appelez la police! — a·play la po·lees

Call a doctor!
Appelez un médecin! — a·play un mayd·sun

I'm sick.
Je suis malade. — zher swee ma·lad

I'm lost.
Je suis perdu/perdue. (m/f) — zhe swee pair·dew

Where are the toilets?
Où sont les toilettes? — oo son lay twa·let

Time & Numbers

What time is it?
Quelle heure est-il? — kel er ay til

It's (eight) o'clock.
Il est (huit) heures. — il ay (weet) er

It's half past (10).
Il est (dix) heures et demie. — il ay (deez) er ay day·mee

morning	*matin*	ma·tun
afternoon	*après-midi*	a·pray·mee·dee
evening	*soir*	swar
yesterday	*hier*	yair
today	*aujourd'hui*	o·zhoor·dwee
tomorrow	*demain*	der·mun

Monday	*lundi*	lun·dee
Tuesday	*mardi*	mar·dee
Wednesday	*mercredi*	mair·krer·dee
Thursday	*jeudi*	zher·dee
Friday	*vendredi*	von·drer·dee
Saturday	*samedi*	sam·dee
Sunday	*dimanche*	dee·monsh

1	*un*	un
2	*deux*	der
3	*trois*	trwa
4	*quatre*	ka·trer
5	*cinq*	sungk
6	*six*	sees
7	*sept*	set
8	*huit*	weet
9	*neuf*	nerf
10	*dix*	dees
100	*cent*	son
1000	*mille*	meel

Transport & Directions

Where's ...?
Où est ...? — oo ay ...

What's the address?
Quelle est l'adresse? — kel ay la·dres

Can you show me (on the map)?
Pouvez-vous m'indiquer (sur la carte)? — poo·vay·voo mun·dee·kay (sewr la kart)

I want to go to ...
Je voudrais aller à ... — zher voo·dray a·lay a ...

Does it stop at (Amboise)?
Est-ce qu'il s'arrête à (Amboise)? — es·kil sa·ret a (om·bwaz)

I want to get off here.
Je veux descendre ici. — zher ver day·son·drer ee·see

Behind the Scenes

Send Us Your Feedback

We love to hear from travellers – your comments help make our books better. We read every word, and we guarantee that your feedback goes straight to the authors. Visit **lonelyplanet.com/contact** to submit your updates and suggestions.

Note: We may edit, reproduce and incorporate your comments in Lonely Planet products such as guidebooks, websites and digital products, so let us know if you don't want your comments reproduced or your name acknowledged. For a copy of our privacy policy visit lonelyplanet.com/privacy.

Our Readers

Many thanks to the travellers who used the last edition and wrote to us with helpful hints, useful advice and interesting anecdotes:

Caroline Horn, Geoff Grimes, Laura Minniti, Lauranne Longuet, Mark Dukas, Mick Thompson, Robert & Janedy Buchanan

Catherine's Thanks

Un grand merci to my *Paris* co-writers Chris and Nicola. *Merci mille fois* to Julian, and all of the innumerable

Parisians who offered insights and inspiration. In particular, *merci beaucoup* to Laurent for going above and beyond, and to Laurence for the same. Huge thanks also to Helen Elfer, Kate Morgan and everyone at Lonely Planet. A heartfelt *merci encore* to my parents, brother, *belle-sœur* and *neveu* for sustaining my lifelong love of Paris.

Acknowledgements

Cover photograph: Eiffel Tower, Luigi Vaccarella/4Corners ©

This Book

This 5th edition of Lonely Planet's *Pocket Paris* guidebook was curated by Catherine Le Nevez and researched and written by Catherine, Christopher Pitts and Nicola Williams. This guidebook was produced by the following:

Destination Editor Helen Elfer

Product Editor Joel Cotterell

Senior Cartographer Valentina Kremenchutskaya

Book Designers Virginia Moreno, Wendy Wright

Assisting Editor Gabrielle Stefanos

Cover Researcher Naomi Parker

Thanks to Bridget Blair, Andi Jones, Lauren Keith, Anne Mason, Kate Mathews, Wayne Murphy, Claire Naylor, Karyn Noble, Alison Ridgway

Index

See also separate subindexes for:

⊗ **Eating p221**
⊙ **Drinking p221**
✪ **Entertainment p222**
🔒 **Shopping p222**

A

accommodation 204-5
airports 17
ambulance 211
amusement parks 191
Aquarium de Paris Cinéaqua 45
Arc de Triomphe 9, 38-9
architecture 180-1
area codes 212
Arènes de Lutèce 135
art galleries 178-9
art nouveau 180
axe historique 39

B

ballet 194
bathrooms 213
belle époque 79
Bercy Village 145
Bibliothèque Nationale de France 145
bicycle travel 201, 208
boat travel 185, 201, 208-9
books 159, 172-3
bouquinistes 163
bus travel 187, 201, 209
business hours 210-11

Sights 000
Map Pages **000**

buskers 122
Butte aux Cailles 145

C

cabarets 194, 195
Canal St-Martin 84-5, **84**
cathedrals 186
cell phones 16
cemeteries 183
Centre Pompidou 10, 88-9
Champs-Élysées area 36-47, **40-1**
    drinking 46-7
    food 45-6
    itineraries 37
    shopping 47
    sights 38-9, 42-5
    transport 37
children, travel with 191
churches 186
Cimetière de Montmartre 77
Cimetière du Montparnasse 156
Cinémathèque Française 145
Cité de l'Architecture et du Patrimoine 42
climate 204
Clos Montmartre 75
cocktails 192, 193
coffee 192, 193
community life 98
Conciergerie 118

cooking courses 202
costs 16, 178, 211
Cour du Commerce St-André 152
covered passages 176-7, **177**
crêpes 160
cruises 185, 201
Crypte Archéologique 115
currency 16
cycling 201, 208

D

dangers 212
de Gaulle, Charles 33, 137
Degas, Edgar 149
disabilities, travellers with 214
Docks en Seine 145
drinking & nightlife 192-5, *see also individual neighbourhoods,* Drinking *subindex*

E

Église de la Madeleine 60
Église du Dôme 30
Église St-Eustache 61
Église St-Germain des Prés 157
Église St-Sulpice 158
Eiffel, Gustave 24, 25
Eiffel Tower 8, 24-5

electricity 16, 211
emergencies 211
entertainment, *see individual neighbourhoods,* Entertainment *subindex*
Espace Dalí 77
etiquette 213
Eurostar 208

F

fashion 198-9
films 159, 194, 201
fire 211
Fondation Cartier pour l'Art Contemporain 158
Fondation Henri Cartier-Bresson 158
food 188-9, *see also individual neighbourhoods,* Eating *subindex*
free attractions 197
French language 215-16
French Revolution 120, 182, 183

G

Galerie Colbert 176
Galerie Véro Dodat 176
Galerie Vivienne 176
galleries 178-9
gardens 184
gay travellers 101, 196

Ginsberg, Allen 172
Golden Triangle 46
Grand Palais 42
Grande Arche 181
grands projets 181
Guimard, Hector 75, 97

H
Halle St-Pierre 78
Haussman, Georges-Eugène 180
Haut Marais 90-1, **90**
Hemingway, Ernest 159, 173
highlights 8-11, 12-13
history 33, 120, 182-3
holidays 212
Hôtel de Ville 96
Hôtel des Invalides 30
Hugo, Victor 96, 159

I
Île aux Cygnes 30
Île de la Cité & Île St-Louis 108-25, **116-17**
drinking 123-4
food 119-23
itineraries 109
shopping 124-5
sights 110-15, 118-19
transport 109
impressionism 148-9, 178
Info Défense 181
Institut du Monde Arabe 134
internet access 211-12
itineraries 14-15, 172-7, *see also individual neighbourhoods*

J
Jardin de la Nouvelle France 44
Jardin des Plantes 134
Jardin des Tuileries 60

Jardin du Luxembourg 10, 150-1
Jardin du Palais Royal 62
jazz 194, 195
Jeu de Paume 60
Joyce, James 172

K
Kerouac, Jack 172
Kiss, The 27

L
La Défense 181
La Pinacothèque 61
language 16, 140, 215-16
Latin Quarter 126-43, **130**, **132-3**
drinking 140-1
entertainment 141
food 136-40
itineraries 130
shopping 142
sights 128-9, 134-6
transport 127
Left Bank 172-3, **173**
Les Berges de Seine 156
Les Catacombes 156
Les Halles 56-7, **56**
Les Invalides area 22-35, **28-9**
drinking 35
food 32-4
itineraries 23
sights 24-7, 30-2
transport 23
LGBT travellers 101, 196
lifestyle 98
literature 159, 172-3
local life 12-13, 98
Louis XIV 166-7
Louis XVI 120, 166-7
Louvre 9, 50-5, 55

M
Maison de Victor Hugo 96
Marais 86-103, **92-3**
drinking 100-2
entertainment 102-3
food 97-100
itineraries 90
shopping 102, 103
sights 88-9, 94-7
transport 87
Marie Antoinette 120, 166, 169
markets 190
Mémorial de la Shoah 94
Mémorial des Martyrs de la Déportation 118
metro travel 209
Metropolitain sign 75
Miller, Henry 173
mobile phones 16
Mona Lisa 52
Monet, Claude 179
money 16, 211, 212
Montmartre 70-83, **74, 76**
drinking 80-2
entertainment 82-3
food 78-9
itineraries 71
shopping 83
sights 72-3, 77-8
transport 71
Montparnasse, *see* St-Germain des Prés
Morrison, Jim 106
Mosquée de Paris 134
Moulin Blute-Fin 75
Moulin Radet 75
Moulin Rouge 82
multiculturalism 200
Musée Cognacq-Jay 96

Musée d'Art et d'Histoire du Judaïsme 97
Musée d'Art Moderne de la Ville de Paris 44
Musée de la Mode de la Ville de Paris 44
Musée de l'Armée 31
Musée de la Sculpture en Plein Air 135
Musée de la Vie Romantique 77
Musée de l'Érotisme 78
Musée de l'Orangerie 60
Musée de Montmartre 75
Musée des Arts et Métiers 94
Musée des Égouts de Paris 32
Musée des Lettres et Manuscrits 158
Musée d'Orsay 10, 148-9
Musée du Luxembourg 151
Musée du Quai Branly 30
Musée Grévin 177
Musée Guimet des Arts Asiatiques 42
Musée Jacquemart-André 42
Musée Marmottan 179
Musée Maxim's 45
Musée National d'Art Moderne 89
Musée National du Moyen Âge 11, 128-9
Musée National Eugène Delacroix 157
Musée National Picasso 94
Musée Rodin 11, 26-7

Muséum National d'Histoire Naturelle 136
museums 178-9
music 122, 194-5

N
Napoléon 30, 38, 120
nightclubs 194-5
nightlife, see drinking & nightlife
Notre Dame 9, 110-15, 113
Nouveau Musée du Parfum 62
Nouvel, Jean 180, 181

O
opening hours 210-11
opera 194
Opéra area, see Tuileries area
Orwell, George 159, 172

P
Palais de Chaillot 44
Palais de Tokyo 43
Palais du Luxembourg 151
Palais Garnier 61
Panthéon 134
Parc des Buttes Chaumont 85
Parc du Champ de Mars 31
Paris Plages 185
parks 184
Passage Choiseul 176
Passage des Panoramas 177
Passage Jouffroy 177

Sights 000
Map Pages **000**

passages couverts 176-7, **177**
Passage Verdeau 177
Passerelle Simone de Beauvoir 145
Perec, Georges 159
Père Lachaise 11, 104-7
Périphérique 98
Petit Palais 43
photography 179, 187
Piaf, Édith 105, 159
Picasso, Pablo 94
Piscine Joséphine Baker 145
Place de la Bastille 94
Place de la Concorde 60-1
Place de la Madeleine 68
Place des Vosges 96
Place du Tertre 75
Pletzl 97
police 211
politics 33, 138
Pont Neuf 118
Pound, Ezra 173
Promenade Plantée 95
public holidays 212

R
redevelopment 98
Rodin, Auguste 26-7
Rue Cler 34
Rue Daguerre 164
Rue d'Alésia 199
Rue de Lappe 100
Rue des Martyrs 80
Rue Mouffetard 130-1, **130**

S
Sacré-Cœur 10, 72-3
safety 212

Sainte-Chapelle 118
scams 212
sculpture 179
Seine 174-5, 185, 208-9, **175**
shopping 176-7, 198-9, see also individual neighbourhoods, Shopping subindex
Sorbonne 136
Southeastern Paris 144-5, **144**
Square du Vert-Galant 119
Square René Viviani 136
Statue of Liberty replica 30
Stein, Gertrude 173
St-Germain des Prés 146-65, **152**, **154-5**
drinking 162
entertainment 163
food 160-2
itineraries 147, 152-3
shopping 152-3, 164-5
sights 148-51, 156-60
transport 147

T
taxis 209-10
telephone services 16, 212
theatre 194
Thinker, The 27
time 16
tipping 16
toilets 213
Tomb of the Unknown Soldier 39
top sights 8-11
Tour Montparnasse 156
Tour St-Jacques 95

tourist information 213-14
tours 201
train travel 209
transport 17, 205-10
Tuileries area 48-69, **58-9**
drinking 65-6
entertainment 66-7
food 62-5
itineraries 49
shopping 68-9
sights 50-5, 60-2
transport 49

V
Van Gogh, Vincent 74
Van Gogh's House 74
Vélib' bicycle share scheme 208
Verlaine, Paul 172
Versailles 11, 166-9, 168
views 187
visas 16, 214

W
walks 172-7, 201
Canal St-Martin 84-5, **84**
Haut Marais 90-1, **90**
Left Bank 172-3, **173**
Les Halles 56-7, **56**
Montmartre 74-5, **74**
Right Bank Covered Passages 176-7, **177**
Rue Mouffetard 130-1, **130**
Seine-Side 174-5, **175**
Southeastern Paris 144-5, **144**
St-Germain des Prés 152-3, **152**
weather 204

websites 16, 205
Wilde, Oscar 105, 173
wine 192, 193
wine-tasting courses 202
WWII 33

⊗ Eating

58 Tour Eiffel 25

A

À la Petite Chaise 27
A Noste 63
Abri 78
Angelina 66, 151, 167
Arnaud Delmontel 80
Au Pied de Fouet 161
Au Rocher de Cancale 57

B

Berthillon 119
Besnier 27
Bouillon Racine 160
Brasserie Bofinger 100
Breizh Café 99

C

Café Campana 149
Café de la Nouvelle Mairie 138
Café La Fusée 89
Café Saint Régis 121
Candelaria 100
Chambelland 99
Chatomat 85
Chez Dumonet 161
Chez Françoise 33
Chez Marianne 97
Chez Nathalie 145
Chez Nicos 131
Chez Toinette 79
Crêperie Josselin 160

D

Dame Tartine 89
Dersou 97

E

Ellsworth 65

F

Floquifil 63
Framboise 46
Frenchie 62

G

Gelati d'Alberto 131
Goût de Brioche 162

H

Hugo Desnoyer 189
Huré 123

J

Jeanne B 78

L

La Closerie des Lilas 162
La Gauloise 34
La Tour d'Argent 138
La Tour de Montlhéry – Chez Denise 63
Ladurée 45
L'AOC 138
L'As du Fallafel 97
Lasserre 45
L'Avant Comptoir de la Mer 160
La Véraison 34
Le Bistrot Paul Bert 97
Le Casse Noix 32
Le Caveau du Palais 121
Le Clos Y 160
Le Comptoir du Panthéon 139

Le Coupe-Chou 138
Le Garde Temps 79
Le Grand Véfour 64
Le Hide 45
Le Jules Verne 25
Le Miroir 80
Le Pantruche 78
Le Pré Verre 129
Le Procope 152
Le Tambour 57
Le Train Bleu 145
Les Climats 161
Les Fables de la Fontaine 33
Les Pipos 138
Les Voyelles 122
L'Été en Pente Douce 73
L'Îlot Vache 122

M

Ma Salle à Manger 122
Marché Bastille 99
Marché des Enfants Rouges 91
Mon Vieil Ami 121

N

Noglu 64

O

Odette 139

P

Passage 53 64
Pink Flamingo 85
Pirouette 64
Poilâne 153
Polidor 151
Prosper et Fortunée 139
Publicis Drugstore 39

R

Racines 2 51

Restaurant AT 137
Restaurant David Toutain 32
Restaurant Musée d'Orsay 149
Richer 63

S

Septime 99
Shakespeare & Company Café 136
Sola 137
Stohrer 57

T

Truffes Folies 34

Y

Yam'Tcha 63
Yard 105

⊗ Drinking

3w Kafé 101
52 Faubourg St-Denis 85

A

Artisan 81
Au P'tit Douai 82
Au Sauvignon 162

B

Blaine 46
Boot Café 91

C

Café Charbon 85
Café de Flore 163
Café des Anges 100
Café des Deux Moulins 74
Chez Prune 85
Coutume 35

E

Experimental Cocktail Club 65

H

Hardware Société 80
Harry's New York Bar 66
Holybelly 85

L

La Caféothèque 101
La Fée Verte 101
La Fourmi 82
La Machine du Moulin Rouge 81
L'Atmosphere 85
Le Baron Rouge 102
Le Batofar 145
Le Cap Horn 102
Le Conchon à l'Oreille 57
Le Crocodile 141
Le Garde Robe 65
Le Mary Céleste 91
Le Petit Trianon 82
Le Progrès 80
Le Pub St-Hilaire 140
Le Pure Café 102
Le Rex Club 66
Le Tango 101
Le Très Particulier 80
Les Deux Magots 162
Les Jardins du Pont-Neuf 124
Le Vieux Chêne 131
Little Bastards 140
Lockwood 65
Lulu White 80

Sights 000
Map Pages **000**

O

Open Café 101

P

PasDeLoup 101

Q

Queen 47
Quetzal 101

S

Showcase 46
Social Club 66
Strada Café 141

T

Taverne Henri IV 123
Tiger Bar 163

W

Wild & the Moon 101

Z

Zig Zag Club 46

☺ Entertainment

Au Lapin Agile 75
Au Limonaire 67
Badaboum 102
Bus Palladium 82
Café Universel 141
Caveau de la Huchette 141
Comédie Française 67
Forum des Images 67
Kiosque Théâtre Madeleine 194
La Chapelle des Lombards 100
La Cigale 82
Le Baiser Salé 67
Le Balajo 100

Le Carreau du Temple 91
Le Champo 141
Le Divan du Monde 80
Le Grand Rex 67
Le Lucernaire 163
Le Nouveau Casino 85
L'Epée de Bois 131
Moulin Rouge 82
Opéra Bastille 102
Palais Garnier 66
Point Éphémère 85
Rosa Bonheur 85
Sunset & Sunside 67
Théâtre des Bouffes Parisiens 177

☺ Shopping

38 Saint Louis 124

A

Abbey Bookshop 142
Album 143
Alexandra Sojfer 153
Androuet 131
Arnaud Magistry 177
Au Plat d'Étain 153
Au Vieux Campeur 143

B

Belle du Jour 83
Bières Cultes 142
bouquinistes 163
Boutique Maille 68

C

Chocolats Mococha 131
Cire Trudon 153
Clair de Rêve 124
Colette 69
Comptoir de la Gastronomie 57
Crocodisc 142

D

Delizius 131
Deyrolle 153
Didier Ludot 68

E

E Dehillerin 56
Emilio Robba 176

F

Fauchon 68
Fermob 165
Forum des Halles 62
Frivoli 85

G

Gab & Jo 164
Galeries Lafayette 68
Guerlain 47

H

Hédiard 68

I

Il Campiello 125

J

JB Guanti 164
Jeremie Barthod 83

K

Kiliwatch 69

L

La Boutique Extraordinaire 91
La Grande Épicerie de Paris 153
La Maison de la Truffe 68
La Maison de Poupée 153
La Maison du Miel 69

La Manufacture de Chocolat 103
Le Bain Rose 153
Le Bon Marché 153
Le Bonbon au Palais 142
Le Printemps 69
Legrand Filles & Fils 68
L'Habilleur 91
Librairie Gourmande 57
Librairie Ulysse 125
L'Îles aux Images 125

M

Magasin Sennelier 164
Maison Kitsuné 83
Marché aux Fleurs Reine Elizabeth II 124
Marché aux Puces d'Aligre 102
Marché aux Puces de St-Ouen 190
Marché Beauvau 102
Marché d'Aligre 102
Marché Mouffetard 130

Marie Mercié 164
Merci 90
M&G Segas 177

P

Paris Rendez-Vous 103
passages couverts 176-7
Patrick Roger 68
Pauline Pin 91
Pierre Hermé 165
Pigalle 83

S

Shakespeare & Company 142
Spree 83

V

Viaduc des Arts 103

W

Wolff et Descourtis 176

Our Writers

Catherine Le Nevez

An award-winning, Paris-based travel writer, Catherine first lived in the French capital aged four and has been hitting the road at every opportunity, completing her Doctorate of Creative Arts in Writing, Masters in Professional Writing, and postgrad qualifications in editing and publishing along the way. Over the last dozen-plus years she's written scores of Lonely Planet guides, along with numerous print and online articles, covering Paris, France, Europe and far beyond. Wanderlust aside, Paris remains her favourite city on earth.

Contributing Writers

Christopher Pitts contributed to Louvre, Tuileries & Opéra; Sacre-Cœur & Montmartre; and the Latin Quarter.

Nicola Williams contributed to Eiffel Tower & Les Invalides, Arc de Triomphe & Champs-Élysées, Centre Pompidou & Le Marais and Notre Dame & the Islands.

Published by Lonely Planet Global Limited
CRN 554153
5th edition – Jan 2017
ISBN 978 1 78657 222 6
© Lonely Planet 2017 Photographs © as indicated 2017
10 9 8 7 6 5 4 3 2 1
Printed in China